SELF-STUDY PROBLEMS/SOLUTIONS BOOK I
CHAPTERS 1–14
TO ACCOMPANY

■ —————— SEVENTH EDITION —————— ■

INTERMEDIATE ACCOUNTING

MARILYN F. HUNT, M.A., C.P.A.

University of Central Florida
Orlando, Florida

DONALD E. KIESO, PH.D., C.P.A.

KPMG Peat Marwick Professor of Accounting
Northern Illinois University
DeKalb, Illinois

JERRY J. WEYGANDT, PH.D., C.P.A.

Arthur Andersen Alumni Professor of Accounting
University of Wisconsin
Madison, Wisconsin

practice

JOHN WILEY & SONS, INC.
NEW YORK ■ CHICHESTER ■ BRISBANE ■ TORONTO ■ SINGAPORE

ISBN 0-471-57032-X

Printed in the United States of America
Printed and bound by Port City Press, Inc.
10 9 8 7 6 5

PREFACE: To the Student

The purpose of this self-study tutorial is to help you to improve your success rate in solving intermediate accounting homework assignments and in answering financial accounting exam questions. For each chapter we provide you with:

OVERVIEW	To briefly introduce the chapter topics and their importance.
TIPS	To alert you to common pitfalls and misconceptions and to remind you of important terminology, concepts, and relationships that are relevant to answering specific questions or solving certain problems.
EXERCISES AND CASES	To provide you with a selection of problems which are representative of homework assignments which an intermediate accounting student may encounter.
MULTIPLE CHOICE	To provide you with a selection of multiple-choice questions which are representative of common exam questions covering topics in the chapter.
PURPOSES	To identify the essence of each question, case, or exercise and to link them to learning objectives.
SOLUTIONS	To show you the appropriate solution for each exercise, case, and multiple choice question presented.
EXPLANATIONS	To give you the details of how selected solutions were derived and to explain why things are done as shown.
APPROACHES _practice_	To coach you on the particular model, computational format, or other strategy to be used to solve particular problems. To teach you how to analyze and solve multiple-choice questions.
MORE TIPS	To help you to understand the intricacies of a problematic situation and to tell you what to do in similar circumstances.

This book should be a welcome teaching/learning aid because it provides you with the opportunity to solve financial accounting problems in addition to the ones assigned by your instructor without having to rely on your teacher for solutions. Many of the exercises and cases contained herein are very similar to items in your intermediate accounting textbook; the difference is, the ones in this book are accompanied with detailed clearly-laid out solutions.

The use of the multiple choice questions in this volume and the related suggestions on how to approach them can easily increase your ability (and confidence in your ability) to deal with exam questions of this variety.

We are grateful to Jennifer Chudoba of the University of Central Florida, Dennis C. Wolff, Jr. of Northern Illinois University, and Professor Wayne Higley of Buena Vista College for their constructive suggestions and editorial comments. Also thanks to Chelsea Hunt, Annabelle and M.F. Specie for their assistance. Our appreciation to Mary Ann Benson and Donna R. Kieso who prepared the manuscript and performed the composition of this book.

Marilyn F. Hunt
Donald E. Kieso
Jerry J. Weygandt

CONTENTS

CHAPTER 1

THE ENVIRONMENT OF FINANCIAL ACCOUNTING AND THE DEVELOPMENT OF ACCOUNTING STANDARDS

OVERVIEW

Accounting is the language of business. It collects and communicates economic information about a business enterprise or other entity to a wide variety of persons. To be useful, financial statements must be clearly understandable and comparable so that users may compare the performance of one business with the performance of the same business for a prior period or with the performance of another similar business. Therefore, all general purpose financial statements should be prepared in accordance with the same uniform guidelines. In this chapter, we will examine the history and sources of current financial accounting standards (generally accepted accounting principles).

TIPS ON CHAPTER TOPICS

TIP: Note the major differences between the Financial Accounting Standards Board (FASB) and its predecessor, the Accounting Principles Board (APB):

1. **Smaller Membership.** The FASB is composed of 7 members, replacing the relatively large 18-member APB.

2. **Full-time, Remunerated Membership.** FASB members are well-paid, full-time members appointed for renewable five-year terms, whereas the APB members were unpaid and part-time.

3. **Greater Autonomy.** The APB was a senior committee of the AICPA, whereas the FASB is not an organ of any single professional organization. It is appointed by and answerable only to the Financial Accounting Foundation.

4. **Increased Independence.** APB members retained their private positions with firms, companies, or institutions; FASB members must sever all such ties.

5. **Broader Representation.** All APB members were required to be CPAs and members of the AICPA; currently, it is not necessary to be a CPA to be a member of the FASB.

CASE 1-1

Purpose: This case will identify the organizations responsible for various accounting documents.

Presented below are a number of accounting organizations and the type of documents they have issued. Match the appropriate document to the organization involved. Note that more than one document may be issued by the same organization. If no document is provided for an organization, write in "0."

Organization	Document
1. _____ Internal Revenue Service	(a) Opinions
2. _____ Committee on Accounting Procedure	(b) Invitations to Comment
3. _____ Financial Accounting Standards Board	(c) Practice Bulletins
4. _____ Securities and Exchange Commission	(d) Accounting Research Bulletins
5. _____ Accounting Standards Executive Committee	(e) Financial Reporting Releases
	(f) Financial Accounting Standards
6. _____ Accounting Principles Board	(g) Statements of Position
	(h) Technical Bulletins

SOLUTION TO CASE 1-1

1. 0	3. b, f, h	5. c, g
2. d	4. e	6. a

CASE 1-2

Purpose: This case discusses the organizations involved in the development of accounting standards and the evolution of the standard-setting process.

Sandra Gargas, a new staff accountant is confused during her first few months on the job because of the complexities involved in accounting standard-setting. Specifically, she is perplexed by the number of bodies issuing financial reporting standards of one kind or another and the level of authoritative support that can be attached to these reporting standards. Sandra decides that she must review the environment in which accounting standards are set, if she is to increase her understanding of the accounting profession.

Instructions
(a) Help Sandra by identifying key organizations involved in accounting standard-setting.
(b) In what ways is accounting involved in the environment as Sandra refers to it? That is, what environmental factors influence accounting and how does accounting influence its environment?

(c) Sandra asks for guidance regarding authoritative support. Please assist her by explaining what is meant by authoritative support.

(d) Give Sandra an historical overview of how standard-setting has evolved.

(e) What authority for compliance with GAAP has existed throughout the period of standard-setting?

SOLUTION TO CASE 1-2

(a) The key organizations involved in standard-setting are the AICPA, FASB, GASB, SEC, AAA, and IMA. See also (d).

(b) Modern financial accounting is the product of many influences and conditions. Accounting recognizes that people live in a world of scarce means and resources, and it helps identify efficient and inefficient users of resources. As a result, investors and lenders are able to assess the relative return and risks associated with investment opportunities.

Second, accounting recognizes and accepts society's current legal and ethical concepts of property and other rights as standards in determining equity among the varying interests in the entity. Accounting looks to its environment for its standards in regard to what property rights society protects, what society recognizes as value, and what society acknowledges as equitable and fair.

Third, accounting recognizes that economic activity is conducted by separately identifiable units--business enterprises. Accounting accumulates and reports economic activity as it affects the elements of each business enterprise.

Fourth, accounting recognizes that in highly developed, complex economic systems, some owners and investors entrust the custodianship of and control over property to managers. Accounting has become responsible for providing standards that ensure the relevance, reliability, and comparability of information reported to absentee owners.

Finally, accounting provides measures of changes in economic resources, economic obligations, and residual interests of a business enterprise in terms of money because in most economies money serves as the measure of these qualitative and quantitative attributes.

On the other hand, accounting also influences its environment by playing a key role in the conduct of economic, social, political, legal, and organizational decisions and actions. Accounting is an information system which feeds back this information to organizations and individuals, which they can use to reshape their environment.

(c) Different authoritative literature pertaining to the methods of recording accounting transactions exist today. Some authoritative literature has received more support from the profession than other literature and should be followed when recording accounting transactions. These standards and procedures are called generally accepted accounting principles (GAAP). There are three different levels of GAAP. The first level is the one with the most authoritative support. It consists of FASB Standards and Interpretations, APB Opinions and Interpretations, and CAP Accounting Research Bulletins. The second level consists of AICPA Accounting and Auditing Guides, AICPA Statements of Position, and FASB Technical Bulletins. The third level consists of AICPA Issues Papers and Practice Bulletins, FASB Concepts Statements, and other authoritative pronouncements.

Note: Between the second and third level is sometimes identified as an additional level which consists of practices or pronouncements that are widely recognized as being generally accepted because they represent prevalent practice in a particular industry or the knowledgeable application to specific circumstances of pronouncements that are generally accepted.

(d) Standard setting has evolved through the work of the following organizations:

1. American Institute of Certified Public Accountants (AICPA)--it is a national professional organization of practicing Certified Public Accountants (CPAs). Outgrowths of the AICPA have been the Committee on Accounting Procedure (CAP) and the Accounting Principles Board (APB) whose major purposes were to advance written expression of accounting principles, determine appropriate practices, and narrow the areas of difference and inconsistency in practice.

2. Financial Accounting Standards Board (FASB)--the mission of the FASB is to establish and improve standards of financial accounting and reporting for the guidance and education of the public, including issuers, auditors, and users of the financial information.

3. Governmental Accounting Standards Board (GASB)--the GASB addresses state and local governmental reporting issues.

4. Securities and Exchange Commission (SEC)--the SEC is an independent regulatory agency of the United States government which administers the Securities Act of 1933, the Securities Exchange Act of 1934, and several other acts. The SEC has broad power to prescribe the accounting practices and standards to be employed by companies that fall within its jurisdiction.

5. American Accounting Association (AAA)--the AAA is an organization of college professors and practicing accountants. Its objective is to influence the development of accounting theory by encouraging and sponsoring accounting research.

6. Institute of Management Accountants (IMA) (formerly the National Association of Accountants)--the IMA is interested in research primarily in cost and managerial accounting.

(e) The SEC and the AICPA have been the authority for compliance with GAAP. The SEC has indicated that financial statements conforming to standards set by the FASB will be presumed to have authoritative support. The AICPA, in Rule 203 of the Code of Professional Ethics, requires that members prepare financial statements in accordance with GAAP. Failure to follow Rule 203 can lead to the loss of a CPA's license to practice.

ANALYSIS OF MULTIPLE-CHOICE TYPE QUESTIONS

Question
1. The most significant current source of generally accepted accounting principles in the nongovernmental sector is the
    a. NYSE.
    b. SEC.
    c. APB.
    d. FASB.

Solution = d.

Explanation: The mission of the Financial Accounting Standards Board (FASB) is to establish and improve standards of financial accounting and reporting. The Governmental Accounting Standards Board (GASB) is responsible for developing standards to regulate state and local government reporting. The Accounting Principles Board (APB) was the predecessor of the FASB. The New York Stock Exchange has nothing to do with the development of generally accepted accounting principles.

Question
2. Members of the Financial Accounting Standards Board are
    a. employed by the American Institute of Certified Public Accountants.
    b. part-time employees.
    c. required to hold a CPA certificate.
    d. independent of any other organization.

Solution = d.

Explanation: The members of the FASB are well-paid, full-time members. The FASB is not affiliated with the AICPA; it is not an organ of any single professional organization. The FASB is answerable only to the Financial Accounting Foundation. It is not necessary to be a CPA or a member of the AICPA to be a member of the FASB. FASB members must sever all ties with CPA firms, companies, or institutions.

Question
3. Which of the following pronouncements were issued by the Accounting Principles Board?
    a. Accounting Research Bulletins.
    b. Opinions.
    c. Statements of Position.
    d. Statements on Financial Accounting Concepts.

Solution = b.

Explanation: The Accounting Principles Board issued 31 APB Opinions between the years 1962-1973. Accounting Research Bulletins (51 of them) were issued by the Committee on Accounting Procedure between 1953 and 1959. Statements of Position are issued by the AICPA (but not the APB). The FASB issues Statements on Financial Accounting Concepts (there are 6 of these to date).

Question

4.   Which of the following is less authoritative than the others?
      a.   FASB Statements on Financial Accounting Standards.
      b.   FASB Statements on Financial Accounting Concepts.
      c.   FASB Interpretations.
      d.   APB Opinions.

Solution = b.

Explanation and Approach: Think of the various levels of the authoritative literature and of the items that are included on the first, most authoritative level.

    Level One (most authoritative):
            FASB Statements on Financial Accounting Standards
            FASB Interpretations
            APB Opinions
            APB Interpretations
            CAP Accounting Research Bulletins
    Level Two
            AICPA Accounting Guides
            AICPA Auditing Guides
            AICPA Statements of Position
            FASB Technical Bulletins
    Level Three
            AICPA Issues Papers and Practice Bulletins
            FASB Statements on Financial Accounting Concepts
            Other Authoritative Pronouncements

A quick mental review of the items on these levels **before** reading the alternative answer selections should make it easy to successfully answer the question. All of the items are Level One except for the FASB Statements on Financial Accounting Concepts which are Level Three.

Question

5.   All of the following organizations are directly involved in the development of financial accounting standards (GAAP) in the United States except the
      a.   Internal Revenue Service.
      b.   Financial Accounting Standards Board.
      c.   American Institute of Certified Public Accountants.
      d.   Securities and Exchange Commission.

Solution = a.

Explanation: The Internal Revenue Service (IRS) is responsible for tax rules and administration. Although the IRS and its Internal Revenue Code are influences on accounting practice, they are not directly involved in the development of accounting standards (for financial statements) as are the other organizations listed.

CHAPTER 2

CONCEPTUAL FRAMEWORK
UNDERLYING FINANCIAL ACCOUNTING

OVERVIEW

To be useful, financial statements must be relevant and reliable so that the information is pertinent to the user's decisions and the information may be relied on to faithfully represent the business. In this chapter, we will examine the FASB's conceptual framework, basic accounting concepts, assumptions, and principles.

TIPS ON CHAPTER TOPICS

TIP: Although it can sometimes be confusing, accountants often use the terms assumptions, concepts, principles, conventions, constraints, and standards interchangeably. Regardless of the particular term used, they are all a part of GAAP (generally accepted accounting principles).

TIP: The revenue recognition principle is applied before the matching principle. The revenue recognition principle gives guidance in determining what revenues belong in a given period. The matching principle then gives guidance in what expenses to recognize during the period. According to the revenue principle, revenues are to be recognized in the period earned. Per the matching principle, expenses are to be recognized in the same period as the revenues they helped generate.

TIP: The term **recognition** refers to the process of formally recording or incorporating an item in the accounts and financial statements of an entity.

TIP: You should study **Illustration 2-1** on the hierarchy of accounting qualities until you can close your eyes and visualize that diagram on the back of your eyelids. A lot of exam questions over *SFAC No. 2* can be answered by describing what is on that diagram.

ILLUSTRATION 2-1
A HIERARCHY OF ACCOUNTING QUALITIES

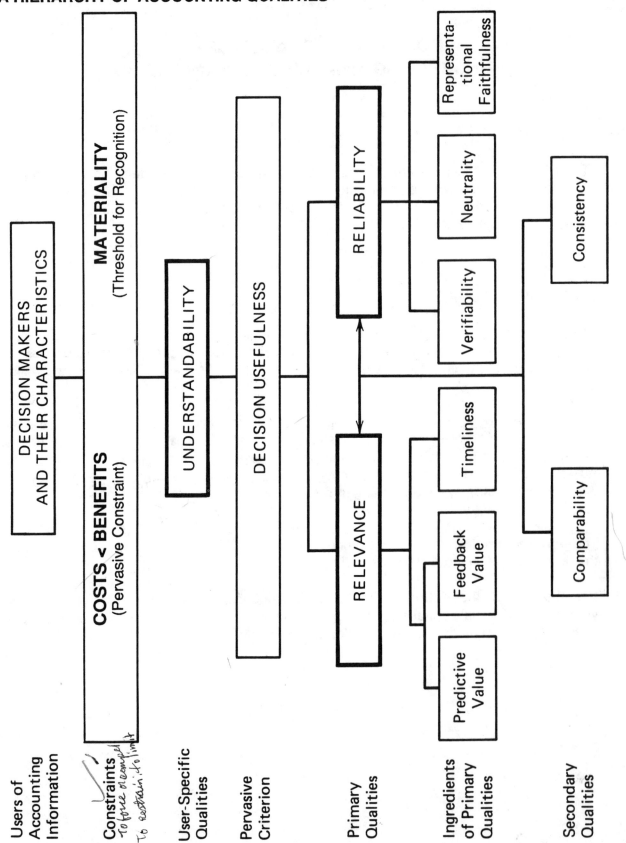

Source: FASB, *Statement of Financial Accounting Concepts No. 2,* "Qualitative Characteristics of Accounting Information."

EXERCISE 2-1

Purpose: This exercise is designed to review the qualitative characteristics that make accounting information useful for decision-making purposes (per *SFAC No. 2*).

The qualitative characteristics that make accounting information useful for decision-making purposes are as follows:

Relevance	Verifiability
Reliability	Neutrality
Predictive value	Representational faithfulness
Feedback value	Comparability
Timeliness	Consistency

Instructions
Fill in the blank to identify the appropriate qualitative characteristic(s) to be used given the information provided below.

_____   1.   Predictive value is an ingredient of this primary quality of information.

_____   2.   Two qualitative characteristics that are related to both relevance and reliability.

_____   3.   Neutrality is an ingredient of this primary quality of accounting information.

_____   4.   Two primary qualities that make accounting information useful for decision-making purposes.

_____   5.   Issuance of interim reports is an example of this secondary quality of financial information.

_____   6.   Qualitative characteristic being employed when companies in the same industry are using the same accounting principles.

_____   7.   Quality of information that confirms users' earlier expectations.

_____   8.   Imperative for providing comparisons of a firm from period to period.

_____   9.   Requires information to be free of personal and data bias.

_____   10.   Requires a high degree of consensus among individuals on a given measurement.

assumption
Broad principle
most underlying conventions - conservatism material
sub stan over fm

SOLUTION TO EXERCISE 2-1

1. Relevance.
2. Comparability and Consistency.
3. Reliability.
4. Relevance and Reliability.
5. Timeliness.

6. Comparability.
7. Feedback value.
8. Consistency.
9. Neutrality.
10. Verifiability.

Approach: Before beginning to fill in the ten blanks required, visualize the diagram for the hierarchy of accounting qualities (**Illustration 2-1**). Also, take a few minutes to individually consider the ten characteristics listed and think of the key phrases involved in describing those items. Such as:

assumption
Economic periodicity concept and cir
Going concern

Relevance--capable of making a difference in a decision.

Reliability--users can depend on information to represent what it purports to represent.

Predictive value--helps users make predictions about the outcome of past, present, and future events.

Feedback value--helps to confirm or correct prior expectations.

Timeliness--information must be available to decision makers before it loses its capacity to influence their decisions.

Verifiability--is demonstrated when a high degree of consensus can be secured among independent measurers using the same measurement methods.

Neutrality--information is not to be selected to favor one set of interested parties over another.

Representational faithfulness--correspondence or agreement between the accounting numbers and descriptions and the resources or events that these numbers and descriptions purport to represent.

Comparability--information that has been measured and reported in a similar manner for different enterprises is considered comparable.

Consistency--a company is to apply the same methods to similar accountable events from period to period.

Exercise 2-2

Purpose: This exercise will test your comprehension of the essence and significance of basic accounting assumptions, principles, and constraints.

Instructions

For each of the following phrases and statements identify (by letter) the basic accounting assumption, principle, or constraint that is **most directly** related to the given phrase. Each code letter may be used more than once.

Assumptions, Principles, and Constraints

a. Economic entity assumption.
b. Going concern assumption.
c. Monetary unit assumption.
d. Periodicity assumption.
e. Historical cost principle.
f. Revenue recognition principle.

g. Matching principle.
h. Full disclosure principle.
i. Materiality constraint.
j. Cost-benefit relationship.
k. Conservatism constraint.
l. Industry practices constraint.

Approach: Before you begin to read and answer the items listed, it would be helpful to briefly think about what you know about each of them.

Statements

_____   1. Acquisition cost is the appropriate basis for both the initial recording of assets and the subsequent accounting for those assets.

_____   2. Revenue should be recognized when it is earned, which is usually at the point of sale.

_____   3. All information necessary to ensure that the statements are not misleading should be reported.

_____   4. Anticipate no profits, but provide for all losses.

_____   5. An enterprise is separate from its owners.

_____   6. This concept eliminates the "liquidation concept" in viewing business affairs.

_____   7. Measurement of the standing and progress of entities should be made at regular intervals rather than at the end of the business life.

_____   8. Although an item such as a wastebasket may be of service for eight years, the total cost of the item may be expensed when it is purchased, because the amount is too insignificant to warrant the strict treatment of depreciation over the eight years.

_____   9. The lower-of-cost-or-market rule is an application of this concept.

_____   10. The recorded value of an acquired item should be the fair market value of what was given or the fair market value of what was received in the exchange, whichever can be more objectively determined.

_____   11. There must be complete and understandable reporting on financial statements.

_____   12. The president of a business should not loan his wife the company's credit card for personal gasoline purchases.

_____   13. In matters of doubt or uncertainty, select the accounting treatment that will result in the lowest figure for net income, assets, and owners' equity.

_____   14. Expenses should be recognized in the same period that the related revenues are recognized.

_____   15. This concept is often exemplified by numerous notes to the financial statements.

_____   16. If revenue is deferred to a future period, the related costs of generating that revenue should be deferred to the same future period.

_____   17. This concept includes a set of rules concerning when to recognize revenue and how to measure its $ amount.

_____ 18. Assets and equities are expressed in terms of a common denominator.

_____ 19. Avoid overstatement of assets, net income, and owners' equity, but do not intentionally understate them.

_____ 20. It is assumed that an organization will remain in business long enough to recover the cost of its assets.

_____ 21. Changes in the purchasing power of the dollar are so small from one period to the next that they are ignored in preparing the financial statements.

_____ 22. Items whose $ amounts are very small relative to other $ amounts on the financial statements may be accounted for in the most expedient manner, rather than requiring strict accounting treatment.

_____ 23. The cost of an item should be measured by the $ amount of the resources expended to acquire it.

_____ 24. Accruals and deferrals are often necessary in order to report revenues and expenses in the proper time periods.

_____ 25. Each accounting unit is considered separate from other accounting units.

_____ 26. An accountant assumes that a business will continue indefinitely.

_____ 27. End-of-the-period adjustments are often necessary in order to report items on the income statement in the appropriate time period(s).

_____ 28. Assets are not reported at their current worth subsequent to acquisition.

_____ 29. Depreciation of a long-term tangible asset is based on the original acquisition cost.

_____ 30. All relevant information pertaining to a business unit must be included in its financial statements.

_____ 31. If an item will not affect any business decisions, it need not be separately reported in the financial statements.

_____ 32. In order to justify requiring a particular measurement or disclosure, the benefits perceived to be derived from it must exceed the costs to be associated with it.

_____ 33. Intangibles are capitalized and amortized over periods benefited.

_____ 34. Repair tools are expensed when purchased even though they may be of use for more than one period.

_____ 35. Brokerage firms use market value for purposes of valuation of all marketable securities.

_____ 36. Each enterprise is kept as a unit distinct from its owner or owners.

_____ 37. All significant postbalance sheet events are reported.

_____ 38. Revenue is recorded at the point of sale.

_____ 39. All important aspects of bond indentures (contracts) are presented in financial statements.

_____ 40. Rationale for accrual accounting is stated.

_____ 41. Reporting must be done at defined time intervals.

_____ 42. An allowance for doubtful accounts is established.

_____ 43. All payments out of petty cash are charged to Miscellaneous Expense even though some expenditures will benefit the following period. (Do not use conservatism.)

_____ 44. No profits are anticipated but all possible losses are recognized.

_____ 45. A company charges its sales commission costs to expense.

_____ 46. Lower of cost or market is used to value inventories.

_____ 47. Financial information is presented so that reasonably prudent investors will not be misled.

SOLUTION TO EXERCISE 2-2

1.	e	9.	k	17.	f	25.	a	33.	g	41.	d
2.	f	10.	e	18.	c	26.	b	34.	i	42.	g
3.	h	11.	h	19.	k	27.	g	35.	l	43.	i
4.	k	12.	a	20.	b	28.	e	36.	a	44.	k
5.	a	13.	k	21.	c	29.	e	37.	h	45.	g
6.	b	14.	g	22.	i	30.	h	38.	f	46.	k
7.	d	15.	h	23.	e	31.	i	39.	h	47.	h
8.	i	16.	g	24.	g	32.	j	40.	g		

CASE 2-1

Purpose: This case is designed to review the FASB's conceptual framework and *SFAC No. 2.*

The Financial Accounting Standards Board (FASB) has been working on a conceptual framework for financial accounting and reporting. The FASB has issued six *Statements of Financial Accounting Concepts.* These statements are intended to set forth objectives and fundamentals that will be the basis for developing financial accounting and reporting standards. The objectives identify the goals and purposes of financial reporting. The fundamentals are the underlying concepts of financial accounting--concepts that guide the selection of transactions, events, and circumstances to be accounted for; their recognition and measurement; and the means of summarizing and communicating them to interested parties.

The purpose of *Statements of Financial Accounting Concepts No. 2*, "Qualitative Characteristics of Accounting Information," is to examine the characteristics that make accounting information useful. The characteristics or qualities of information discussed in *SFAC No. 2* are the ingredients that make information useful and the qualities to be sought when accounting choices are made.

Instructions

(a)   Identify and discuss the benefits that can be expected to be derived from the FASB's conceptual framework study.

(b)   What is the most important quality for accounting information as identified in *Statement of Financial Accounting Concepts No. 2*. Explain why it is the most important.

(c)   *Statement of Financial Accounting Concepts No. 2* describes a number of key characteristics or qualities for accounting information. Briefly discuss the importance of any three of these qualities for financial reporting purposes.

SOLUTION TO CASE 2-1

(a)   The FASB's conceptual framework study should provide benefits to the accounting community such as
   1.   guiding the FASB in establishing accounting standards on a consistent basis.
   2.   determining bounds for judgment in preparing financial statements by prescribing the nature, functions, and limits of financial accounting and reporting.
   3.   increasing users' understanding of and confidence in financial reporting.

(b)   *Statement of Financial Accounting Concepts No. 2* identifies the most important quality for accounting information as usefulness for decision-making. Relevance and reliability are the primary qualities leading to this decision usefulness. Usefulness is the most important quality because, without usefulness, there would be no benefits from information to set against its costs.

(c)   A number of key characteristics or qualities that make accounting information desirable are described in the *Statement of Financial Accounting Concepts No. 2*. They are discussed below.
   1.   **Understandability**--information provided by financial reporting should be comprehensible to those who have a reasonable understanding of business and economic activities and are willing to study the information with reasonable diligence. Financial information is a tool and, like most tools, cannot be of much direct help to those who are unable or unwilling to use it or who misuse it.
   2.   **Relevance**--accounting information is capable of making a difference in a decision by helping users to form predictions about the outcomes of past, present, and future events or to confirm or correct expectations.
   3.   **Reliability**--the reliability of a measure rests on the faithfulness with which it represents what it purports to represent, coupled with an assurance for the user, which comes through verification, that it has representational quality.
   4.   **Predictive value**--relevant information helps users make predictions about the outcome of past, present, and future events.
   5.   **Feedback value**--relevant information helps users confirm or correct prior expectations.
   6.   **Timeliness**--to be relevant, accounting information must be available to decision makers before it loses its capacity to influence their decisions.
   7.   **Verifiability**--information can be said to be verifiable when a large number of independent observers derive similar results using the same measurement methods.

8. **Neutrality**--neutrality means that the information is free from bias towards a predetermined result.
9. **Representational faithfulness**--means correspondence or agreement between the accounting numbers and descriptions and the resources or events that these numbers and descriptions purport to represent.
10. **Comparability**--accounting information that has been measured and reported in a similar manner for different enterprises is considered comparable.
11. **Consistency**--accounting information is consistent when an entity applies the same accounting treatment from period to period to similar accountable events.

CASE 2-2

Purpose: This case is designed to review the three methods of matching expenses with revenues and examples of each.

An unexpired cost represents probable future benefits and hence is accounted for as an asset. An expired cost represents an expiration of benefits and hence is accounted for as an expense or a loss. There are three common bases of expense recognition: (1) cause and effect, (2) systematic and rational allocation, and (3) immediate recognition.

Instructions
Describe each of the three bases of expense recognition and give a few examples of each for a retail establishment.

SOLUTION TO CASE 2-2

1. **Cause and effect.**
   When there is a direct association between a cost and a particular revenue transaction, the expense recognition should accompany the revenue recognition; that is, the cost is expensed in the same time period that the related specific revenue is recognized.
   Examples: Cost of goods sold, sales commissions, transportation-out.

2. **Systematic and rational allocation.**
   This basis is used when although a cost benefits the revenue generating process of two or more accounting periods, the cost cannot be related to particular revenue transactions. Even though a close cause-and-effect relationship between revenue and cost cannot be determined, this relationship is assumed to exist. The cost is thus initially accounted for as an asset and then allocated to the periods benefited (as an expense) in a systematic and rational manner. The allocation method used should appear reasonable to an unbiased observer and should be consistently applied from period to period.
   Examples: Depreciation of plant assets, amortization of intangibles, amortization of prepaids (such as rent and insurance).

3. **Immediate recognition.**
   This basis is used for costs that fall in the following categories:
   (a) their incurrence during the period provides no discernible future benefits.
   (b) they must be incurred each accounting period, and no build-up of expected future benefits occurs.

(c) by their nature they relate to current revenues even though they cannot be directly associated with any specific revenues.

(d) the amount of cost to be deferred can be measured only in an arbitrary manner or great uncertainty exists regarding the realization of future benefits.

(e) uncertainty exists regarding whether allocating them to current and future periods will serve any useful purpose.

(f) they are measures of asset costs recorded in prior periods from which no future benefits are now discernible.

Examples: Sales salaries, office salaries, utilities, repairs, advertising, accounting and legal, research and development, postage.

ANALYSIS OF MULTIPLE-CHOICE TYPE QUESTIONS

Question
1. According to *Statement of Financial Accounting Concepts No. 2*, timeliness is an ingredient of

	Relevance	Reliability
a.	Yes	Yes
b.	Yes	No
c.	No	No
d.	No	Yes

Solution = b.

Explanation: In the diagram of the hierarchy of accounting qualities, timeliness is linked to the relevance box and not the reliability box. Therefore, we want to respond "Yes" to the relevance column and "No" to the reliability column.

Approach: In answering this question, read the stem and answer "Yes" (true) or "No" (false) when completing the statement with the word **relevance.** Then reread the stem and answer "Yes" or "No" when completing the statement with the word **reliability.** Then look for the corresponding combination of "Yes" and "No" to select your answer.

Question
2. According to **Statement of Financial Accounting Concepts No. 2,** which of the following is considered a pervasive constraint?
   a. Representational faithfulness.
   b. Verifiability.
   c. Comparability.
   d. Costs < Benefits.

Solution = d.

Explanation: Selections a. and b. are incorrect because representational faithfulness and verifiability are both ingredients of primary qualities of accounting information. Selection c. is incorrect because comparability is a secondary quality of accounting information. Selection d. is correct because *SFAS*

No. 2 states that "in order to justify requiring a particular measurement or disclosure, the benefits perceived to be derived from it must exceed the costs perceived to be associated with it."

<u>Approach:</u> In visualizing the diagram for a hierarchy of accounting qualities (**Illustration 2-1**), it is an easy task to identify why costs < benefits is the pervasive constraint in question and why the other selections can be eliminated in selecting the correct response.

Question

3. If the LIFO inventory method was used last period, it should be used for the current and following periods because of
    a. materiality.
    b. verifiability.
    c. timeliness.
    d. consistency.

Solution = d.

<u>Explanation:</u> Selection a. is incorrect because materiality refers to a constraint whereby an item is to be given strict accounting treatment unless it is insignificant. Verifiability refers to an ingredient of reliability (it is demonstrated when a high degree of consensus can be secured among independent measurers using the same measurement methods). Timeliness is an ingredient of relevance which indicates that for information to be relevant, it must be prepared on a timely basis. Selection d. is correct because consistency is a secondary quality of accounting information. To be useful, financial statements should reflect consistent application of generally accepted accounting principles. This means that a company should apply the same methods to similar accountable events from period to period.

<u>Approach:</u> In reading the stem of the question, cover up the answer selections. Anticipate the correct answer by attempting to complete the statement given. This process should yield the answer of "consistency." If you cannot think of the word to complete the statement, then take each answer selection and write down what each means. You should then be able to match up the question with answer selection d.

Question

4. Pluto Magazine Company sells space to advertisers. The company requires an advertiser to pay for services one month before publication. Advertising revenue should be recognized when
    a. an advertiser places an order.
    b. a bill is sent to an advertiser.
    c. the related cash is received.
    d. the related ad is published.

Solution = d.

<u>Explanation:</u> At the points where an order is placed and a bill is sent to an advertiser, revenue has neither been realized nor earned. At the point when the cash is received in advance of the publication, the revenue is realized but not earned. The revenue is earned when the related ad is published and, thus, should be recognized then.

Approach: Read the last sentence of the stem. We want to know the point at which revenue should be recognized. Write down what you know from the revenue recognition principle. Revenue is generally recognized when (1) realized or realizable, and (2) earned. Read the stem and think of how to apply the revenue recognition principle to the facts given.

Question
5. The assumption that a business enterprise will remain in business indefinitely and will not liquidate in the near future is called the
   a. economic entity assumption.
   b. going concern assumption.
   c. monetary unit assumption.
   d. periodicity assumption.

Solution = b.

Explanation: Answer selection a. is incorrect because the economic entity assumption indicates that the activities of an accounting entity should be kept separate from all other accounting entities. Selection c. is incorrect because the monetary unit assumption indicates that all transactions and events can be measured in terms of a common denominator--units of money. Selection d. is incorrect because the periodicity assumption indicates that the economic activities of an enterprise can be divided into equally spaced artificial time periods. Selection b. is correct because the going concern assumption implies that an enterprise will continue in business and will not liquidate within the foreseeable future.

Approach: Read the stem (while covering up the answer selections) and attempt to complete the statement. Compare your attempt with the selections. Hopefully, you anticipated the answer of "going concern assumption." If your attempt does not match any of the selections given, take each selection and write down the key words in the definitions of the term. This process should lead you to the correct response.

CHAPTER 3

A REVIEW OF THE ACCOUNTING PROCESS

OVERVIEW

Accounting information must be accumulated and summarized before it can be communicated and analyzed. In this chapter we will discuss the steps involved in the accounting cycle. We will emphasize the subject of adjusting entries. Adjusting entries are required so that revenues and expenses are reflected on an accrual basis of accounting. Adjusting entries are simply entries required to bring account balances up to date. The failure to record proper adjustments will cause errors on both the income statement and the balance sheet.

This chapter is an extremely important one. A good understanding of this chapter and an ability to think and work quickly with the concepts incorporated herein are necessary for comprehending subsequent chapters. Although adjusting entries were introduced in your principles course, you are likely to discover new dimensions to this subject in your intermediate accounting course. Pay close attention when studying this chapter.

TIPS ON CHAPTER TOPICS

TIP: **None** of the adjusting entries discussed in Chapter 3 involve the **Cash** account. Therefore, if you are instructed to record **adjusting entries,** double check your work when it is completed. If you have used the Cash account in any adjusting entry, it is very likely in error. (The only time Cash belongs in an adjusting entry is when a bank reconciliation discloses a need to adjust the Cash account--see Chapter 7 for this--or when an error has been made that involves the Cash account, in which case a correcting entry is required.)

TIP: Each adjusting entry discussed in this chapter involves a balance sheet account (a real account) and an income statement account (a nominal account).

TIP: Keep in mind that for accrued items (accrued revenues and accrued expenses), the related cash flow follows the adjusting entry; whereas, with deferred items (unearned revenues and prepaid expenses), the related cash flow precedes the adjusting entry.

TIP: In an adjusting entry for an accrual (accrued revenue or accrued expense), the word "accrued" is **not** needed in either account title. If you choose to use the word "accrued" in an account title, it is appropriate to do so **only** in the balance sheet account title. For example, the entry to record accrued salaries of $1,000 is as follows:

Salaries Expense	1,000	
Salaries Payable		1,000

The word "accrued" is not needed in either account title, but it could be used in the liability account title if desired (the account title would then be Accrued Salaries Payable). It would be wrong to insert the word "accrued" in the expense account title. Some people simply call the credit account "Accrued Salaries" but we advise that you include the key word "Payable" and omit the unnecessary "Accrued."

TIP: If cash is **received** in a rental situation, the amount will be recorded in either an earned rental revenue account or an unearned rental revenue account, **not** in an expense or a prepaid expense account. Cash received for rent relates to revenue or unearned revenue. If cash is **paid** in a rental situation, the amount will be recorded in either an expense or a prepaid expense account.

TIP: An interest rate is an annual rate unless otherwise indicated. For preparing an adjusting entry involving interest, compute interest assuming the rate given is for a whole year, unless it is evident that this is not the case. Also, assume a 360 day year, unless otherwise indicated.

TIP:
1. An **accrued revenue** is a revenue that has been earned but has not been received. An adjusting entry for an accrued revenue involves a REVENUE account and an ASSET (receivable) account.
2. An **accrued expense** is an expense that has been incurred but has not been paid. An adjusting entry for an accrued expense involves an EXPENSE account and a LIABILITY (payable) account.
3. A **deferred revenue** (unearned revenue) is a revenue that has been collected but has not been earned. An adjusting entry for a deferred revenue involves a REVENUE account and a LIABILITY (unearned revenue) account.
4. A **deferred expense** (prepaid expense) is an expense that has been paid but has not been incurred. An adjusting entry for a deferred expense involves an EXPENSE account and an ASSET (prepaid expense) account.

TIP: In determining whether it is appropriate or not to reverse an adjusting entry, it can be helpful to write down what the reversing entry would look like and then (1) think about the effects that the reversing entry would have on the account balances in the accounting period that follows the one for which the adjustment was made, and (2) think about whether those effects are appropriate or not.

TIP: It is appropriate to reverse an adjusting entry involving a deferral (prepaid expense or un-earned revenue) **only if** the adjustment increases (rather than decreases) a balance sheet account. It is **always** appropriate to reverse an adjusting entry involving an accrual. It is **never** appropriate to reverse an adjusting entry for depreciation or amortization.

TIP: If the estimate for uncollectible accounts receivable is to be based on a percentage of net sales, the expense figure is a percentage of net sales and any existing balance in the Allowance account will **not** affect the amount of the adjusting entry. If the estimate for uncollectible accounts receivable is to be based on an aging of accounts receivable or a percentage of accounts receivable, the desired ending balance for the Allowance account is determined and any existing balance in the Allowance account **will** affect the amount of the adjusting entry.

TIP: The Cost of Goods Sold account is an expense account; therefore, it is increased by debits and decreased by credits. The normal balance of the Cost of Goods Sold account is a debit balance.

TIP: A deferred expense is so named because the recognition of expense is being deferred (put-off) to a future period; thus a debit is carried on the balance sheet now and will be released to the income statement in a future period when the related benefits are consumed (expense is incurred).

TIP: An unearned revenue is often called deferred revenue because the recognition of revenue is being deferred to a future period; thus a credit is carried on the balance sheet now and will be released to the income statement in a future period when the related revenue is earned.

TIP: In an adjusting entry to record accrued interest revenue (revenue earned but not received), the debit is to an asset account and the credit is to a revenue account. Possible names for that asset account are Interest Receivable and Accrued Interest Receivable. Possible names for the revenue account include Interest Revenue, Interest Income, and Interest Earned.

TIP: In an adjusting entry to record accrued salaries expense (expense incurred, but not paid) the debit is to an expense account and the credit is to a liability account. The expense account is usually titled Salaries Expense. Possible names for the liability account include Salaries Payable and Accrued Salaries Payable.

TIP: An adjusting entry for deferred rent revenue (revenue collected but not earned) involves a revenue account and a liability account. The revenue account is often called Rent Revenue or Rental Income or Rent Earned. Possible titles for the liability account include Unearned Rent Revenue, Unearned Rent, Deferred Rent Revenue, Rent Revenue Received in Advance, and Rental Income Collected in Advance. The use of Prepaid Rent Revenue as an account title is **not** appropriate because the term prepaid usually refers to the payment of cash in advance, not the receipt of cash in advance.

TIP: An adjusting entry for deferred insurance expense (expense paid but not incurred) involves an expense account and an asset account. The expense account is often called Insurance Expense or Expired Insurance. Possible titles for the asset account include Prepaid Insurance, Deferred Insurance Expense, Prepaid Insurance Expense, Deferred Insurance, and Unexpired Insurance.

TIP: A nominal account with a credit balance is closed by a debit to that account and a credit to Income Summary. A nominal account with a debit balance is closed by a credit to that account and a debit to Income Summary. The Income Summary is closed to owners' equity (Retained Earnings for a corporation).

TIP: Closing entries are necessary at the end of an accounting period to prepare the nominal accounts for the recording of transactions of the next accounting period. Closing entries are prepared after the nominal account balances have been used to prepare the income statement. Only nominal accounts are closed. Real accounts are never closed; their balances continue into the next accounting period. **Nominal** accounts are often called **temporary** accounts; **real** accounts are often called **permanent** accounts.

TIP: A **post-closing trial balance** contains only real account because the nominal accounts all have a zero balance after the closing process. A post closing trial balance is prepared to check on the equality of debits and credits after the closing process.

ILLUSTRATION 3-1
REVERSING ENTRIES

JOURNAL ENTRIES

	Accounting System Where Reversing Entries ARE Used	Accounting System Where Reversing Entries are NOT Used
(1) During 1992	Interest Expense.......... 80,000 　　Cash.......... 80,000	Interest Expense.......... 80,000 　　Cash.......... 80,000
(2) 12/31/92 Adjusting	Interest Expense.......... 5,500 　　Interest Payable... 5,500	Interest Expense.......... 5,500 　　Interest Payable... 5,500
(3) 12/31/92 Closing	Income Summary.......... 85,500 　　Interest Expense.. 85,500	Income Summary.......... 85,500 　　Interest Expense.. 85,500
(4) 1/1/93 Reversing	Interest Payable.......... 5,500 　　Interest Expense.. 5,500	No entry.
(5) 1/1/93 Payment	Interest Expense.......... 6,000 　　Cash.......... 6,000	Interest Expense.......... 500 Interest Payable.......... 5,500 　　Cash.......... 6,000

LEDGER ACCOUNT POSTINGS

Accounting System Where Reversing Entries ARE Used

	Interest Expense		Interest Payable	
(1) During 1992	80,000			
(2) 12/31/92 Adjusting	5,500			5,500
(3) 12/31/92 Closing		85,500		
(4) 1/1/93 Reversing		5,500	5,500	
(5) 1/1/93 Payment	6,000			

Accounting System Where Reversing Entries are NOT Used

	Interest Expense		Interest Payable	
(1) During 1992	80,000			
(2) 12/31/92 Adjusting	5,500			5,500
(3) 12/31/92 Closing		85,500		
(4) 1/1/93 Reversing				
(5) 1/1/93 Payment	500		5,500	

FINANCIAL STATEMENTS

	ARE Used	NOT Used
Interest Expense for the year 1992	$85,500	$85,500
Interest Paid in 1992	$80,000	$80,000
Balance of Interest Payable at close of business on 12/31/92	$5,500	$5,500
Interest Expense for the day 1/1/93	$500	$500
Balance of Interest Payable at close of business on 1/1/93	$ 0	$ 0

EXERCISE 3-1

Purpose: This exercise will provide you with examples of adjusting entries for the accrual of expenses and revenues.

The following information relates to the Yuppy Clothing Sales Company at the end of 1992. The accounting period is the calendar year. This is the company's first year of operations.

1. Employees are paid every Friday for the five-day work week ending on that day. Salaries amount to $2,400 per week. The accounting period ends on a Thursday.
2. On October 1, 1992, Yuppy borrowed $8,000 cash by signing a note payable due in one year at 8% interest. Interest is due when the principal is due.
3. A note for $2,000 was received from a customer in a sales transaction on May 1, 1992. The note matures in one year and bears 12% interest per annum.
4. A portion of Yuppy's parking lot is used by executives of a neighboring company. A person pays $6 per day for each day's use and the parking fees are due by the fifth business day following the month of use. The fees for December 31, 1992 amount to $1,260.

Instructions
Prepare the necessary adjusting entries at December 31, 1992.

SOLUTION TO EXERCISE 3-1

1. Salaries Expense 1,920
       Salaries Payable 1,920
         ($2,400 ÷ 5 = $480); ($480 X 4 = $1,920)

2. Interest Expense 160
       Interest Payable 160
         ($8,000 X 8% X 3/12 = $160)

3. Interest Receivable 160
       Interest Revenue 160
         ($2,000 X 12% X 8/12 = $160)

4. Parking Fees Receivable 1,260
       Parking Fees Revenue 1,260

Approach An accrued expense is an expense that has been incurred but not paid. The "incurred" part results in an increase in Expense (debit) and the "not paid" part results in an increase in Payable (credit). An accrued revenue is a revenue that has been earned but not received. The earned part results in an increase in a Revenue (credit) and the not received part results in an increase in a Receivable (debit).

EXERCISE 3-2

Purpose: This exercise will provide you with examples of adjusting entries for the:
  (1) Deferral of expense when cash payments are recorded in an asset (real) account.
  (2) Deferral of expense when cash payments are recorded in an expense (nominal) account.
  (3) Deferral of revenue when cash receipts are recorded in a liability (real) account.
  (4) Deferral of revenue when cash receipts are recorded in a revenue (nominal) account.

Each situation described below is independent of the others.

(1) Office supplies are recorded in an asset account when acquired. There were no supplies on hand at the beginning of the period. Cash purchase of office supplies during the period amounted to $900. A count of supplies at the end of the period shows $320 worth to be on hand.

(2) Office supplies are recorded in an asset account when acquired. There were $400 of supplies on hand at the beginning of the period. Cash purchases of office supplies during the period amount to $900. A count of supplies at the end of the period shows $320 worth to be on hand.

(3) Office supplies are recorded in an expense account when acquired. There were no supplies on hand at the beginning of the period. Cash purchases of office supplies during the period amounted to $900. A count of supplies at the end of the period shows $320 worth to be on hand.

(4) Office supplies are recorded in an expense account when acquired. There were $400 of supplies on hand at the beginning of the period. Cash purchases of office supplies during the period amount to $900. A count of supplies at the end of the period shows $320 worth to be on hand. Reversing entries are used when appropriate.

(5) Receipts from customers for magazine subscriptions are recorded as a liability when cash is collected in advance of delivery. There was no beginning balance in the liability account. During the period, $54,000 was received for subscriptions. At the end of the period, it was determined that the balance of the Unearned Subscription Revenue account should be $8,000.

(6) Receipts from customers for magazine subscriptions are recorded as a liability when cash is collected in advance of delivery. The beginning balance in the liability account was $6,700. During the period, $54,000 was received for subscriptions. At the end of the period, it was determined that the balance of the Unearned Subscription Revenue account should be $8,000.

(7) Receipts from customers for magazine subscriptions are recorded as revenue when cash is collected in advance of delivery. There was no balance in the Unearned Subscription Revenue account at the beginning of the period. During the period, $54,000 was received for subscriptions. At the end of the period, it was determined that the balance of the Unearned Subscription Revenue account should be $8,000.

(8) Receipts from customers for magazine subscriptions are recorded as revenue when cash is collected in advance of delivery. The beginning balance in the liability account was $6,700. During the period, $54,000 was received for subscriptions. At the end of the period, it was

3-6

determined that the balance of the Unearned Subscription Revenue account should be $8,000. Reversing entries are used when appropriate.

Instructions

For each of the **independent** situations above:

(a)   Prepare the appropriate adjusting entry in general journal form.
(b)   Indicate the amount of revenue or expense which will appear on the income statement for the period.
(c)   Indicate the balance of the applicable asset or liability account at the end of the period.
(d)   Indicate the amount of cash received or paid during the period.
(e)   Indicate the change in the applicable asset or liability account from the beginning of the period to the end of the period.

HINT: It would be helpful to draw T-accounts for each situation. Enter the information given as it would be, or needs to be, reflected in the accounts. Solve for the adjusting entry that would be necessary to "reconcile" the facts given.

SOLUTION TO EXERCISE 3-2

(1)   (a)   Office Supplies Expense   580
                Office Supplies on Hand   580
(b)   Office Supplies Expense $580
(c)   Office Supplies on Hand $320
(d)   Cash paid $900
(e)   Increase in Office Supplies on Hand $320

Approach:

Office Supplies on Hand		Office Supplies Expense	
Acquisitions 900	(580) ← ENTRY NEEDED TO COMPLETE ACCOUNTS → (580)		
Desired End-ing Balance 320		Ending Balance 580	

(2)   (a)   Office Supplies Expense   980
                Office Supplies on Hand   980
(b)   Office Supplies Expense $980
(c)   Office Supplies on Hand $320
(d)   Cash paid $900
(e)   Decrease in Office Supplies on Hand $80

352,750

210 900

18 0400

Approach:

```
        Office Supplies on Hand                          Office Supplies Expense
────────────────────────────────────        ────────────────────────────────────
Begin. Bal.     400  │ (980)── ENTRY NEEDED TO COMPLETE ACCOUNTS ──▶(980)
Acquisitions    900  │                                    │
Desired End-         │                        Ending      │
  ing Balance  320   │                          Balance    980
```

(3) (a) Office Supplies on Hand 320
             Office Supplies Expense   320
    (b) Office Supplies Expense $580
    (c) Office Supplies on Hand $320
    (d) Cash paid $900
    (e) Increase in Office Supplies on Hand $320

Approach:

```
        Office Supplies Expense                          Office Supplies on Hand
────────────────────────────────────        ────────────────────────────────────
Acquisitions   900   │ (320)── ENTRY NEEDED TO COMPLETE ACCOUNTS ──▶(320)
                     │                                    │
Ending Bal.    580   │                        Desired End-│
                     │                          ing Bal.    320
```

(4) (a) Office Supplies on Hand 320
             Office Supplies Expense   320
    (b) Office Supplies Expense $980
    (c) Office Supplies on Hand $320
    (d) Cash paid $900
    (e) Decrease in Office Supplies on Hand $80

Approach:

```
        Office Supplies Expense                          Office Supplies on Hand
────────────────────────────────────        ────────────────────────────────────
                                              Beginning
Reversing      400   │                          Bal.        400   │
Acquisitions   900   │                                            │
              (320)── ENTRY NEEDED TO COMPLETE ACCOUNTS ──▶(320)  │ Reversing   400
────────────────────────────────────        ──────────────────────────────────────
Ending Bal.    980   │                        Desired End-
                                                ing Balance  320
```

(5)   (a)   Unearned Subscription Revenue   46,000
                 Subscription Revenue   46,000

      (b)   Subscription Revenue $46,000
      (c)   Unearned Subscription Revenue $8,000
      (d)   Cash received $54,000
      (e)   Increase in Unearned Subscription Revenue $8,000

Approach:

Subscription Revenue	Unearned Subscription Revenue
	Receipts 54,000
(46,000) ←ENTRY NEEDED TO COMPLETE ACCOUNTS→ (46,000)	
Ending Bal. 46,000	Desired End Bal. 8,000

(6)   (a)   Unearned Subscription Revenue   52,700
                 Subscription Revenue   52,700

      (b)   Subscription Revenue $52,700
      (c)   Unearned Subscription Revenue $8,000
      (d)   Cash received $54,000
      (e)   Increase in Unearned Subscription Revenue $1,300

Approach:

Subscription Revenue	Unearned Subscription Revenue
	Beg. Bal. 6,700 Receipts 54,000
(52,700) ←ENTRY NEEDED TO COMPLETE ACCOUNTS→ (52,700)	
Ending Bal. 52,700	Desired End. Bal. 8,000

(7)   (a)   Subscription Revenue   8,000
                 Unearned Subscription Revenue   8,000

      (b)   Subscription Revenue $46,000
      (c)   Unearned Subscription Revenue $8,000
      (d)   Cash received $54,000
      (e)   Increase in Unearned Subscription Revenue $8,000

Approach:

Unearned Subscription Revenue	Subscription Revenue
	Receipts 54,000
(8,000) ←ENTRY NEEDED TO COMPLETE ACCOUNTS→ (8,000)	
Desired End. Bal. 8,000	Ending Balance 46,000

(8)	(a)	Subscription Revenue	8,000	
		Unearned Subscription Revenue		8,000
	(b)	Subscription Revenue	$52,700	
	(c)	Unearned Subscription Revenue	$8,000	
	(d)	Cash received	$54,000	
	(e)	Increase in Unearned Subscription Revenue	$1,300	

Approach:

Unearned Subscription Revenue				Subscription Revenue	
	Beg. Bal. 6,700				Reversing 6,700
Reversing 6,700					Receipts 54,000
	8,000	ENTRY NEEDED TO COMPLETE ACCOUNTS	8,000		
	Desired End. Bal. 8,000				End. Bal. 52,700

EXERCISE 3-3

Purpose: This exercise will illustrate the preparation of adjusting entries from an unadjusted trial balance and additional data.

The following list of accounts and their balances represents the unadjusted trial balance of Tami Corp. at December 31, 1992.

	Dr.	Cr.
Cash	$ 6,000	
Accounts Receivable	49,000	
Allowance for Doubtful Accounts		$ 750
Inventory	58,000	
Prepaid Insurance	2,940	
Prepaid Rent	13,200	
Investment in Dukakis Corp. Bonds	18,000	
Land	10,000	
Plant and Equipment	104,000	
Accumulated Depreciation		18,000
Accounts Payable		9,310
Bonds Payable		50,000
Discount on Bonds Payable	1,500	
Capital Stock		100,000
Retained Earnings		80,660
Sales		213,310
Rental Revenue		10,200
Purchases	170,000	
Purchase Discounts		2,400
Transportation-Out	9,000	
Transportation-In	3,500	
Salaries and Wages	35,000	
Interest Expense	3,600	
Miscellaneous Expense	890	
	$484,630	$484,630

Additional data:

1. On November 1, 1992, Tami received $10,200 rent from its lessee for a 12-month lease beginning on that date, crediting Rent Revenue.
2. Tami estimates that 4% of the Accounts Receivable balances on December 31, 1992, will become uncollectible. On December 28, 1992, the bookkeeper incorrectly credited Sales for a collection of cash on a customer's account receivable in the amount of $1,000. This error had not yet been corrected on December 31.
3. Per a physical count, inventory on hand at December 31, 1992, was $65,000. Record the adjusting entry for inventory by using a Cost of Goods Sold account.
4. Prepaid Insurance contains the premium costs of two policies: Policy A, cost of $1,320, 2-year term, taken out on September 1, 1992, Policy B, cost of $1,620, 3-year term, taken out on April 1, 1992.
5. The regular rate of depreciation is 10% per year. Acquisitions and retirements during a year are depreciated at half this rate. There were no retirements during the year. On December 31, 1991, the balance of Plant and Equipment was $90,000.
6. On April 1, 1992, Tami issued 50 $1,000, 10% bonds, maturing on April 1, 2002, at 97% of par value. Interest payment dates are April 1 and October 1. The straight-line method is used to amortize any bond premium or discount. Amortization is recorded only at year-end.
7. On August 1, 1992, Tami purchased 18 $1,000, 10% Dukakis Corp. bonds, maturing on July 31, 1994, at par value. Interest payment dates are July 31 and January 31.
8. On May 30, 1992, Tami rented a warehouse for $1,100 per month, paying $13,200 in advance, debiting Prepaid Rent.

Instructions

(a) Prepare the year-end adjusting and correcting entries in general journal form using the information above.
(b) Indicate the adjusting entries that could be reversed.

SOLUTION TO EXERCISE 3-3

(a) 1.   Rent Revenue 8,500
              Unearned Rent Revenue 8,500
              ($10,200 X 10/12 = $8,500)

     2a. Sales... 1,000
              Accounts Receivable 1,000

      b. Bad Debt Expense 1,170
              Allowance for Doubtful Accounts 1,170
              [.04 ($49,000 - $1,000) - $750 = $1,170]

     3.   Inventory 65,000
          Purchase Discounts 2,400
          Cost of Goods Sold 164,100
              Inventory 58,000
              Transportation-In 3,500
              Purchases 170,000

4.	Insurance Expense	625	
	Prepaid Insurance		625
	($1,320 X 4/24 = $220); ($1,620 X 9/36 = $405)		
	($220 + $405 = $625)		

5.	Depreciation Expense	9,700	
	Accumulated Depreciation		9,700
	($90,000 X .10 = $9,000); ($14,000 X .05 = $700)		
	($9,000 + $700 = $9,700)		

6a.	Interest Expense	1,250	
	Interest Payable		1,250
	($50,000 X 10% X 3/12 = $1,250)		

b.	Interest Expense	113	
	Discount on Bonds Payable		113
	($1,500/10 X 9/12 = $113)		

7.	Interest Receivable	750	
	Interest Revenue		750
	($18,000 X .10 X 5/12 = $750)		

8.	Rent Expense	7,700	
	Prepaid Rent		7,700
	($13,200 X 7/12 = $7,700)		

(b)   Reverse: 1, 6a, and 7.

Explanation:

(a)   1.   On November 1, 1992, cash was received and recorded as follows:

| Cash .... | 10,200 | |
| Rent Revenue .... | | 10,200 |

At December 31, 1992, before adjustment, there is no Unearned Rent Revenue account on the trial balance. We need a balance of $8,500 (10 X $10,200 ÷ 12) in Unearned Rent Revenue at the balance sheet date. Therefore, in an adjusting entry, Unearned Rent Revenue is credited for $8,500. The other half of an adjusting entry dealing with Unearned Rent Revenue always has to be Rent Revenue. The debit to Rent Revenue in this exercise will reduce the balance in the earned revenue account to the amount actually earned.

2.   The error must be corrected before the entry can be made for the estimated uncollectible accounts. The desired ending balance for the Allowance for Doubtful Accounts account is 4% of the ending Accounts Receivable balance. The existing balance in the allowance account before adjustment, therefore, will affect the amount required in the adjusting entry.

3.   The beginning inventory amount is removed from the Inventory account by a credit (and added to Cost of Goods Sold by a debit). Purchases and Transportation-In are added to cost of goods sold by transferring the balances of their accounts to the Cost of Goods

Sold account. Purchase discounts are deducted from cost of goods sold. The ending inventory is established in the Inventory account and deducted from cost of goods sold by a debit to Inventory and a credit to Cost of Goods Sold. The foregoing is done in one compound entry in the solution shown. The same things could be accomplished by an alternative equivalent set of four entries as follows:

Cost of Goods Sold	58,000	
Inventory		58,000
Cost of Goods Sold	173,500	
Purchases		3,500
Transportation-In		170,000
Purchase Discounts	2,400	
Cost of Goods Sold		2,400
Inventory	65,000	
Cost of Goods Sold		65,000

4. Before adjustment, the cost of all insurance premiums is in the Prepaid Insurance account. The expired portion must be taken out of Prepaid Insurance (credit) and put into Insurance Expense (debit).

5. Of the $104,000 ending balance in Plant and Equipment, $90,000 represents items held during the whole year and $14,000 represents acquisitions during the year (to be depreciated for only one-half of a year--that is at a 5% rate). A 10% rate of depreciation per year is equivalent to depreciating assets over a 10-year period using the straight-line method.

6. Interest must be accrued since the last interest payment date (October 1) so three months of interest belong in the accrual entry. The discount (3% of the par value) is to be amortized on a straight-line basis from the date of issuance (April 1, 1992) to the date of maturity (April 1, 2002) which is a ten year period.

7. Interest must be accrued since the last interest payment date, which is five months. The 10% interest rate stated is expressed on an annual basis.

8. The advance payment was for twelve months. At December 31, 1992, seven months have passed for which the rent was paid, so the expired portion of the rent must be removed from the Prepaid Rent (asset) account and put into the Rent Expense account.

(b) Accrual type adjusting entries can always be reversed. Therefore, items 6a. and 7 can be reversed. Estimated items such as depreciation of plant assets, the recognition of bad debts, and amortization of intangibles and discounts and premiums on receivables and payables should **never** be reversed. Therefore, items 2b., 5, and 6b. should **not** be reversed. The entry to adjust the Inventory account and to record cost of goods sold is **never** to be reversed, so item 3 is not reversed. Adjustments involving deferrals can be reversed if the original cash entry involved a nominal account (revenue or expense account) rather than a prepaid or unearned account (a real account) and the adjustment **increases** a prepaid expense or unearned revenue account. Therefore, item 1 **can be** reversed but items 4 and 8 should **not** be reversed.

EXERCISE 3-4

Purpose: This exercise will help you develop skill in recognizing circumstances which involve:
(a)   An accrual, or
(b)   A deferral, or
(c)   Neither an accrual nor a deferral.

Instructions

Assume it is now Thursday, December 31, 1992. For each of the situations below, indicate whether (a) an accrual, or (b) a deferral, or (c) neither an accrual nor deferral is involved. You may use the designated letters (a), (b), and (c) to indicate your answers. The accounting period is the calendar year of 1992.

Answers   Situations

_____   1.   A check was written on June 2, 1992, for $6,000 to pay for an insurance policy which covers the period June 1, 1992 through May 31, 1993. An asset was debited.

_____   2.   At December 31, 1992, the company reviews tenants' records and notes that rent of $3,000 has been earned but not received.

_____   3.   The company has some revenue that has been received but has not been earned as of December 31, 1992.

_____   4.   Property taxes for the period July 1, 1992 through June 30, 1993 amount to $9,000 and are due by July 31, 1993.

_____   5. $1,200 was received from a tenant on December 20, 1992, to cover the months of Dec., Jan., and Feb.

_____   6.   At Jan. 1, 1992, office supplies on hand were valued at $220. During the year, purchases of office supplies amounted to $800. On Dec. 31, a count of supplies discloses $230 worth to be on hand.

_____   7.   The company wrote a check on Dec. 14 for $100 to pay for an ad which appeared in the Dec. 10 newspaper.

_____   8.   The company employs an office clerk and pays him $150 every Friday for the week's work.

_____   9.   Charges for local telephone service were paid on Dec. 1 for the month of December. Another payment is due on Jan. 1 for local telephone service for January.

_____   10.   An employee was hired on December 31, 1992, and is to begin work on Jan. 2.

SOLUTION TO EXERCISE 3-4

1.   b   6.   b
2.   a   7.   c
3.   b   8.   a
4.   a   9.   c
5.   b   10.   c

Item 2 involves an accrued revenue.
Items 4 and 8 involve accrued expenses.
Items 1 and 6 involve prepaid expenses.
Items 3 and 5 involve unearned revenues.

EXERCISE 3-5

Purpose: This exercise reviews the procedures involved in the accounting cycle.

Instructions
Arrange the nine procedures carried out in the accounting cycle in the order in which they should be performed by numbering them "1," "2," and so forth in the spaces provided. As you work through this exercise, concentrate on the logical step progression and the flow of information in the data gathering process.

_____   a.   Journalize and post closing entries.

_____   b.   Prepare financial statements from the work sheet.

_____   c.   Prepare a post-closing trial balance.

_____   d.   Balance the ledger accounts and prepare a trial balance.

_____   e.   Journalize and post adjustments made on the work sheet.

_____   f.   Record transactions in the journals.

_____   g.   Journalize and post reversing entries.

_____   h.   Post from journals to the ledgers.

_____   i.   Prepare a work sheet.

SOLUTION TO EXERCISE 3-5

a.   7
b.   6 or 5
c.   8
d.   3
e.   5 or 6
f.   1
g.   9
h.   2
i.   4

ILLUSTRATION 3-2
CONVERSION OF CASH BASIS TO ACCRUAL BASIS

Cash Basis ➤	➤ ➤	Accrual Basis
Receipts	- Beginning accounts receivable +Ending accounts receivable	= Net sales
Rent receipts	+ Beginning unearned rent - Ending unearned rent - Beginning rent receivable + Ending rent receivable	= Rent revenue
Payment for goods	+ Beginning inventory - Ending inventory - Beginning accounts payable + Ending accounts payable	= Cost of goods sold
Payments for expenses	+ Beginning prepaid expenses - Ending prepaid expenses - Beginning accrued expenses + Ending accrued expenses	= Operating expenses (except depreciation and similar write-offs)
Payments for property, plant, and equipment	- Cash payments for property, plant, and equipment + Periodic write-off of the asset cost through some formula(s)	= Depreciation or amortization expense

EXERCISE 3-6

<u>Purpose:</u> This exercise will allow you to quickly check your knowledge of how items are extended on a work sheet.

Instructions

Place an "X" in the appropriate columns to indicate the proper work sheet treatment of the balance in each of the accounts listed. (The accounts are **not** listed in their usual order, the work sheet is only partially illustrated, and the Trial Balance and Adjustments columns have been omitted.)

HANDY DANDY HARDWARE
Work Sheet
For the Year Ended December 31, 1992

Account	Adjusted Trial Balance		Income Statement		Balance Sheet	
	Debit	Credit	Debit	Credit	Debit	Credit
Advertising Expense	✓					
Depreciation Expense	✓					
Land	✓					
Store Equipment	✓					
Wages and Salaries Expense	✓					
Mortgage Payable		✓				
Cash	✓					
Salaries Payable		✓				
Prepaid Insurance	✓					
Delivery Equipment	✓					
Accumulated Depreciation		✓				
Revenue Received in Advance		✓				
Rent Expense	✓					
Sales Revenue						
Prepaid Rent	✓					
Dividends Declared	✓					
Repairs Expense	✓					
Wages Payable		✓				
Interest Receivable	✓					
Accounts Receivable	✓					
Net Income						

3-17

SOLUTION TO EXERCISE 3-6

HANDY DANDY HARDWARE
Work Sheet
For the Year Ended December 31, 1992

Account	Adjusted Trial Balance		Income Statement		Balance Sheet	
	Debit	Credit	Debit	Credit	Debit	Credit
Advertising Expense	X		X			
Depreciation Expense	X		X			
Land	X				X	
Store Equipment	X				X	
Wages and Salaries Expense	X		X			
Mortgage Payable		X				X
Cash	X				X	
Salaries Payable		X				X
Prepaid Insurance	X				X	
Delivery Equipment	X				X	
Accumulated Depreciation		X				X
Revenue Received in Advance		X				X
Rent Expense	X		X			
Sales Revenue		X		X		
Prepaid Rent	X				X	
Dividends Declared	X				X	
Repairs Expense	X		X			
Wages Payable		X				X
Interest Receivable	X				X	
Accounts Receivable	X				X	
Net Income			X			X

EXERCISE 3-7

Purpose: This exercise will provide practice in determining which adjusting entries may be reversed.

The following represent adjusting entries prepared for the Bent Tree Company at December 31, 1992 (end of the accounting period). The company has the policy of using reversing entries when appropriate. For each adjusting entry below, indicate if it would be appropriate to reverse it at the beginning of 1993. Indicate your answer by writing "yes" or "no" in the space provided.

_____ 1. Deferred Advertising Expense 4,500
                Advertising Expense 4,500

_____ 2. Interest Expense 800
                Discount on Bonds Payable 800

_____	3. Interest Receivable	690	
	Interest Revenue		690
_____	4. Unearned Rental Income	900	
	Rental Income		900
_____	5. Insurance Expense	1,600	
	Prepaid Insurance		1,600
_____	6. Salaries Expense	1,100	
	Salaries Payable		1,100

SOLUTION TO EXERCISE 3-7

1. Yes   3. Yes   5. No
2. No   4. No   6. Yes

Explanation:
1. An adjustment for a deferred expense can be reversed if the adjustment increases an asset or liability account. This adjustment increases a prepaid expense account.
2. Never reverse an adjustment for amortization of a discount.
3. An accrual type adjustment can always be reversed.
4. A reversal of this entry would put back into the Unearned Rental Revenue account the amount that the adjustment indicated has been earned.
5. An adjustment for a deferral can be reversed only if it increases a balance sheet account. This adjustment decreases an asset account.
6. An accrual type adjustment can always be reversed. You can tell the entry is for an accrued expense because the debit is to an expense account and the credit is to a payable account.

EXERCISE 3-8

Purpose: This exercise will illustrate the process of converting cash information to accrual amounts.

Dash and Crash, attorneys, summarize income on a cash basis. Their cash basis income for 1992 is calculated to be $15,900. Although accruals and deferrals and estimated items are not formally recognized in the accounts, the following data are available:

	Jan. 1, 1992	Dec. 31, 1992	Increase (Decrease)
Receivables from clients	$12,000	$9,250	$(2,750)
Office supplies on hand	310	360	50
Unearned retainer income	1,600	3,000	1,400
Miscellaneous accrued payables	450	200	(250)
Depreciation expense		1,200	1,200

Instructions
Answer the following questions. Show your computations.
(1) If cash of $103,000 was received during 1992 from clients, what was the total fee revenue earned on the accrual basis?

3-19

(2) If cash of $1,275 was paid for office supplies during the period, what was the amount of office supplies expense incurred on an accrual basis?

(3) If cash of $1,720 was paid for miscellaneous expense items, what was the amount of miscellaneous office expense on an accrual basis?

(4) What net income would they have shown for the year if income had been calculated on the accrual basis?

SOLUTION TO EXERCISE 3-8

(1)		
	Cash receipts	$103,000
	Beginning receivables	(12,000)
	Ending receivables	9,250
	Beginning unearned income	1,600
	Ending unearned income	(3,000)
	Fee revenue earned	$ 98,850

(2)		
	Cash payments for office supplies	$1,275
	Beginning office supplies on hand	310
	Ending office supplies on hand	(360)
	Office supplies expense incurred	$1,225

(3)		
	Cash payments for miscellaneous items	$1,720
	Beginning miscellaneous accrued payables	(450)
	Ending miscellaneous accrued payables	200
	Miscellaneous office expense incurred	$1,470

(4)		
	Cash basis income	$15,900
	Beginning receivables	(12,000)
	Ending receivables	9,250
	Beginning unearned income	1,600
	Ending unearned income	(3,000)
	Beginning office supplies on hand	(310)
	Ending office supplies on hand	360
	Beginning miscellaneous accrued payables	450
	Ending miscellaneous accrued payables	(200)
	Depreciation expense	(1,200)
	Net income on an accrual basis	$10,850

Explanation:

(1) A decrease in receivables during a period indicates that the amount of cash collections from clients exceeds the amount of revenue earned by $2,750. An increase in unearned income also indicates that cash collections exceed revenue earned by $1,400. The beginning receivables amount of $12,000 was earned prior to 1992 but was received in 1992. The ending receivables amount of $9,250 was earned in 1992 but won't be received until a future period.

(2) An increase in a prepaid expense causes cash paid to exceed expense incurred. The beginning prepaid amount was paid in a prior period (and thus is not part of the $1,275 paid in 1992) but was consumed and, therefore, incurred during 1992. The ending prepaid amount was paid during the current period but should not be included in the expense total.

(3) A decrease in an accrued payable indicates that cash paid exceeds the amount of expense incurred. The beginning payable relates to an expense incurred in a period prior to 1992 but paid in 1992. The ending payable arises from an expense incurred in 1992 that will be paid in a future period.

(4) To solve part (4), you use the same thought processes you used for items (1) through (3) above, **but** you take everything a step further and think in terms of a **net** result. Notice the items added to arrive at the answer to part (1) are also added to arrive at the answer to part (4). However, the items added to arrive at answers to parts (2) and (3) are deducted to arrive at the answer to part (4). The reason for this is that item (1) deals with revenues and items (2) and (3) deal with expenses. Revenues are a positive component in arriving at net income; whereas, expenses are a negative component of net income. Thus, as revenues increase, net income also increases; whereas, if expenses increase, net income decreases.

EXERCISE 3-9

Purpose: This exercise will point out the relationships that exist between cash data and accrual amounts when certain balance sheet accounts increase during the period.

Instructions
Complete each of the following blanks with one of the following, whichever is appropriate.

>   symbol for is greater than
<   symbol for is less than
or   =   symbol for equals

1. On a comparative balance sheet, if an accrued receivable increased, then revenue earned _____ cash received so net income on the accrual basis _____ income on a cash basis.

2. On a comparative balance sheet, if an unearned revenue increased, then revenue earned _____ cash received so net income on the accrual basis _____ income on a cash basis.

3. On a comparative balance sheet, if a prepaid expense increased, then expense incurred _____ cash paid so net income on the accrual basis _____ income on a cash basis.

4. On a comparative balance sheet, if an accrued payable increased, then expense incurred _____ cash paid so net income on the accrual basis _____ income on a cash basis.

SOLUTION TO EXERCISE 3-9

1. >   3. <
    >   >

2. <   4. >
    <   <

Note: The signs are the same in the answers to 1 and 2 but the signs are different in the answers to 3 and 4. The reason is that revenue is a positive component of income and expense is a negative component of income.

EXERCISE 3-10

Purpose: This exercise will require you to use your knowledge of the accrual basis of accounting to solve for an unknown amount.

The Doors Corporation, which uses the accrual basis of accounting, reported interest expense of $86,110 in its 1992 income statement. Accrued interest at December 31, 1992 amounted to $20,000; cash paid for interest during 1992 totaled $77,930. There was no prepaid interest either at the beginning or at the end of 1992.

Instructions
What was the amount, if any, of accrued interest at January 1, 1992? Show computations.

SOLUTION TO EXERCISE 3-10

Accrued interest, December 31, 1992		$20,000
Increase in accrued interest during 1992:		
Interest expense for 1992 (accrual basis)	$86,110	
Cash paid for interest in 1992	77,930	
Excess of reported expense over cash paid for interest		(8,180)
Accrued interest, January 1, 1992		$11,820

OR

Interest Expense

Cash paid 1992	77,930	1/1/92 Reversing entry	X
12/31/92 accrual	20,000		
12/31/92 Balance	86,110		

$$\$77,930 + \$20,000 - X = \$86,110$$
$$-X = \$86,110 - \$77,930 - \$20,000$$
$$X = \$11,820$$

ANALYSIS OF MULTIPLE-CHOICE TYPE QUESTIONS

Question

1. In reviewing some adjusting entries, you observe an entry which contains a debit to Prepaid Insurance and a credit to Insurance Expense. The purpose of this journal entry is to record a(n)
   a. accrued expense.
   b. deferred expense.
   c. expired cost.
   d. prepaid revenue.

Solution = b.

Explanation: A debit to Prepaid Insurance records an increase in a prepaid expense. A prepaid expense is an expense that has been paid but has not been incurred. Another name for a prepaid expense is deferred expense. A deferred expense is an expense whose recognition is being deferred (put off) until a future period.

Approach: Write down the entry so you can see what the entry does. Notice the entry records a prepaid expense (an asset). Then examine each answer selection one at a time. An accrued expense is an expense incurred, but not paid. An expired cost is an expense or a loss. Prepaid revenue is a bad term for unearned revenue (or deferred revenue). Deferred expense is an expense paid, but not incurred.

Question

2.   The Office Supplies account had a balance at the beginning of year 3 of $1,600. Payments for office supplies during year 3 amounted to $10,000 and were recorded as expense. A physical count at the end of year 3 revealed supplies costing $1,900 were on hand. Reversing entries are used by this company. The required adjusting entry at the end of year 3 will include a debit to
   a.   Office Supplies Expense for $300.
   b.   Office Supplies for $300.
   c.   Office Supplies Expense for $9,700.
   d.   Office Supplies for $1,900.

Solution = d.

Explanation and Approach: Draw T accounts. Enter the data given and solve for the adjusting entry. Compare each alternative answer to the adjusting entry you have sketched in the accounts.

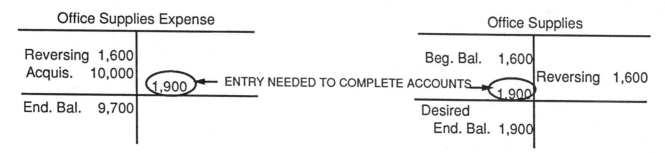

Question

3.   The purpose of recording closing entries is to
   a.   reduce the number of nominal accounts.
   b.   enable the accountant to prepare financial statements at the end of an accounting period.
   c.   prepare revenue and expense accounts for the recording of the next period's revenues and expenses.
   d.   establish new balances in some asset and liability accounts.

Solution = c.

Explanation: Closing entries clear out the balances of revenue and expense accounts so that the accounts are ready to accumulate data for a new accounting period.

Approach: Cover up the answer selections while you read the question. Attempt to complete the statement started by the stem of the question. Think about when closing entries are made and what they do. Then go through the selections using a process of elimination approach. Selection a. is incorrect, closing entries do not change the number of accounts. Selection b. is incorrect. Financial statements are prepared before closing entries are done. If closing entries were posted first, the income statement would include nothing but zero amounts. Selection d. is incorrect. Closing entries will affect only nominal accounts and owners' equity. Selection c. is correct.

Question
4. Which of the following is a nominal account?
    a. Prepaid Insurance.
    b. Unearned Revenue.
    c. Insurance Expense.
    d. Interest Receivable.

Solution = c.

Explanation and Approach: Read the question. Before looking at the answer selections, write down the meaning of the term nominal account. Then answer "true" or "false" as you ask whether each answer selection is a nominal account. A nominal account is an account whose balance is closed at the end of an accounting period. Revenue and expense accounts are closed; real accounts (including asset and liability accounts) are never closed. Prepaid Insurance and Interest Receivable are asset accounts. Unearned Revenue is a liability account. Insurance Expense is a nominal account.

Question
5. If ending accounts receivable exceeds the beginning accounts receivable,
    a. cash collections during the period exceed the amount of revenue earned.
    b. net income for the period exceeds the amount of cash basis income.
    c. no cash was collected during the period.
    d. cash collections during the year are less than the amount of revenue earned.

Solution = d.

Explanation: An increase in accounts receivable indicates that the amount of revenue earned (and recognized) exceeds the amount of cash collected.

Approach: Write down the format for reconciling the amount of cash receipts to the amount of revenue earned.

Cash receipts	$
Beginning accounts receivable	( )
Ending accounts receivable	+
Revenue earned	$

Fill in what you know from the question.

Cash receipts	$ X	
Beginning accounts receivable	( )	
Ending accounts receivable	+	More than beginning receivable
Revenue earned	$	Greater than X

CHAPTER 4

STATEMENT OF INCOME AND RETAINED EARNINGS

OVERVIEW

An income statement reports on the results of operations of an entity for a period of time. It is important to classify revenues, expenses, gains, and losses properly on the income statement. In this chapter, we discuss the income statement classifications and the content of the statement of retained earnings along with related disclosure issues. It is imperative that charges and credits that represent elements of income determination be properly reflected in the financial statements. Errors in the determination of income cause errors on the statement of retained earnings and balance sheet.

TIPS ON CHAPTER TOPICS

TIP: The income statement is often referred to as the statement of operations or the operating statement because it reports on the results of operations for a period of time. Other names include the earnings statement, statement of earnings, and profit and loss statement (or P & L statement).

TIP: The income statement is often referred to as a link between balance sheets because it explains one major reason why the balance of owners' equity changed during the period. Owners' equity at the beginning of the period can be reconciled with ending owners' equity as follows:

	Owners' equity at the beginning of the period
+	Additional owner investments during the period
-	Owner withdrawals during the period
±	<u>Results of operations for the period (net income or net loss)</u>
=	Owners' equity at the end of the period

TIP: $A = L + OE$ at a point in time

$\Delta A = \Delta L + \Delta OE$ for a period of time (Δ = changes in)

Reasons for changes in owners' equity include:
- (1) additional owner investments
- (2) owner withdrawals
- (3) results of operations (net income or net loss)

TIP: A contra revenue item has the same effect on net income as that of an expense. Contra revenue accounts include Sales Discounts and Sales Returns and Allowances.

TIP: It is often helpful to form an acronym when attempting to remember a list of items. In looking at the order of the things that can appear after the "Income from Continuing Operations" line on an income statement, you might come up with **DEC** to help you to remember the exact order of these items:

Discontinued operations
Extraordinary items
Cumulative effect of changes in accounting principles

TIP: The income tax consequences of all items appearing above the line "Income from continuing operations before income taxes" are summarized in the line "Income taxes." Revenues cause an increase in income taxes and expenses cause a decrease in income taxes. The income tax consequences of items appearing below the "Income from continuing operations" line are reported right along with the items (hence, these items are reported "net of tax").

EXERCISE 4-1

Purpose: This exercise reviews the basic accounting formula (A = L + OE) and the connection between the income statement and the balance sheet (which is a change in owners' equity due to the net income or net loss for the period).

The following data were extracted from the records of Dora Loesing's Cookies, a sole proprietorship:

Total assets, beginning of the period	$100,000
Total liabilities, beginning of the period	36,000
Owner withdrawals during the period	30,000
Total assets, end of the period	108,000
Total liabilities, end of the period	38,000
Owner's contributions during the period	10,000

Instructions
Compute the amount of net income (or loss) for the period. Show computations.

SOLUTION TO EXERCISE 4-1

Approach: The question asks you to solve for net income; however, no information is given regarding revenues and expenses for the period. Only balance sheet data and transactions affecting owner's equity are given. Net income (or net loss) for a period is one reason for a change in the balance of owner's equity. Write down the items that reconcile the beginning owner's equity balance with the ending owner's equity balance, enter the amounts known, compute beginning and ending owner's equity balances by use of the basic accounting equation, and then solve for the amount of net income.

Beginning owner's equity	$64,000[a]
Additional owner contributions	10,000
Owner withdrawals during the period	(30,000)
Subtotal	44,000
Net income (loss) for the period	+ X
Ending owner's equity	$70,000[b]
Solving for X, net income =	$26,000

[a]$A = L + OE$
  $100,000 = 36,000 + ?$
  Beginning owner's equity = $64,000

[b]$A = L + OE$
  $108,000 = 38,000 + ?$
  Ending owner's equity = $70,000

EXERCISE 4-2

Purpose: This exercise will allow you to contrast the multiple-step format and the single-step format for the income statement.

The accountant for Mike Cuzak Shoe Co. has compiled the following information from the company's records as a basis for an income statement for the year ended 12/31/92.

Rental revenue	$ 29,000
Interest on notes payable	18,000
Market appreciation on temporary investments above cost	31,000
Merchandise purchases	409,000
Transportation-in--merchandise	37,000
Wages and salaries--sales	114,800
Materials and supplies--sales	17,600
Common stock outstanding (no. of shares)	10,000*
Income taxes	66,400
Wages and salaries--administrative	135,900
Other administrative expense	51,700
Merchandise inventory, January 1, 1992	92,000
Merchandise inventory, December 31, 1992	81,000
Purchase returns and allowances	11,000
Net sales	980,000
Depreciation on plant assets (70% selling, 30% administrative)	65,000
Dividends declared	16,000

*Remained unchanged all year.

Instructions
(a) Prepare a multiple-step income statement.
(b) Prepare a single-step income statement.

SOLUTION TO EXERCISE 4-2

(a)

Mike Cuzak Shoe Co.
Income Statement
For the Year Ending December 31, 1992

Net sales			$980,000
Cost of Goods Sold			
Merchandise inventory, Jan. 1, 1992		$ 92,000	
Purchases	$409,000		
Less purchase returns & allowances	11,000		
Net purchases	398,000		
Transportation-in	37,000	435,000	
Total merchandise available for sale		527,000	
Less merchandise inventory, Dec. 31, 1992		81,000	
Cost of goods sold			446,000
Gross profit			534,000
Operating Expenses			
Selling expenses			
Wages and salaries	114,800		
Materials and supplies	17,600		
Depreciation (70% X $65,000)	45,500	177,900	
Administrative expenses			
Wages and salaries	135,900		
Depreciation (30% X $65,000)	19,500		
Other administrative expenses	51,700	207,100	385,000
Income from operations			149,000
Other Revenues and Gains			
Rental revenue			29,000
			178,000
Other Expenses and Losses			
Interest expense			18,000
Income before taxes			160,000
Income taxes			66,400
Net income			$ 93,600
Earnings per share ($93,600 ÷ 10,000)			$9.36

(b)

Mike Cuzak Shoe Co.
Income Statement
For the Year Ending December 31, 1992

Net sales	$ 980,000
Rental revenue	29,000
Total revenue	1,009,000
Expenses	
Cost of goods sold	446,000
Selling expenses	177,900
Administrative expenses	207,100
Interest expense	18,000
Total expenses	849,000
Income before taxes	160,000
Income taxes	66,400
Net income	$ 93,600
Earnings per share	$9.36

EXERCISE 4-3

<u>Purpose:</u> This exercise will give you practice in identifying components of net income and the order of items appearing on a single-step version of a combined statement of income and retained earnings.

Presented below is the trial balance of Arthur Ites Corporation at December 31, 1992. The account titles and balances are **not** in the customary order.

Arthur Ites Corporation
TRIAL BALANCE
December 31, 1992

	Debits	Credits
Purchase discounts		$ 10,000
Cash	$ 210,100	
Accounts receivable	105,000	
Rent revenue		18,000
Retained earnings		260,000
Salaries payable		18,000
Sales		1,000,000
Notes receivable	110,000	
Accounts payable		49,000
Accumulated depreciation--equipment		28,000
Sales discounts	14,500	
Sales returns	17,500	
Notes payable		70,000
Selling expenses	232,000	
Administrative expenses	99,000	
Common stock		300,000
Income tax expense	38,500	
Cash dividends	60,000	
Allowance for doubtful accounts		5,000
Supplies	14,000	
Freight-in	20,000	
Land	70,000	
Equipment	140,000	
Bonds payable		100,000
Gain on sale of land		30,000
Accumulated depreciation--building		19,600
Merchandise inventory	89,000	
Building	98,000	
Purchases	590,000	
Totals	$1,907,600	$1,907,600

A physical count of inventory on December 31 resulted in an inventory amount of $124,000.

Instructions
Prepare a combined statement of income and retained earnings using the single-step form. Assume that the only changes in retained earnings during the current year were from net income and dividends. Ten thousand shares of common stock were outstanding the entire year.

SOLUTION TO EXERCISE 4-3

Arthur Ites Corporation
Combined Statement of Income and Retained Earnings
For the Year Ending December 31, 1992

Revenues		
Net sales*		$ 968,000
Gain on sale of land		30,000
Rent revenue		18,000
Total revenues		1,016,000
Expenses		
Cost of goods sold**		565,000
Selling expenses		232,000
Administrative expenses		99,000
Total expenses		896,000
Income before taxes		120,000
Income taxes		38,500
Net income (per common share, $8.15)		81,500
Retained earnings at beginning of the year		260,000
		341,500
Cash dividends declared and paid		60,000
Retained earnings at end of the year		$ 281,500

*Net sales:			
Sales			$1,000,000
Less: Sales discounts		$14,500	
Sales returns		17,500	32,000
Net sales			$ 968,000
**Cost of goods sold:			
Merchandise inventory, January 1			$ 89,000
Purchases		$590,000	
Less purchase discounts		10,000	
Net purchases			580,000
Add freight-in			20,000
Merchandise available for sale			689,000
Less merchandise inventory, December 31			124,000
Cost of merchandise sold			$565,000

Approach:
  (1) Go through the trial balance and lightly cross through any account title that does **not** pertain to the computation of net income. With the exception of the balance of Merchandise Inventory, balance sheet account balances are not used in determining net income.
  (2) Compute intermediate subtotals for items such as (a) net sales, (b) cost of goods sold, (c) selling expenses, and (d) administrative expenses. Show your computations for these subtotals. (In this particular exercise, selling expenses and administrative expenses are already summarized.)
  (3) Identify revenue and gain items.
  (4) Identify expense and loss items.

(5) Identify income taxes for the period.
(6) Identify any discontinued operations, extraordinary items, and cumulative effect on prior periods of a change in accounting principle (none of these appear in this exercise).
(7) Compute net income.
(8) Add beginning retained earnings.
(9) Include any prior period adjustments (none identified in this exercise).
(10) Deduct dividends declared.
(11) Arrive at ending retained earnings.

EXERCISE 4-4

Purpose: This exercise is designed to give you practice in preparing a condensed multiple-step income statement and a statement of retained earnings.

Presented below is information related to Jill Eikenberry Corp., for the year 1992.

Net sales	$1,300,000
Cost of goods sold	800,000
Selling expenses	65,000
Administrative expenses	48,000
Dividend revenue	20,000
Interest revenue	7,000
Write-off of inventory due to obsolescence	80,000
Depreciation expense omitted by accident in 1991	40,000
Casualty loss (extraordinary item)	50,000
Dividends declared	45,000
Retained earnings at December 31, 1991	2,000,000
Federal tax rate of 34% on all items	

Instructions

(a) Prepare a multiple-step income statement for 1992. Assume that 70,000 shares of common stock are outstanding.
(b) Prepare a separate statement of retained earnings for 1992.

SOLUTION TO EXERCISE 4-4

(a)

Jill Eikenberry Corp.

Income Statement

For the Year Ended December 31, 1992

Net sales		$1,300,000
Cost of goods sold		800,000
Gross profit		500,000
Operating expenses		
Selling expenses	$65,000	
Administrative expenses	48,000	113,000
Income from operations		387,000
Other revenues and gains		
Dividend revenue	20,000	
Interest revenue	7,000	27,000
		414,000
Other expenses and losses		
Loss due to inventory obsolescence		80,000
Income before taxes and extraordinary item		334,000
Income taxes		113,560
Income before extraordinary item		220,440
Extraordinary item		
Casualty loss	50,000	
Less applicable income tax reduction	17,000	33,000
Net income		$ 187,440

Per share of common stock:	
Income before extraordinary item ($220,440 ÷ 70,000 shares)	$3.15
Extraordinary item (net of tax) ($33,000 ÷ 70,000)	(.47)
Net income ($187,440 ÷ 70,000)	$2.68

TIP: Regarding the earnings per share (EPS) presentations: The EPS figures for "income before extraordinary item" and "net income" are required. The EPS figure for an extraordinary item is optional, but it is usually presented.

TIP: The loss due to inventory obsolescence is sometimes reported along with cost of goods sold or right below cost of goods sold (i.e., included in "gross profit").

(b)

Jill Eikenberry Corp.

Statement of Retained Earnings

For the Year Ended December 31, 1992

Retained earnings, January 1, 1992, as previously reported	$2,000,000
Depreciation error (net of $13,600 tax)	(26,400)
Adjusted balance of retained earnings at January 1, 1992	1,973,600
Net income	187,440
	2,161,040
Dividends declared	45,000
Retained earnings, December 31, 1992	$2,116,040

EXERCISE 4-5

Purpose: This exercise will test your knowledge of the elements and arrangement of the major sections of the income statement.

Instructions

The following list represents captions that would appear on an income statement (single-step format) for a company reporting an extraordinary gain, losses from discontinued operations, and a change in depreciation method as well as the results of continuing operations for the period. You are to "unjumble" the list and prepare a skeleton income statement using the captions given. (If you do not wish to write out each caption above, you may still test your knowledge by listing the appropriate letters in the correct order.

(a)   Income before extraordinary item and cumulative effect of a change in accounting principle.
(b)   Revenues.
(c)   Cumulative effect on prior years of a change in depreciation method (net of tax).
(d)   Income taxes.
(e)   Discontinued operations:
(f)   Extraordinary gain (net of tax).
(g)   Expenses.
(h)   Loss from disposal of assets of discontinued segment of business (net of tax).
(i)   Net income.
(j)   Income from continuing operations before taxes.
(k)   Loss from operations of discontinued segment of business (net of tax).
(l)   Income from continuing operations.

SOLUTION TO EXERCISE 4-5

Company Name
Income Statement
For the Year Ended December 31, 19XX

(b)   Revenues
(g)   Expenses
(j)   Income from continuing operations before taxes
(d)   Income taxes
(l)   Income from continuing operations
(e)   Discontinued operations:
(k)   Loss from operations of discontinued segment of business (net of tax)
(h)   Loss from disposal of assets of discontinued segment of business (net of tax)
(a)   Income before extraordinary item and cumulative effect of a change in accounting principle
(f)   Extraordinary gain (net of tax)
(c)   Cumulative effect on prior years of a change in depreciation method (net of tax)
(i)   Net income

EXERCISE 4-6

<u>Purpose:</u> This exercise will enable you to practice identifying the proper classification for items on an income statement. It will also give you an example of how the tax effects of various items are reflected in the income statement.

Louise E. Anna, Inc. reported income from continuing operations before taxes during 1992 of $790,000. Additional transactions occurring in 1992 but **not** considered in the $790,000 are as follows:

1. The corporation experienced an uninsured flood loss (extraordinary) in the amount of $60,000 during the year. The tax rate on this item is 46%.

2. At the beginning of 1990, the corporation purchased a machine for $54,000 (salvage value of $9,000) that has a useful life of six years. The bookkeeper used straight-line depreciation for 1990, 1991, and 1992 but failed to deduct the salvage value in computing the depreciation base.

3. Sale of securities held as a part of Anna's portfolio resulted in a loss of $75,500 (pretax).

4. When its president died, the corporation realized $110,000 from an insurance policy. The cash surrender value of this policy had been carried on the books as an investment in the amount of $46,000 (the gain is nontaxable).

5. The corporation disposed of its recreational division at a loss of $115,000 before taxes. Assume that this transaction meets the criteria for being classified as discontinued operations. There were no results of operations for this division during 1992.

6. The corporation decided to change its method of inventory pricing from average cost to the FIFO method. The effect of this change on prior years would be to increase 1990 income by $60,000 and decrease 1991 income by $20,000 before taxes. The FIFO method has been used for 1992. The tax rate on these items is 40%.

Instructions
Prepare part of a corrected income statement for the year 1992 starting with "Income from continuing operations before taxes." Compute earnings per share as it should be shown on the face of the income statement. There were 25,000 shares of common stock outstanding for the year. (Assume a tax rate of 30% on all items, unless indicated otherwise.)

TIP: An extraordinary item is reported "net of tax" by deducting the tax effect from the related gain or loss. For example, if the tax rate is 30%, an extraordinary gain of $400,000 will be reported at $280,000 net of tax. Likewise, an extraordinary loss of $400,000 will be reported at $280,000 net of tax. The gain situation increases net income whereas the loss reduces it.

SOLUTION TO EXERCISE 4-6

Louise E. Anna, Inc.
Income Statement (Partial)
For the Year Ended December 31, 1992

Income from continuing operations before taxes		$780,000*
Income taxes		214,800**
Income from continuing operations		565,200
Discontinued operations:		
Loss from disposal of recreational division	$(115,000)	
Less applicable income tax reduction	34,500	(80,500)
Income before extraordinary item and cumulative effect of a change in accounting principle		484,700
Extraordinary item:		
Major casualty loss--uninsured flood loss	(60,000)	
Less applicable income tax reduction	27,600	(32,400)
Cumulative effect on prior years of retroactive application of new inventory method	40,000	
Less applicable income taxes	16,000	24,000
Net income		$476,300

Per share of common stock:

Income from continuing operations ($565,200 ÷ $25,000)	$22.61
Discontinued operations, net of tax	(3.22)
Income before extraordinary items and cumulative effect of accounting change	19.39
Extraordinary item, net of tax	(1.30)
Change in accounting principle, net of tax	.96
Net income ($476,300 ÷ 25,000)	$19.05

* Computation of income from continuing operations before taxes:

As previously stated		$790,000
Loss on sale of securities		(75,500)
Gain on proceeds of life insurance policy ($110,000 - $46,000)		64,000
Error in computation of depreciation for the current year		
As computed ($54,000 ÷ 6)	$9,000	
Corrected ($54,000 - $9,000) ÷ 6	(7,500)	1,500
As restated		$780,000

** Computation of income tax:

Income from continuing operations before income tax	$780,000
Nontaxable income (gain on life insurance)	(64,000)
Taxable income	716,000
Tax rate	X .30
Income tax expense	$214,800

TIP: The effect of the depreciation error on prior periods ($1,500 for 1990 plus $1,500 for 1991) is to be reported as a deduction from the beginning retained earnings balance on the statement of retained earnings for 1992.

EXERCISE 4-7

Purpose: This exercise will give you examples of the various situations possible [realized gains (losses) and expected gains (losses)] when you have an extended phase-out period for discontinued operations.

Koon Company has discontinued operations. The basic facts are as follows:
   Measurement date: October 1, 1992.
   Disposal is expected to be completed by May 1, 1993.
   Accounting period ends December 31, 1992.

Instructions

For each of the following **independent** cases, indicate the amount of "gain (loss) on disposal of segment" to be reported on the 1992 and 1993 income statements by filling in the blanks provided.

	Realized Income (Loss) on Operations Oct. 1, 1992 - Dec. 31, 1992	Realized Gain (Loss) on Sale of Assets Oct. 1, 1992 - Dec. 31, 1992	Expected Income (Loss) on Operations Jan. 1, 1993 - May 1, 1993	Expected Gain (Loss) on Sale of Assets Jan. 1, 1993 - May 1, 1993	Gain (Loss) on Disposal of Segment
Case 1	(144,000)	(52,500)	(117,600)	(88,200)	1992 _____
					1993 _____
Case 2	300,000	(52,500)	(117,600)	(88,200)	1992 _____
					1993 _____
Case 3	(144,000)	(52,500)	324,000	(88,200)	1992 _____
					1993 _____
Case 4	(144,000)	(52,500)	(117,600)	360,000	1992 _____
					1993 _____
Case 5	300,000	(52,500)	324,000	(88,200)	1992 _____
					1993 _____

SOLUTION TO EXERCISE 4-7

	1992	1993
Case 1	(402,300)	-0-
Case 2	41,700	-0-
Case 3	-0-	39,300
Case 4	-0-	45,900
Case 5	247,500	235,800

Approach: To compute the amount to report as the gain or loss on disposal of a segment:
(1) Compute the net realized items.
(2) Compute the net estimated items.
(3) Follow the rules for handling the income (loss) on operations and the gains and losses on disposal of assets estimated in the phase-out of discontinued operations:
   (a) Accrue net estimated losses in total (so they add to net realized losses or offset net realized gains).
   (b) Defer net estimated gains **except** may use them to offset a net realized loss.

Explanation:

	Net Realized Items	Net Estimated Items	Treatment
Case 1	$(196,500)	$(205,800)	Accrue net estimated losses to 1992.
Case 2	$247,500	$(205,800)	Accrue net estimated losses to 1992.
Case 3	$(196,500)	$235,800	Use some estimated gains to offset net realized losses; defer the rest.
Case 4	$(196,500)	$242,400	Use some estimated gains to offset net realized losses; defer the rest.
Case 5	$247,500	$235,800	Do not reflect any estimated gains in 1992; there are no realized losses to offset.

EXERCISE 4-8

Purpose: This exercise will allow you to practice dealing with discontinued operations when there is an extended phase-out period.

Assume that Hunt Enterprises Inc. decides to sell its sporting goods division in 1992. This sale qualifies for discontinued operations treatment. Pertinent data at December 31, 1992 regarding the operations of the sporting goods division are as follows:

Loss from operations from beginning of 1992 to measurement date, $1,000,000 (net of tax).
Realized loss from operations from measurement date to end of 1992, $700,000 (net of tax).
Estimated income from operations from end of year to disposal date of June 1, 1993, $350,000 (net of tax).
Estimated gain on sale of the division's assets on June 1, 1993, $150,000 (net of tax).

Instructions
(a) What is the gain (loss) on the disposal of the segment to be reported in 1992? In 1993?
(b) If the sporting goods division had realized income of $100,000 (net of tax) instead of a realized loss from the measurement date to the end of 1992, what is the gain or loss on the disposal of the segment to be reported in 1992? In 1993?

SOLUTION TO EXERCISE 4-8

(a) Realized loss from operations from measurement date to end of 1992, net of tax $(700,000)

Estimated income from operations from end of year to disposal date of
June 1, 1993, net of tax   350,000

Estimated gain on sale of net assets on June 1, 1993 of $150,000 net of tax   150,000

Loss on disposal of the segment to be reported in 1992 $(200,000)

No gain or loss on disposal is to be reported in 1993. $ -0-

(b) Gain on disposal of the segment to be reported in 1992. $100,000

Estimated income from operations from beginning of year to
disposal date of June 1, 1993, net of tax $350,000

Estimated gain on sale of assets on June 1, 1993, net of tax   150,000

Gain on disposal of segment to be reported in 1993 $500,000

Approach: Use the same approach as was designated for Exercise 4-7. Notice that the answers for 1993 in both exercises assume that in 1993, operations and disposal transactions resulted in exactly the amounts that had been estimated at December 31, 1992.

ANALYSIS OF MULTIPLE-CHOICE TYPE QUESTIONS

Question
1.   A loss from the disposal of a segment of business should be reported in the income statement
   a.   after extraordinary items and before cumulative effect of an accounting change.
   b.   before extraordinary items and after cumulative effect of an accounting change.
   c.   after extraordinary items and cumulative effect of an accounting change.
   d.   before extraordinary items and cumulative effect of an accounting change.

Solution = d.

Explanation: The correct order of the items involved in the question is as follows:
   (1)   **D**iscontinued operations
   (2)   **E**xtraordinary items
   (3)   **C**umulative effect of an accounting change.

Approach: Keep in mind the acronym **DEC.** Write the items down in the proper order. Read each answer response to see if it properly describes the order in which you have listed the items.

Question
2.   A material loss should be presented separately as a component of income from continuing operations when it is
   a.   unusual in nature and infrequent in occurrence.
   b.   unusual in nature but **not** infrequent in occurrence.
   c.   an extraordinary loss.
   d.   a cumulative effect of an accounting change.

Solution = b.

Explanation: A material loss that is (1) unusual in nature **and** (2) infrequent in occurrence should be reported as an extraordinary item. A loss that meets one of the criteria for being classified as extraordinary, but not both, should be separately disclosed as a component of income from continuing operations. An extraordinary item and a cumulative effect of a change in accounting principle are to be reported **after** (and not part of) income from continuing operations.

Approach: Visualize an income statement and mentally identify the section that reports income from continuing operations. Read one answer at a time and determine if it correctly describes how the statement in the question stem can be completed.

Question

3.   The following expenses were among those incurred by Mitzer Company during 1992:

Rent for office space	$660,000
Loss on sale of office furniture	55,000
Interest	132,000
Accounting and legal fees	352,000
Freight-out	70,000

One-half of the rented premises is occupied by the sales department. How much of the items listed above should be classified as general and administrative expenses in Mitzer's income statement for 1992?

a. $682,000.
b. $869,000.
c. $884,000.
d. $939,000.

Solution = a.

Explanation:		
	One-half of office space (.5 X $660,000)	$330,000
	Accounting and legal fees	352,000
	General and administrative expenses	$682,000

Approach: For each item listed, identify where it is reported. Then collect together the ones that you identify as general and administrative (G & A) expenses.

Rent for office space	--	One-half selling; one-half G & A
Loss on sale of equipment	--	Other expenses and losses
Interest	--	Other expenses and losses
Accounting and legal fees	--	G & A expenses
Freight-out	--	Selling expenses

Question

4.   During the year ended December 31, 1992, Schmelya Corporation incurred the following infrequent losses:
1.   A factory was shutdown during a major strike by employees; costs were $120,000.
2.   A loss of $50,000 was incurred on the abandonment of computer equipment used in the business.
3.   A loss of $82,000 was incurred as a result of flood damage to a warehouse.
How much total loss should Schmelya report in the extraordinary item section of its 1992

4-16

income statement?
- a. $82,000.
- b. $120,000.
- c. $202,000.
- d. $252,000.

Solution = a.

Explanation: To be classified as extraordinary, an item needs to be unusual in nature and infrequent in occurrence. However, there are certain items that do **not** constitute extraordinary items. A listing of these include:
- (a) Write-down or write-off of receivables, inventories, equipment leased to others, deferred research and development costs, or other intangible assets.
- (b) Gains or losses from exchange or translation of foreign currencies, including those relating to major devaluations and revaluations.
- (c) Gains or losses on disposal of a segment of a business.
- (d) Other gains or losses from sale or abandonment of property, plant, or equipment used in the business.
- (e) Effects of a strike, including those against competitors and major suppliers.
- (f) Adjustment of accruals on long-term contracts.

Approach: It is wise to review the list of items above (that the APB said are not extraordinary items) until you can readily recognize items that appear in the list. In the question at hand, the first two items are on the list of items that are **not** extraordinary. Therefore, the only possible one being extraordinary is the loss from flood damage. A flood would be considered infrequent in some locations but not others. Because there is no answer selection of $0, the flood is apparently deemed infrequent for Schmelya.

Question

5. When a segment of a business has been discontinued during the year, that segment's operating losses of the current year after the measurement date should be included in the
- a. income statement as part of the income (loss) from operations of the discontinued segment.
- b. income statement as part of the gain (loss) on disposal of the discontinued segment.
- c. income statement as part of the income (loss) from continuing operations.
- d. statement of retained earnings as a direct decrease in retained earnings.

Solution = b.

Explanation: There are two lines in the "discontinued operations" section of the income statement: (1) Income (loss) from operations of discontinued segment, and (2) Gain or loss on disposal of discontinued segment. The results of operations of the discontinued segment from the beginning of the year up to the measurement date are to be reported in the first line. The results of operations of the discontinued segment after the measurement date go in the second line.

Approach: Read the question and write down the two captions used to report discontinued operations and also write down a brief description of what goes in each category. Read each answer selection and answer **True** or **False** whether it correctly completes the statement in the stem.

CHAPTER 5

BALANCE SHEET AND STATEMENT OF CASH FLOWS

OVERVIEW

A balance sheet reports on the financial position of an entity at a point in time. A statement of cash flows reports reasons for cash receipts and cash payments during the period. In this chapter, we discuss the classifications of a balance sheet and a statement of cash flows along with related disclosure issues. It is extremely important that items are properly classified. Errors in classification will result in incorrect ratio analyses which can lead to misinterpretations of the meaning of the information conveyed. This can affect the decisions that are being made based on that information.

TIPS ON CHAPTER TOPICS

TIP: Memorize the definition of current assets. Current assets are cash and other assets that are expected to be converted into cash, sold, or consumed within the year or operating cycle that immediately follows the balance sheet date, whichever is longer. Think about how various examples of current assets meet this definition.

Unless otherwise indicated, always assume the operating cycle is less than a year so the one-year test is used as the cutoff between current and noncurrent.

TIP: Memorize the definition of current liabilities. Current liabilities are obligations which are expected to require the use of current assets or the incurrence of other current liabilities. A liability may be coming due within a year of the balance sheet date and **not** be a current liability. An example is a debt that is coming due in six months that will be liquidated by use of a noncurrent asset.

TIP: Any asset that is not classified as a current asset is a noncurrent asset. There are four noncurrent asset classifications: long-term investments, property, plant and equipment, intangible assets, and other assets.

TIP: The term **current** is synonymous with **short-term** and **noncurrent** is synonymous with **long-term.** Thus, we may refer to the liability classifications as "current and noncurrent" or "short-term and long-term" or "short-term and noncurrent" or "current and long-term."

TIP: An investment may be classified as a current asset (if it is a short-term investment) or as a noncurrent asset (if it is a long-term investment). For an investment to be classified as current: (1) it should be readily marketable, and (2) there should be a lack of management intent to hold it for a long-term purpose.

TIP: If an account title starts with "Allowance for . . .", then it generally is a contra balance sheet account.

TIP: If an account title starts with "Provision for . . .", it is generally an income statement account.

TIP: An appropriation of retained earnings is a positive component of total retained earnings. An appropriation of retained earnings refers to a portion of retained earnings which for one reason or another is restricted, which simply means it can not be used as a basis for the declaration of dividends.

TIP: A **valuation account** is an account whose balance is needed to properly value the item to which the valuation account relates. A **contra account** is a valuation account whose normal balance (debit versus credit) is opposite of the normal balance of the account to which the valuation account relates. An **adjunct** account is a valuation account whose normal balance is the same as the normal balance of the account to which it relates.

TIP: Interest on debt is due annually or more frequently (semi-annually or monthly, for example). Therefore, interest accrued on long-term debt is generally classified as a current liability. Likewise, interest receivable stemming from the accrual of interest on long-term receivables is generally classified as a current asset.

TIP: Current assets are listed in the order of liquidity with the most liquid first. Property, plant and equipment items are listed in order of length of life with the longest life first.

TIP: A fund can consist of restricted cash or noncash assets such as stocks and bonds of other companies. Funds are reported in the long-term investment classification.

TIP: In answering questions regarding the classification of items on a balance sheet, always assume an individual item is material unless it is apparent otherwise.

ILLUSTRATION 5-1
BALANCE SHEET CLASSIFICATIONS

Current assets--includes cash and items which are expected to be converted to cash or sold or consumed within the next year or operating cycle, whichever is longer.

Long-term investments--includes long-term receivables, restricted funds, investment in stocks and bonds of others, land held for future plant site.

Property, plant and equipment--includes long-lived tangible assets (land, building, equipment, and machinery) that is currently being used in operations (used to produce goods and services for customers).

Intangible assets--includes assets that lack physical substance, such as patent, copyright, franchise, goodwill.

Other assets--includes assets that by common practice don't fit elsewhere.

Current liabilities--obligations that are due within a year and are expected to require the use of current assets or the incurrence of other current liabilities to liquidate them.

Long-term debt--obligations that do not meet the criterion to be classified as current.

Capital stock--the par or stated value of shares issued or about to be issued.

Additional paid-in capital--excess of issuance price over par or stated value.

Retained earnings--excess of net incomes over net losses and dividend distributions since inception of the business. An appropriation of retained earnings is a restricted portion of the total retained earnings figure.

EXERCISE 5-1

Purpose: This exercise lists examples of balance sheet accounts and enables you to practice determining where they are classified.

Instructions
Indicate which balance sheet classification is the most appropriate for reporting each account listed below by selecting the abbreviation of the corresponding section.

CA	Current Assets	CL	Current Liabilities
INV	Long-term Investments	LTL	Long-term Liabilities
PPE	Property, Plant, and Equipment	CS	Capital Stock
ITG	Intangible Assets	APC	Additional Paid-in Capital
OA	Other Assets	RE	Retained Earnings

If the account is a contra account, indicate that fact by putting the abbreviation in parenthesis. If the exact classification depends on facts which are not given, indicate your answer of "depends on" by the abbreviation **DEP** and the possible classifications. If the account is reported on the income statement rather than the balance sheet, indicate that fact with an **IS.** Assume all items are material.

Classification		Account
_____	1.	Accounts Payable.
_____	2.	Accounts Receivable.
_____	3.	Accrued Interest Receivable on Long-term Debt.
_____	4.	Accrued Interest Payable.
_____	5.	Accrued Taxes Payable.
_____	6.	Accumulated Depreciation-- Building.
_____	7.	Accumulated Depreciation-- Machinery.
_____	8.	Mineral Reserves.
_____	9.	Advances by Customers.
_____	10.	Advances to Vendors.
_____	11.	Advertising Expense.
_____	12.	Allowance for Bad Debts.
_____	13.	Allowance for Depreciation.
_____	14.	Allowance for Doubtful Accounts.
_____	15.	Allowance for Excess of Cost Over Market Value of Short-term Marketable Equity Securities.
_____	16.	Allowance for Inventory Price Declines.
_____	17.	Allowance for Price Declines in Short-term Marketable Securities.

Classification		Account
_____	18.	Allowance for Purchases Discounts.
_____	19.	Allowance for Sales Discounts.
_____	20.	Allowance for Uncollectible Accounts.
_____	21.	Appropriation for Bond Sinking Fund.
_____	22.	Appropriation for Contingencies.
_____	23.	Appropriation for Future Plant Expansion.
_____	24.	Appropriation for Treasury Stock Purchased.
_____	25.	Bank Overdraft.
_____	26.	Bond Interest Payable.
_____	27.	Bond Interest Receivable.
_____	28.	Bond Sinking Fund.
_____	29.	Building.
_____	30.	Cash.
_____	31.	Cash in Preferred Stock Redemption Fund.
_____	32.	Cash Surrender Value of Life Insurance.
_____	33.	Certificate of Deposit.
_____	34.	Common Stock.
_____	35.	Construction in Process (entity's new plant under construction).

Classification		Account
_____	36.	Creditors' accounts with debit balances.
_____	37.	Current Maturities of Bonds Payable (to be paid from Bond Sinking Fund).
_____	38.	Current Maturities of Bonds Payable (to be paid from general cash account).
_____	39.	Current Portion of Mortgage Payable.
_____	40.	Current Portion of Long-term Debt.
_____	41.	Customers' accounts with credit balances.
_____	42.	Customers' Deposits.
_____	43.	Deferred Income Tax Asset.
_____	44.	Deferred Income Tax Liability.
_____	45.	Deferred Property Tax Expense.
_____	46.	Deferred Office Supplies.
_____	47.	Deferred Rental Income.
_____	48.	Deferred Subscription Revenue.
_____	49.	Deferred Service Contract Revenue.
_____	50.	Deposits on Equipment Purchases.
_____	51.	Depreciation of Equipment.
_____	52.	Discount on Bonds Payable.
_____	53.	Discount on Common Stock.

Classification		Account
_____	54.	Discount on Notes Payable.
_____	55.	Discount on Notes Receivable.
_____	56.	Dishonored Notes Receivable.
_____	57.	Dividend Payable in Cash.
_____	58.	Dividend Payable in Common Stock.
_____	59.	Earned Rental Revenue.
_____	60.	Accrued Pension Liability.
_____	61.	Estimated Liability for Income Taxes.
_____	62.	Estimated Liability for Warranties.
_____	63.	Estimated Premium Claims Outstanding.
_____	64.	Factory Supplies.
_____	65.	Finished Goods Inventory.
_____	66.	Furniture and Fixtures.
_____	67.	Gain on Sale of Equipment.
_____	68.	General and Administrative Expenses.
_____	69.	Goodwill.
_____	70.	Income Tax Payable.
_____	71.	Income Tax Refund Receivable.
_____	72.	Income Tax Withheld (from employees).
_____	73.	Interest Payable.
_____	74.	Interest Receivable.

Classification	Account	Classification	Account
_____	75. Interest Revenue.	_____	97. Organization Costs.
_____	76. Investment in General Motors Stock.	_____	98. Patents.
_____	77. Investment in U.S. Gov. Bonds.	_____	99. Petty Cash Fund.
_____	78. Investment in Unconsolidated Subsidiary.	_____	100. Plant and Equipment.
_____	79. Land.	_____	101. Preferred Stock Redemption Fund.
_____	80. Land Held for Future Plant Site.	_____	102. Premium on Bonds Payable.
_____	81. Land Used for Parking Lot.	_____	103. Premium on Common Stock.
_____	82. Leasehold Improvements.	_____	104. Prepaid Advertising.
_____	83. Leasehold Costs.	_____	105. Prepaid Insurance.
_____	84. Loss on Price Decline of Marketable Securities.	_____	106. Prepaid Insurance Expense.
_____	85. Machinery and Equipment.	_____	107. Prepaid Office Supplies.
_____	86. Machinery and Equipment Sitting Idle.	_____	108. Prepaid Royalty Payments.
_____	87. Marketable Securities.	_____	109. Prepaid Property Taxes.
_____	88. Merchandise Inventory.	_____	110. Provision for Bad Debts.
_____	89. Mortgage Payable.	_____	111. Provision for Income Taxes.
_____	90. Notes Payable.	_____	112. Rental Revenue.
_____	91. Notes Payable to Banks.	_____	113. Salaries Payable.
_____	92. Notes Receivable.	_____	114. Sales Discounts and Allowances.
_____	93. Notes Receivable Discounted.	_____	115. Selling Expense Control.
_____	94. Office Supplies on Hand.	_____	116. Stock Dividends Distributable.
_____	95. Office Supplies Prepaid.	_____	117. Stock Dividends Payable.
_____	96. Office Supplies Used.	_____	118. Store Supplies.
		_____	119. Store Supplies Used.

Classifica- tion	Account	Classifica- tion	Account
_____	120. Tools and Dies (5-year life).	_____	126. Unearned Royalties.
_____	121. Tools and Dies (6-mos. life).	_____	127. Unearned Subscription Income.
_____	122. Treasury Stock Common (at cost).	_____	128. Unexpired Insurance.
_____	123. Unamortized Bond Issue Costs.	_____	129. Vacation Pay Payable.
_____	124. Unamortized Organization Costs.	_____	130. Vouchers Payable.
_____	125. Unearned Rental Income	_____	131. Work in Process.

SOLUTION TO EXERCISE 5-1

Item #	Solution	Explanation and/or Comment
1.	CL	These are trade payables usually due within 60 days.
2.	CA	These are trade receivables usually due within 60 days.
3.	CA	Interest is due annually or more frequently.
4.	CL	A better title is simply Interest Payable (item 73).
5.	CL	A better title is simply Taxes Payable.
6.	(PPE)	This is a contra account. It is another title for item 13 (item 6 is used more frequently).
7.	(PPE)	This is a contra account and an alternative title for item 13.
8.	PPE	Tracks of natural resources are classified in PPE.
9.	DEP: CL or LTL	These advances refer to revenue amounts received in advance from customers.
10.	DEP: CA or INV or OA	These advances can be prepayments or loans.
11.	IS	
12.	(CA)	This is another title for Allowance for Doubtful Accounts.
13.	(PPE)	This is another title for Accumulated Depreciation (items 6 and 7).
14.	(CA)	This is Contra to Accounts Receivable.
15.	(CA)	This account arises because of the use of the lower of cost or market rule.
16.	(CA)	This is contra to Inventory.
17.	(CA)	This is another title for item 15.
18.	(CL)	This account reflects amounts included in Accounts Payable that will not be paid because of purchase discounts to be taken.
19.	(CA)	This account reflects amounts included in Accounts Receivable that will not be collected because of sales discounts allowed.
20.	(CA)	This is another title for Allowance for Doubtful Accounts.
21.	RE	This is a restriction on retained earnings (portion of total retained earnings).
22.	RE	This is a restriction on retained earnings (portion of total retained earnings).

Item #	Solution	Explanation and/or Comment
23.	RE	This is a restriction on retained earnings (portion of total retained earnings).
24.	RE	This is a restriction on retained earnings (portion of total retained earnings).
25.	CL	This is usually listed as the first item under current liabilities.
26.	CL	
27.	CA	
28.	INV	A fund can be comprised of cash or securities.
29.	PPE	
30.	CA	
31.	INV	
32.	INV	
33.	DEP: CA or INV	Some CDs are for 90 days, 180 days, 30 months or 60 months.
34.	CS	
35.	PPE	This is one of two exceptions to the general guidelines for items to be included in the PPE classification.
36.	CA	
37.	LTL	This answer assumes that the Bond Sinking Fund is classified under long-term investments.
38.	CL	
39.	CL	"Current portion" refers to the portion that is coming due within a year of the balance sheet date.
40.	CL	
41.	CL	
42.	DEP: CL or LTL	
43.	DEP: CA or OA	
44.	DEP: CL or LTL	
45.	CA	This is another title for item 109.
46.	CA	This is another title for items 94, 95, and 107.
47.	DEP: CL or LTL	This is another title for item 125.
48.	DEP: CL or LTL	Some subscriptions are for one year, others are for two or more years. This is another title for item 127.
49.	DEP: CL or LTL	
50.	PPE	This is the second of two exceptions to the general guidelines for items to be included in the PPE classification.
51.	IS	
52.	(LTL)	In the rare instance where the bonds payable are classified as current, the discount would be current also.
53.	(CS)	
54.	DEP: (CL) or (LTL)	
55.	DEP: (CA) or (INV)	
56.	CA	
57.	CL	
58.	CS	This is a bad title for Stock Dividend Distributable.
59.	IS	
60.	LTL	
61.	CL	
62.	DEP: CL or LTL	Some warranties are for more than one year.
63.	DEP: CL or LTL	Premiums in this context are similar to prizes.

Item #	Solution	Explanation and/or Comment
64.	CA	
65.	CA	
66.	PPE	
67.	IS	
68.	IS	
69.	ITG	
70.	CL	
71.	CA	
72.	CL	
73.	CL	This is another title for item 4 (item 73 is the preferable title).
74.	CA	
75.	IS	
76.	CA	This answer assumes there is no reason to hold the stock for a long-term purpose.
77.	DEP: CA or INV	
78.	INV	The fact that the investee is a subsidiary means there is an intention to hold the investee's stock for a long-term purpose.
79.	PPE	
80.	INV	
81.	PPE	
82.	PPE	
83.	ITG	
84.	IS	
85.	PPE	
86.	OA	
87.	CA	This is a title often used to refer to short-term investments.
88.	CA	
89.	LTL	The portion of this balance due within the next year will be reclassified and reported as a current liability.
90.	DEP: CL or LTL	
91.	DEP: CL or LTL	
92.	DEP: CA or INV	
93.	DEP: (CA) or (INV)	
94.	CA	This is another title for items 46, 95, and 107.
95.	CA	This is another title for items 46, 94, and 107.
96.	IS	
97.	ITG	This is another title for item 124 (item 97 is the more commonly used title).
98.	ITG	
99.	CA	
100.	PPE	
101.	INV	
102.	LTL	This is an adjunct type valuation account.
103.	APC	This is an adjunct type valuation account.
104.	CA	
105.	CA	This is another title for items 106 and 128.
106.	CA	This is another title for items 105 and 128.
107.	CA	This is another title for items 46, 94, and 95.
108.	CA	

Item #	Solution	Explanation and/or Comment
109.	CA	This is another title for item 45.
110.	IS	This is another title for Uncollectible Accounts Expense or Bad Debt Expense.
111.	IS	This is another title for Income Tax Expense.
112.	IS	
113.	CL	This is another title for Accrued Salaries or Accrued Salaries Payable. Salaries Payable is the preferred title.
114.	IS	This is a contra sales revenue item.
115.	IS	This is an account in the general ledger for which the details appear in a subsidiary ledger.
116.	CS	This is another title for items 58 and 117. The title in item 116 is the preferable title.
117.	CS	This is another title for items 58 and 116. This is a misleading title because the word payable suggests a liability which a stock dividend is not.
118.	CA	
119.	IS	
120.	PPE	
121.	IS	
122.	(CS + APC + RE)	Treasury Stock is contra to the total of all other stockholder equity items when the cost method is used to account for it.
123.	OA	This is usually called Bond Issue Costs.
124.	ITG	This is usually called Organization Costs. It is the same as item 97.
125.	DEP: CL or LTL	This is another title for item 47.
126.	DEP: CL or LTL	
127.	DEP: CL or LTL	This is another title for item 48.
128.	CA	This is another title for items 105 and 106.
129.	CL	
130.	CL	This is another title for Accounts Payable when a voucher system is in use.
131.	CA	This is an inventory account for a manufacturer.

Approach: For each balance sheet classification, write down a definition or description of what is to be reported in that classification. Refer to those notes as you go down the list of items to be classified. Your notes should contain the guidelines summarized in **Illustration 5-1.**

EXERCISE 5-2

Purpose: This exercise will enable you to practice identifying errors and other deficiencies in a balance sheet.

Keith Sweat Company has decided to expand their operations. The bookkeeper recently completed the balance sheet presented below to submit to the bank in order to obtain additional funds for expansion.

Instructions

Prepare a revised balance sheet in good form. Correct any errors and weaknesses you find in the presentation below. Assume that the accumulated depreciation balance for the buildings is $140,000 and for the office equipment, $95,000. The allowance for doubtful accounts has a balance of $10,000. The pension obligation is considered to be a long-term liability.

Keith Sweat Company
BALANCE SHEET
For the Year Ended 1992

Current assets	
Cash (net of bank overdraft of $30,000)	$200,000
Accounts receivable (net)	340,000
Inventories at lower of average cost or market	385,000
Marketable securities--at market (cost $120,000)	140,000
Property, plant, and equipment	
Building (net)	570,000
Office equipment (net)	160,000
Land held for future use	175,000
Intangible assets	
Goodwill	80,000
Cash surrender value of life insurance	90,000
Prepaid expenses	5,000
Current liabilities	
Accounts payable	105,000
Notes payable (due next year)	125,000
Pension obligation	82,000
Rent payable	55,000
Premium on bonds payable	53,000
Long-term liabilities	
Bonds payable	500,000
Appropriation for plant expansion	92,000
Stockholders' equity	
Common stock, $1.00 par, authorized	
400,000 shares, issued 290,000	290,000
Additional paid-in capital	160,000
Unappropriated retained earnings	683,000

SOLUTION TO EXERCISE 5-2

Keith Sweat Company
Balance Sheet
December 31, 1992
Assets

Current assets			
Cash			$ 230,000
Marketable securities, at cost (market value is $140,000)			120,000
Accounts receivable		$350,000	
Less allowance for doubtful accounts		10,000	340,000
Inventories, at lower of average cost or market			385,000
Prepaid expenses			5,000
Total current assets			1,080,000
Long-term investments			
Land held for future use		175,000	
Cash surrender value of life insurance		90,000	
Total long-term investments			265,000
Property, plant, and equipment			
Building		$710,000	
Less accumulated depreciation--building		140,000	570,000
Office equipment		255,000	
Less accumulated depreciation--office equip.		95,000	160,000
Total property, plant, and equipment			730,000
Intangible assets			
Goodwill			80,000
Total assets			$2,155,000

Liabilities and Stockholders' Equity

Current liabilities			
Bank overdraft			$ 30,000
Notes payable			125,000
Accounts payable			105,000
Rent payable			55,000
Total current liabilities			315,000
Long-term liabilities			
Bonds payable		$500,000	
Add premium on bonds payable		53,000	$553,000
Pension obligation			82,000
Total long-term liabilities			635,000
Total liabilities			950,000
Stockholders' equity			
Paid-in capital			
Common stock, $1 par, authorized 400,000 shares, issued 290,000 shares		290,000	
Additional paid-in capital		160,000	450,000
Retained earnings			
Appropriation for plant expansion		92,000	
Unappropriated		663,000	755,000
Total stockholders' equity			1,205,000
Total liabilities and stockholders' equity			$2,155,000

Explanation:
1. A bank overdraft in one bank account should not be reflected as an offset to positive cash items (such as a positive balance in another account). A bank overdraft must be reported as a current liability. (The one exception to this rule is as follows: if an account with a positive balance exists in the same bank as the overdraft, the overdraft can be reflected as an offset to the extent of that positive balance).

2. Because the marketable securities were being reported at their market value of $140,000 which is in excess of their cost, this means that a debit had erroneously been made to the asset account for Marketable Securities for $20,000 to write the securities up to market value. A corresponding credit for $20,000 is, therefore, inappropriately included in Retained Earnings and must be removed from there. Marketable securities are to be reported at the lower of cost or market value. What the bookkeeper did was a violation of both the historical cost and the revenue recognition principles.

3. Land held for future use is not to be classified in the property, plant, and equipment section because the land is not currently being used in operations.

4. Cash surrender value of life insurance is an intangible item in a legal sense (because it lacks physical substance), but it is classified as a long-term investment for accounting purposes.

5. Prepaid expenses represent prepayments that relate to benefits that are expected to be consumed within the year that follows the balance sheet date. Hence, they are current assets.

6. A pension obligation is generally not expected to become due in the near future and, therefore, is not expected to require the use of current assets within a year of the balance sheet date. Hence, it is a long-term liability.

7. Rent is normally paid in advance. In this exercise, the rent payment is due after the relevant time period has lapsed. The rent payable is a current liability.

8. Premium on Bonds Payable is an adjunct type valuation account. A valuation account should always be reported with the account to which it relates.

9. Bonds payable are always assumed to be a long-term liabilities unless the facts make them appear to meet the definition for a current liability.

10. An Appropriation for Plant Expansion is an appropriation of retained earnings so retained earnings must be shown in two portions--appropriated and unappropriated.

EXERCISE 5-3

Purpose: This exercise will enable you to practice identifying errors and other deficiencies in a balance sheet.

Presented below is a balance sheet for the George Strait Corporation.

George Strait Corporation
BALANCE SHEET
December 31, 1992

Current assets	$ 435,000	Current liabilities	$ 380,000
Investments	640,000	Long-term liabilities	1,000,000
Property, plant, and equipment	1,720,000	Stockholders' equity	1,720,000
Intangible assets	305,000		
	$3,100,000		$3,100,000

The following information is presented:

1.   The current asset section includes: cash $100,000, accounts receivable $170,000 less $10,000 for allowance for doubtful accounts, inventories $180,000, and prepaid revenue $5,000. The cash balance is composed of $116,000, less a bank overdraft of $16,000. Inventories are stated on the lower of FIFO cost or market.

2.   The investments section includes the cash surrender value of a life insurance contract $40,000, investments in common stock, short-term $80,000 and long-term $140,000, bond sinking fund $200,000, and organization costs $180,000.

3.   Property, plant, and equipment includes buildings $1,040,000 less accumulated depreciation $360,000, equipment $420,000 less accumulated depreciation $180,000, land $500,000, and land held for future use $300,000.

4.   Intangible assets include a franchise $165,000, goodwill $100,000, and discount on bonds payable $40,000.

5.   Current liabilities include accounts payable $90,000, notes payable--short-term $120,000 notes payable--long-term $80,000, taxes payable $40,000, and appropriation for short-term contingencies $50,000.

6.   Long-term liabilities are composed solely of 10% bonds payable due in the year 2000.

7.   Stockholders' equity includes preferred stock, no par value, 200,000 shares authorized with 70,000 shares issued for $450,000, and common stock, $1.00 par value, 400,000 shares authorized with 100,000 shares issued at an average price of $10. In addition, the corporation has unappropriated retained earnings of $270,000.

Instructions
Prepare a balance sheet in good form.

SOLUTION TO EXERCISE 5-3

George Strait Corporation
Balance Sheet
December 31, 1992

Assets

Current assets			
Cash			$ 116,000
Marketable securities			80,000
Accounts receivable		$170,000	
Less allowance for doubtful accounts		10,000	160,000
Inventories, at lower of FIFO cost or market			180,000
Total current assets			536,000
Investments			
Investments in common stock		140,000	
Bond sinking fund		200,000	
Cash surrender value of life insurance		40,000	
Land held for future use		300,000	
Total long-term investments			680,000
Property, plant, and equipment			
Land		500,000	
Buildings	$1,040,000		
Less accumulated depreciation--building	360,000	680,000	
Equipment	420,000		
Less accumulated depreciation--equipment	180,000	240,000	
Total property, plant, and equipment			1,420,000
Intangible assets			
Organization costs		180,000	
Franchise		165,000	
Goodwill		100,000	
Total intangible assets			445,000
Total assets			$3,081,000

Liabilities and Stockholders' Equity

Current liabilities			
Bank overdraft			$ 16,000
Notes payable			120,000
Accounts payable			90,000
Taxes payable			40,000
Unearned revenue			5,000
Total current liabilities			271,000
Long-term liabilities			
Notes payable		$ 80,000	
10% bonds payable, due 2000	$1,000,000		
Less discount on bonds payable	40,000	960,000	
Total long-term liabilities			1,040,000
Total liabilities			1,311,000
Stockholders' equity			
Paid-in capital			
Preferred stock, no par value; 200,000 shares authorized, 70,000 issued	450,000		
Common stock, $1 par value; 400,000 shares authorized, 100,000 issued	100,000		
Paid-in capital in excess of par on common stock	900,000*	1,450,000	
Retained earnings			
Appropriated for contingencies	50,000		
Unappropriated	270,000	320,000	
Total stockholders' equity			1,770,000
Total liabilities and stockholders' equity			$3,081,000

*100,000 shares X ($10.00 - $1.00) = $900,000.

5-15

EXERCISE 5-4

Purpose: This exercise will enable you to practice preparing a balance sheet in good form from a trial balance.

The post-closing trial balance of Tiffany Company and other related information for the year 1992 is presented below.

Tiffany Company
Post-closing Trial Balance
December 31, 1992

Cash	$ 41,000	
Accounts Receivable	163,500	
Allowance for Doubtful Accounts		$ 6,700
Prepaid Expenses	5,900	
Inventory	308,500	
Long-term Investments	349,000	
Land	85,000	
Construction Work in Progress	124,000	
Patents	26,000	
Equipment	400,000	
Accumulated Depreciation of Equipment		142,000
Unamortized Discount on Bonds Payable	20,000	
Accounts Payable		148,000
Accrued Expenses		38,200
Notes Payable		94,000
Bonds Payable		400,000
Common Stock		500,000
Premium on Capital Stock		45,000
Retained Earnings		75,000
Reserve for Future Plant Expansion		74,000
	$1,522,900	$1,522,900

Additional information:
1. The inventory has a replacement value of $353,000. The LIFO method of inventory pricing is used.
2. Long-term investments consist of stock and bonds with a market value of $380,000.
3. The amount of the Construction Work in Progress account represents the costs expended to date on a building in the process of construction. (The company rents factory space at the present time.) The land on which the building is being constructed cost $85,000, as shown in the trial balance.
4. The patents were purchased by the company at a cost of $36,000 and are being amortized on a straight-line basis.
5. Of the unamortized discount on bonds payable, $2,000 will be amortized in 1993.
6. The notes payable represent bank loans that are secured by long-term investments which are carried at a cost of $120,000 and have a market value of $148,000. These bank loans are due in 1993.
7. The bonds payable bear interest at 11% and are due January 1, 2003.
8. Six hundred thousand shares of common stock of a par value of $1.00 are authorized, of which 500,000 shares are issued and are outstanding.
9. The Reserve for Future Plant Expansion was created by action of the board of directors.

Instructions--Prepare a balance sheet as of December 31, 1992 so that all important information is appropriately disclosed.

SOLUTION TO EXERCISE 5-4

Tiffany Company
Balance Sheet
December 31, 1992
<u>Assets</u>

<u>Current assets</u>

Cash		$ 41,000
Accounts receivable	$163,500	
Less allowance for doubtful accounts	6,700	156,800
Inventory--at LIFO cost		308,500
Prepaid expenses		5,900
Total current assets		$ 512,200

<u>Long-term investments</u>

Miscellaneous stocks and bonds, of which investments costing $120,000 have been pledged as security for notes payable-- at cost (market value, $380,000)	349,000

Property, plant, and equipment

Land		85,000
Building in process of construction		124,000
Equipment	400,000	
Less accumulated depreciation	142,000	258,000
Total property, plant, and equipment		467,000

<u>Intangible assets</u>

Patents	26,000
Total assets	$1,354,200

<u>Liabilities and Stockholders' Equity</u>

<u>Current liabilities</u>

Bank loans payable, secured by investments with a cost of $120,000 and a market value of $148,000	$ 94,000
Accounts payable	148,000
Accrued expenses	38,200
Total current liabilities	$ 280,200

<u>Long-term liabilities</u>

11% bonds payable, due January 1, 2003	400,000	
Less unamortized discount on bonds payable	20,000	
Total long-term liabilities		380,000
Total liabilities		660,200

<u>Stockholders' equity</u>

Paid-in capital

Common stock, $1 par, authorized 600,000 shares; issued and outstanding, 500,000 shares	$500,000		
Additional paid-in capital	45,000	545,000	
Retained earnings			
Appropriation for plant expansion	74,000		
Unappropriated	75,000	149,000	694,000
Total liabilities and stockholders' equity			$1,354,200

5-17

EXERCISE 5-5

Purpose: This exercise enables you to practice identifying investing and financing activities.

Instructions
Place the appropriate code in the blanks to identify each of the following transactions as giving rise to an:

Code
II   inflow of cash due to an investing activity, or
IO   outflow of cash due to an investing activity, or
FI   inflow of cash due to a financing activity, or
FO   outflow of cash due to a financing activity.

Transactions

_____ 1. Sell common stock to new stockholders.

_____ 2. Purchase treasury stock.

_____ 3. Borrow money from bank by issuance of short-term note.

_____ 4. Repay money borrowed from bank.

_____ 5. Purchase bonds as an investment.

_____ 6. Sell investment in real estate.

_____ 7. Loan money to an affiliate.

_____ 8. Collect on loan to affiliate.

_____ 9. Buy equipment.

_____ 10. Sell a plant asset.

_____ 11. Pay cash dividends to stockholders.

SOLUTION TO EXERCISE 5-5

1.	FI	4.	FO	7.	IO	10.	II
2.	FO	5.	IO	8.	II	11.	FO
3.	FI	6.	II	9.	IO		

Approach:
1. Reconstruct journal entries for the transactions. Examine each entry to identify if there is an inflow of cash (debit to Cash) or an outflow of cash (credit to Cash).
2. Write down the definitions for investing activities and financing activities. Analyze each transaction to see if it fits one of these definitions.
3. Assume purchases and sales of items are for cash unless otherwise indicated.

Definitions:
Investing activities--include (a) making and collecting loans, (b) acquiring and disposing of debt and equity instruments, and (c) acquiring and disposing of property, plant, and equipment.
Financing activities--include (a) obtaining capital from owners and providing them with a return on and a return of their investment, and (b) borrowing money from creditors and repaying the amounts borrowed.

TIP: The journal entry to record a transaction that is an investing activity which results in a cash flow will involve: (1) Cash and (2) an asset account other than Cash, such as Investment (short-term or long-term), Land, Building, Equipment, Patent, Franchise, etc.

TIP: The journal entry to record a transaction that is a financing activity which results in a cash flow will involve: (1) Cash and (2) a liability account or an owners' equity account such as Bonds Payable, Note Payable, Dividends Payable, Common Stock, Additional Paid-in Capital, Treasury Stock, etc.

EXERCISE 5-6

Purpose: This exercise will enable you to practice reconciling net income with net cash provided by operating activities.

The following data relate to the L. Heckenmueller Co. for 1992:

Net income	$75,000
Increase in accounts receivable	7,000
Decrease in prepaid expenses	3,200
Increase in accounts payable	5,000
Decrease in taxes payable	900
Gain on sale of investment	1,700
Depreciation	3,500
Loss on sale of equipment	600

Instructions
Compute the net cash provided by operating activities for 1992.

SOLUTION TO EXERCISE 5-6

Net income	$75,000
Increase in accounts receivable	(7,000)
Decrease in prepaid expenses	3,200
Increase in accounts payable	5,000
Decrease in taxes payable	(900)
Gain on sale of investment	(1,700)
Depreciation	3,500
Loss on sale of equipment	600
Net cash provided by operating activities	$77,700

Explanation:
1.   Net income is a summary of all revenues earned, all expenses incurred, and all gains and losses recognized for a period. Most revenues earned during the year result in a cash inflow during the same year but there may be some cash and/or revenue flows that do not correspond. Most expenses incurred during the year result in a cash outflow during the same year but there may be some cash and or expense flows that do not correspond.

2.   An increase in accounts receivable indicates that revenues earned exceed cash collected from customers and, therefore, net income exceeds net cash provided by operating activities.

3.   A decrease in prepaid expenses indicates that expenses incurred exceed cash paid and, therefore, net income is less than net cash provided by operating activities.

4. An increase in accounts payable indicates that expenses incurred exceed cash paid and, therefore, net income is less than net cash provided by operating activities.

5. A decrease in taxes payable indicates expenses incurred are less than the cash paid, and, therefore, net income is greater than net cash provided by operating activities.

6. When an investment is sold, the entire proceeds are to be displayed as an investing activity on the statement of cash flows. The gain included in net income must, therefore, be deducted from net income to arrive at the net cash provided by operating activities. If this adjustment was not made, there would be double counting for the gain amount. For example: An investment with a carrying value of $4,000 is sold for $7,000. The entire $7,000 proceeds is an investing inflow; the $7,000 includes the gain of $3,000; the $3,000 gain will be deducted from net income to arrive at the net cash from operating activities figure.

7. Depreciation is a noncash charge (debit) against income. It must be added to net income to arrive at the amount of net cash provided by operating activities.

8. A loss on the sale of equipment does not cause a cash outlay so it is added back to net income to arrive at net cash provided by operating activities.

ANALYSIS OF MULTIPLE-CHOICE TYPE QUESTIONS

Question
1. The Heather Miller Company has the following obligations at December 31, 1992:

I.	Accounts payable	$ 72,000
II.	Taxes payable	60,000
III.	Notes payable issued November 1, 1989, due October 31, 1993	80,000
IV.	Bonds payable issued December 1, 1983, due November 30,1993 (to be paid by use of a sinking fund)	100,000

The amount that should be reported for total current liabilities at December 31, 1992 is
a. $312,000.
b. $212,000.
c. $132,000.
d. $72,000.

Solution = b.

Explanation and Approach: Write down the definition (or key phrases therein) for current liability. A current liability is an obligation which is coming due within a year of the balance sheet date and is expected to require the use of current assets or the incurrence of another current liability to liquidate it. Analyze each of the obligations listed to see if it meets the criteria for being classified as current. Accounts payable and taxes payable will both be due shortly after the balance sheet date and will require cash to liquidate the debts. The notes payable are due within a year of the balance sheet date and there is no evidence to indicate that assets other than current assets will be used for settlement; thus, the notes payable are a current liability. The bonds payable are coming due within a year but they will **not** require the use of current assets to liquidate the debt because a sinking fund (restricted cash or securities classified as a long-term investment) is to be used to extinguish that debt. $72,000 + $60,000 + $80,000 = $212,000.

Question

2. Land held for a future plant site should be classified in the section for
   a. current assets.
   b. long-term investments.
   c. property, plant, and equipment.
   d. intangible assets.

Solution = b.

Approach: Quickly review in your mind the descriptions of what goes in each of the asset classifications. Then read each answer selection and respond **True** or **False** if the selection answers the question. The land is not being used in operations so it doesn't belong in property, plant, and equipment. It is not lacking physical existence so it can't be an intangible. It isn't expected to be converted to cash or sold or consumed within the next year, so it's not a current asset. The item properly belongs in long-term investments.

Question

3. A loss contingency that has a level of likelihood rated as reasonably possible and an amount that can be reasonably estimated should be:

	Accrued	Disclosed
a.	Yes	Yes
b.	Yes	No
c.	No	Yes
d.	No	No

Solution = c.

Explanation: A loss contingency that is probable and estimable should be accrued. A loss contingency that is reasonably possible and estimable should be disclosed only in the notes (and not be accrued). A loss contingency that is only remotely possible can usually be ignored and not disclosed or accrued.

Approach: Read the stem and write down how you would complete the statement in the stem. Then look at the answer selections one at a time to find the one that corresponds with your anticipated response.

Question

4. Which of the following is a contra account?
   a. Premium on bonds payable.
   b. Unearned revenue.
   c. Patents.
   d. Accumulated depreciation.

Solution = d.

Approach and Explanation: After reading the stem and before reading the answer selections, write down the description of the term contra account. A contra account is a valuation account whose normal balance is opposite of the balance of the account to which it relates. Then take each answer selection and answer **True** or **False** whether it meets that description. Premium on bonds payable is a valuation account, but it is an adjunct type (its normal balance is the same as the normal balance of the account to which it relates). Unearned Revenue and Patents are not valuation accounts. Accumulated Depreciation is a valuation account for property, plant, and equipment. The normal balance is a credit and the normal balance of a property, plant, and equipment account is a debit. Hence, Accumulated Depreciation is a contra account.

Question

5. Which of the following should be classified as an inflow of cash in the investing section of a statement of cash flows?
    a. Cash sale of merchandise inventory.
    b. Sale of delivery equipment at book value.
    c. Sale of common stock.
    d. Issuance of a note payable to a bank.

Solution = b.

Approach and Explanation: Read the stem and before reading the answer selections, write down the items that appear in the definition of investing activities. Investing activities include making and collecting loans to others, acquiring and disposing of stocks and bonds of other entities, acquiring and disposing of property, plant, and equipment and other productive assets. Think of the items included in that definition that would produce a cash inflow (collecting loans, disposing of investments and property, plant, and equipment). Look for the answer selection that fits that analysis. As you analyze each answer selection, indicate what kind of activity it represents. A cash sale of merchandise inventory is an operating activity. The sale of common stock is a financing activity. The issuance of a note payable is a financing activity. A sale of equipment is an investing activity.

CHAPTER 6

ACCOUNTING AND THE TIME VALUE OF MONEY

OVERVIEW

Due to the time value of money, a certain sum today is not equal to the same sum at a future point in time. We must consider the compound interest factor for the time between two given dates in order to determine what amount in the future is equivalent to a given sum today or what amount today is equivalent to a given sum in the future. We compound the dollar amount forward in time in the former case and discount the dollar amount from the future to the present time in the latter case. In this chapter we discuss both of these procedures for a single sum and the appropriate procedures for compounding and discounting annuities.

Interest tables appear at the end of this chapter.

TIPS ON CHAPTER TOPICS

TIP: Present value of a single sum is the current worth of a future amount. Future amount of a single sum is the future value of an amount to be put on deposit today (a present value figure).

TIP: The factor for the "present value of 1" is the reciprocal (inverse) of the factor for the "future amount of 1". Thus, if you are given the factor from the Future Amount of 1 Table for n = 3, i = 8% which is 1.25971, you can compute the factor for the "present value of 1" for n = 3, i = 8% by dividing 1 by 1.25971. This division yields a factor of .79383 which does agree with the factor for n = 3, i = 8% in the Present Value of 1 Table.

TIP: Future amount of 1 is often referred to as future value of 1, and future amount of an annuity is often called future value of an annuity.

TIP: The factor for the present value of an ordinary annuity of 1 for n periods is the sum of factors for the present value of 1 for each of the n periods. For example, the factor for the present value of an ordinary annuity of 1 for n = 3, i = 8% (which is 2.57710) is equal to sum of the factors from the 8% column of the Present Value of 1 Table for n = 1, n = 2, n = 3 (.92593 + .85734 + .79383 = 2.57710).

TIP: One payment (or receipt) involved in an annuity is called a **rent.**

TIP: The factor for the future value of an ordinary annuity of 1 for n = 3, i = 8% reflects interest on the first rent for two periods, interest on the second rent for one period, and no interest on the third rent. The factor for the future value of an annuity due of 1 for n = 3, i = 8% reflects interest on the first rent for three periods, interest on the second rent for two periods, and interest for one period on the third rent.

TIP: Referring to the TIP immediately above, we can see that the future value of an annuity due equals the future value of an ordinary annuity multiplied by 1 + i.

TIP: The present value of an annuity due equals the present value of an ordinary annuity multiplied by 1 + i.

TIP: A factor for the present value or the future value of an annuity reflects one rent per period. Therefore, if an annuity involves a delay before the rents begin, the factor for n must be adjusted before the problem can be solved.

TIP: Anytime you have a present value or a future value problem to solve, it is wise to draw a time diagram. This picture will help you to determine:
(1)   if you are given present value or future value data or both.
(2)   if you are dealing with a single sum or an annuity situation.
(3)   what you are to solve for--present value or future value or n or i or rent.

TIP: Any present value or future value problem is an application (or variation) of one or more of the following formulas: (parentheses indicate multiplication)
Future Value of an Amount = Present Value (Future Value of 1 Factor)
Present Value of an Amount = Future Value (Present Value of 1 Factor)
Future Value of an Annuity = Rent (Future Value of an Annuity Factor)
Present Value of an Annuity = Rent (Present Value of an Annuity Factor)

TIP: To convert a factor for n = 3; i = 8% from an ordinary annuity table to a factor for an annuity due for n = 3, i = 8%, simply multiply the factor for n from the ordinary annuity table by (1 + i) **or** follow the rules below:
(1)   For future value: Select factor for ordinary annuity for (n + 1) then deduct 1.00000 from that factor.
(2)   For present value: Select factor for ordinary annuity for (n - 1) then add 1.00000 to that factor.

TIP: The interest rate is often referred to as the discount rate in computing present value.

TIP: The higher the discount rate (interest rate) is, the lower the present value will be.

ILLUSTRATION 6-1
STEPS IN SOLVING FUTURE VALUE AND PRESENT VALUE PROBLEMS

1.   Classify the problem into one of six types:
    (1)   Future value of a single sum.
    (2)   Present value of a single sum.
    (3)   Future value of an ordinary annuity.
    (4)   Present value of an ordinary annuity.
    (5)   Future value of an annuity due.
    (6)   Present value of an annuity due.
2.   Determine n, the number of compounding periods, and i, the interest rate per period.
    a.   Draw a time diagram. This is helpful when the number of periods or number of rents must be figured out from the dates given in the problem.
    b.   If interest is compounded more than once a year--
        (1)   to find n: **multiply** the number of years by the number of compounding periods per year.

        (2)   to find i: **divide** the annual interest rate by the number of compounding periods per year.
3.   Use n and i (if known) to choose the proper interest factor from the interest table indicated in Step 1.
4.   Solve for the missing quantity. A summary of the possibilities appears below. Abbreviations used in this summary are explained at the end of the summary.

ILLUSTRATION 6-2
SUMMARY OF SIX TYPES OF FUTURE VALUE AND PRESENT VALUE PROBLEMS

1.   Future Value of a Single Sum
      a.   Future Value   =   Present Value X FV Factor

      b.   FV Factor   = $\dfrac{\text{Future Value}}{\text{Present Value}}$
             (1)   "i" unknown and "n" known, or   Trace solved factor to Table 6-1.
             (2)   "n" unknown and "i" known   Trace solved factor to Table 6-1.

2.   Present Value of a Single Sum
      a.   Present Value   =   Future Value X PV Factor

      b.   PV Factor   = $\dfrac{\text{Present Value}}{\text{Future Value}}$
             (1)   "i" unknown and "n" known, or   Trace solved factor to Table 6-2.
             (2)   "n" unknown and "i" known   Trace solved factor to Table 6-2.

3.   Future Value of an Ordinary Annuity
      a.   Future Value of an Ordinary Annuity   =   Rent X FVOA Factor

      b.   Rent   = $\dfrac{\text{Future Value of an Ordinary Annuity}}{\text{FVOA Factor}}$

      c.   FVOA Factor   = $\dfrac{\text{Future Value of an Ordinary Annuity}}{\text{Rent}}$
             (1)   "i" unknown and "n" known, **or**   Trace solved factor to Table 6-3.
             (2)   "n" unknown and "i" known   Trace solved factor to Table 6-3.

4.   Present Value of an Ordinary Annuity
      a.   Present Value of an Ordinary Annuity   =   Rent X PVOA Factor

      b.   Rent   = $\dfrac{\text{Present Value of an Ordinary Annuity}}{\text{PVOA Factor}}$

      c.   PVOA Factor   = $\dfrac{\text{Present Value of an Ordinary Annuity}}{\text{Rent}}$
             (1)   "i" unknown and "n" known, **or**   Trace solved factor to Table 6-4.
             (2)   "n" unknown and "i" known   Trace solved factor to Table 6-4.

5. Future Value of an Annuity Due
   a. Future Value of an Annuity Due $\quad = \quad$ Rent X FVAD Factor

   b. Rent $\quad = \quad \dfrac{\text{Future Value of an Annuity Due}}{\text{FVAD Factor}}$

Note: There is no table in this book for Future Amount of an Annuity Due so ordinary annuity factors must be modified as follows:

$$FVAD_n = FVOA_{n+1} - 1.00000$$
$$\textbf{OR}$$
$$FVAD_n = FVOA_n (1 + i)$$

6. Present Value of an Annuity Due
   a. Present Value of an Annuity Due $\quad = \quad$ Rent X PVAD Factor

   b. Rent $\quad = \quad \dfrac{\text{Present Value of an Annuity Due}}{\text{PVAD Factor}}$

   c. PVAD Factor $\quad = \quad \dfrac{\text{Present Value of an Annuity Due}}{\text{Rent}}$

   (1) "i" unknown and "n" known, **or** $\qquad$ Trace solved factor to Table 6-5.
   (2) "n" unknown and "i" known $\qquad$ Trace solved factor to Table 6-5.

Note: Factors for the present value of an annuity due can be derived by adjusting factors from the Table for Present Value of an Ordinary Annuity as follows:

$$PVAD_n = PVOA_{n-1} + 1.00000$$
$$\textbf{OR}$$
$$PVAD_n = PVOA_n (1 + i)$$

Abbreviations:

FV Factor	=	Future Amount of 1 Factor
PV Factor	=	Present Value of 1 Factor
i	=	Interest Rate
n	=	Number of Periods or Rents
FVOA Factor	=	Future Amount of an Ordinary Annuity of 1
PVOA Factor	=	Present Value of an Ordinary Annuity of 1
FVAD Factor	=	Future Amount of an Annuity Due of 1
PVAD Factor	=	Present Value of an Annuity Due of 1

ILLUSTRATION 6-3
STEPS IN SOLVING FUTURE VALUE AND
PRESENT VALUE PROBLEMS ILLUSTRATED

The steps in solving future value and present value problems (listed on page 6-2 and 6-3) are illustrated below and on the following pages:

<u>Problem</u>   <u>Solution</u>

1. If $10,000 is deposited in the bank today at   <u>Step 1:</u> This is a future value of a single sum
    8% interest compounded annually, what   problem.
    will be the balance in 5 years?

                                                     <u>Step 2:</u> n = 5; i = 8%

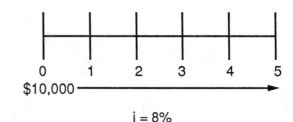

                                                     i = 8%

                                                     <u>Step 3:</u> The interest factor from Table 6-1 is
                                                                1.46933.

                                                     <u>Step 4:</u> Future Value = Present Value X FV
                                                                                        Factor
                                                                Future Value = $10,000 X 1.46933
                                                                Future Value = $14,693.30

2. A company needs $100,000 to retire debt.   <u>Step 1:</u> This is a present value of a single
    What amount must be deposited on Jan. 1,   sum problem.
    1992 at 8% interest compounded quarterly
    in order to accumulate the desired sum by   <u>Step 2:</u> It is 2 years from 1/1/92 to 1/1/94.
    Jan. 1, 1994?   The annual interest rate is 8%. n = 4
                                                                X 2 = 8; i = 8% ÷ 4 = 2%.

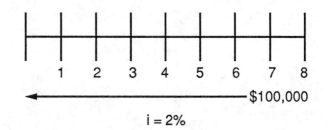

                                                     i = 2%

                                                     <u>Step 3:</u> The interest factor from Table 6-2 is
                                                                .85349.

Step 4:   Present Value = Future Value X PV'
                  Factor
      Present Value = $100,000 X .85349
      Present Value = $85,349.00

3.   If $71,178 can be invested now, what annual interest rate must be earned in order to accumulate $100,000 three years from now?

Step 1:   This can be solved either as a future value or as a present value of a single sum problem. This solution illustrates the present value approach.

Step 2:   n = 3; i must be solved for.

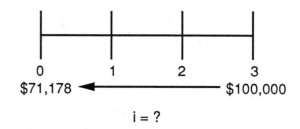

Step 3:   i must be solved for.

Step 4:   Present Value = Future Value X PV
                  Factor
      $71,178 = $100,000 X PV Factor
      $71,178 ÷ 100,000 = PV Factor
      .71178 = PV Factor
      Refer to Table 6-2 in the 3 period row.
        i = 12%

4.   If $1,000 is deposited into an account at the end of every year for six years, what will be the balance in the account after the sixth deposit if all amounts earn 6% interest?

Step 1:   This is a future value of an ordinary annuity problem.

Step 2:   n = 6; i = 6%.

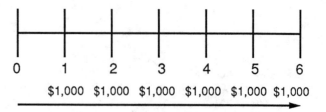

Step 3:   The interest factor from Table 6-3 is 6.97532.

Step 4:   Future Value of an Ordinary Annuity = Rent X FVOA Factor.

Future Value of an Ordinary Annuity =
$1,000 X 6.97532
Future Value of an Ordinary Annuity =
$6,975.32

5. What amount must be deposited at 10% in an account on Jan. 1, 1992 if it is desired to make equal annual withdrawals of $10,000 each, beginning on Jan. 1, 1993 and ending on Jan. 1, 1996?

Step 1: This is a present value of an ordinary annuity problem.

Step 2: The time diagram shows 4 withdrawals.

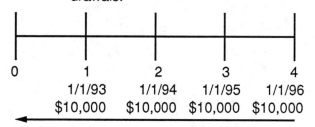

n = 4;   i = 10%.

Step 3: The interest factor from Table 6-3 is 3.16986.

Step 4: Present Value of An Ordinary Annuity = Rent X PVOA Factor.

Present Value of an Ordinary Annuity =
$10,000 X 3.16986
Present Value of Ordinary Annuity = $31,698.60

6. Beginning today, six annual deposits of $1,000 each will be made into an account paying 6%. What will be the balance in the account one year after the sixth deposit is made?

Step 1: This is a future value of an annuity due problem.

Step 2: n = 6; i = 6%.

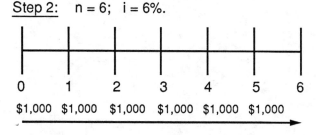

i = 6%

Step 3: Table 6-3 with factors for future value of an ordinary annuity (FVOA) can be used to derive the factor needed here for future value of an annuity due (FVAD). The process is as follows:

FVOA factor for n + 1	8.39384
	- 1.00000
FVAD factor for n	7.39384

Step 4: Future Value of an Annuity Due =
Rent X FVAD Factor
Future Value of Annuity Due = $1,000
X 7.39384 = $7,393.84

Note: Compare the results of this problem with those of problem 4 above.

The solution to problem 4 can be multiplied by (1 + i) to get the answer to number 6.

Proof: $6,975.32 X 1.06 = $7,393.84.

Explanation: Although both situations use the same number of equal rents and the same interest rate, the interest is earned on all of the deposits for one period more under the annuity due situation.

7. What is the present value of four annual payments of $10,000 each if interest is 10% and the first payment is made today?

Step 1: This is a present value of an annuity due problem.

Step 2: n = 4; i = 10%

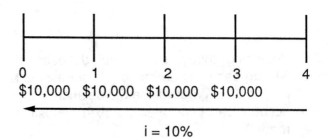

0   1   2   3   4
$10,000 $10,000 $10,000 $10,000

i = 10%

Step 3:
The interest factor from Table 6-5 is 3.48685.

This factor could also be derived by using the present value of an ordinary annuity table (Table 6-4) as follows:

PVOA factor for n - 1 =	2.48685
	+ 1.00000
PVAD factor for n =	3.48685

Step 4: Present Value of an Annuity Due =
Rent X PVAD Factor

Present Value of Annuity Due =
$10,000 X 3.48685
Present Value of Annuity Due =
$34,868.50.

Note: Compare the results of this problem with those of problem 5 above.

The solution to problem 5 can be multiplied by (1 + i) to get the answer to number 7.

Proof: $31,698.60 X 1.10 = $34,868.46. (Difference of $.04 is due to the rounding of the factors.)

Explanation: Although both situations use the same number of equal rents and the same interest rate, the discounting is done on all of the deposits for one period less under the annuity due situation.

8.   What amount must be deposited at the end of each year in an account paying 8% interest if it is desired to have $10,000 at the end of the fifth year?

Step 1:   This is a future value of an ordinary annuity problem.

Step 2:   n = 5; i = 8%.

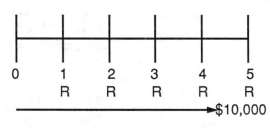

i = 8%

Step 3:   The interest factor from Table 6-3 is 5.86660.

Step 4:   Future Value of an Ordinary Annuity = Rent X FVOA Factor
$10,000 = Rent X 5.86660
$10,000 ÷ 5.86660 = Rent
$1,704.56 = Rent

Note: You can prove this solution by:
$1,704.56 X 5.86660 = $9,999.97

The difference of $.03 is due to rounding.

EXERCISE 6-1

Purpose: This exercise will test your knowledge of the applicability of four of the compound interest tables discussed in this chapter.

Instructions

For each independent situation below, (1) indicate which table you would need to use in order to locate the appropriate factor to solve for the figure requested, and (2) indicate if you divide (D) or multiply (M) by that factor to solve for the figure requested. Use the appropriate numerals and letters to indicate your answer for each.

I.   Amount of 1
II.   Amount of an Ordinary Annuity of 1
III.   Present Value of 1
IV.   Present Value of an Ordinary Annuity of 1

(1)	(2)	
_____	_____	1. $1,000 is put on deposit today to earn 6% interest, compounded annually. How much will be on deposit at the end of 8 years?
_____	_____	2. What amount today is equivalent to receiving $600 at the end of every year for 6 years, assuming interest is compounded annually at the rate of 5%?
_____	_____	3. If you wish to be able to withdraw the sum of $8,000 at the end of 12 years, how much do you have to deposit today, assuming interest is compounded annually at the rate of 6%?
_____	_____	4. If $400 is put in a savings account at the end of every year for 5 years, how much will be accumulated in the account if all amounts that remain on deposit earn 6% interest, compounded annually?
_____	_____	5. What amount today is equivalent to receiving $1,000 ten years from now if interest of 7% is compounded annually?
_____	_____	6. What amount today is equivalent to receiving $1,000 at the end of each year for ten years if interest of 7% is compounded annually?
_____	_____	7. How much must be deposited today to allow for the withdrawal of $1,000 at the end of each year for ten years if interest of 7% is compounded annually?
_____	_____	8. What is the present value of $500 due in 8 years at 6% compounded interest?
_____	_____	9. What is the future value of an ordinary annuity of $100 per period for 6 years at 7% compounded interest?
_____	_____	10. How much money must be deposited today to be able to withdraw $700 at the end of 7 years, assuming 7% compounded interest?

_____ _____ 11. How much money must be deposited today to be able to withdraw $700 at the end of each of 7 years, assuming 7% compounded interest?

_____ _____ 12. What is the discounted value of $700 due in 7 years at a 7% compounded interest rate?

_____ _____ 13. What is the future value of $700 put on deposit now for 7 years at 7% compounded interest?

_____ _____ 14. What is the future value in seven years of $700 put on deposit at the end of each of 7 years if all amounts on deposit earn 7% compound interest?

_____ _____ 15. How much can be withdrawn at the end of 5 years if $1,000 is deposited now at a 6% compound interest rate?

_____ _____ 16. What amount can be withdrawn at the end of each period for five years if $1,000 is deposited now and all amounts on deposit earn 6% interest compounded annually?

_____ _____ 17. If a debt of $5,000 is to be repaid in five equal end-of-year installments, what is the amount of each installment if interest at 7% is charged on the unpaid balance?

_____ _____ 18. What amount must be deposited at the end of each of four years to accumulate a fund of $7,000 at the end of the fourth year, assuming interest at a rate of 6% compounded annually?

SOLUTION TO EXERCISE 6-1

1.	I	M	or	III	D
2.	IV	M			
3.	III	M	or	I	D
4.	II	M			
5.	III	M	or	I	D
6.	IV	M			
7.	IV	M			
8.	III	M	or	I	D
9.	II	M			
10.	III	M	or	I	D
11.	IV	M			
12.	III	M	or	I	D
13.	I	M	or	III	D
14.	II	M			
15.	I	M	or	III	D
16.	IV	D			
17.	IV	D			
18.	II	D			

EXERCISE 6-2

Purpose: This exercise will illustrate some key concepts such as (1) the more frequently interest is compounded, the more interest will accumulate, (2) the greater the interest rate, the lower the present value will be, and (3) there is more interest reflected in an annuity due situation than in an ordinary annuity.

There are a wide variety of situations in which present value and/or future value concepts must be applied. A few of them are illustrated in the questions that follow.

1. If $1,000 is put on deposit today to earn 6% interest, how much will be on deposit at the end of 10 years if interest is compounded annually?

2. If $1,000 is put on deposit today to earn 6% interest, how much will be on deposit at the end of 10 years if interest is compounded semiannually?

3. In comparing questions 1 and 2, which answer would you expect to be the larger? Why?

4. What is the value today of $1,000 due 10 years in the future if the time value of money is 6% and interest is compounded once annually?

5. What is the value today of $1,000 due 10 years in the future if the time value of money is 6% and interest is compounded semiannually?

6. In comparing questions 4 and 5, which answer would you expect to be the larger? Why?

7. What is the present value of $1,000 due in 10 years if interest is compounded annually at 10%?

8. What is the present value of $1,000 due in 10 years if interest is compounded annually at 8%?

9. In comparing questions 7 and 8, which answer would you expect to be the larger? Why?

10. If $1,000 is deposited at the end of each year for 10 years and all amounts on deposit draw 6% interest compounded annually, how much will be on deposit at the end of 10 years?

11. If $1,000 is deposited at the beginning of each year for 10 years and all amounts on deposit draw 6% interest compounded annually, how much will be on deposit at the end of 10 years?

12. In comparing questions 10 and 11, which answer would you expect to be the larger? Why?

Instructions
Answer each of the questions above. Interest tables are included at the end of this chapter. Use the appropriate factors where needed.

SOLUTION TO EXERCISE 6-2

1. (1) This is a future value of a single sum problem.
   (2) n = 10; i = 6%.

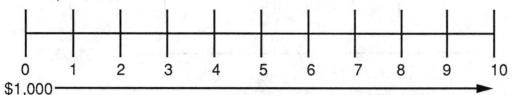

$$i = 6\%$$

   (3) The interest factor from Table 6-1 is 1.79085.
   (4) Future Value = Present Value X FV Factor
   Future Value = $1,000 X 1.79085
   Future Value = <u>$1,790.85</u>

2. (1) This is a future value of a single sum problem.
   (2) n = 10 X 2 = 20; i = 6% ÷ 2 = 3%

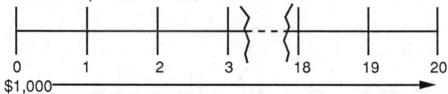

$$i = 3\%$$

   (3) The interest factor from Table 6-1 is 1.80611.
   (4) Future Value = Present Value X FV Factor
   Future Value = $1,000 X 1.80611
   Future Value = <u>$1,806.11</u>

3. We would expect the answer to question 2 to be a little larger than the answer to question 1 because the interest is compounded more frequently in question 2 which means there will be a larger amount of accumulated interest by the end of year 10 in this scenario.

4. (1) This is a present value of a single sum problem.
   (2) n = 10; i = 6%

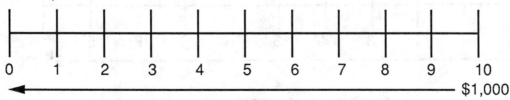

$$i = 6\%$$

   (3) The interest factor from Table 6-2 is .55839.
   (4) Present Value = Future Value X PV Factor.
   Present Value = $1,000 X .55839
   Present Value = <u>$558.39</u>

5. (1) This is a present value of single sum problem.
    (2) n = 2 X 10 = 20; i = 6% ÷ 2 = 3%

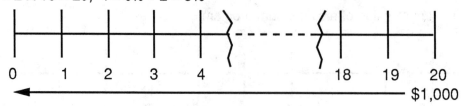

i = 3%
    (3) The interest factor from Table 6-2 is .55368.
    (4) Present Value = Future Value X PV Factor
         Present Value = $1,000 X .55368
         Present Value = $553.68

6. We would expect the answer to question 4 to be the larger because the more frequently that interest is compounded, the more the total interest will be. The greater the interest, the less the present value. Thus, the answer to question 5 has more interest reflected and a lesser present value figure.

7. (1) This is a present value of a single sum problem.
    (2) n = 10; i = 10%

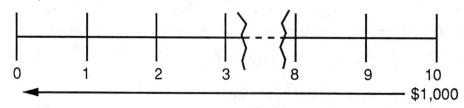

i = 10%
    (3) The interest factor from Table 6-2 is .38554.
    (4) Present Value = Future Value X PV Factor
         Present Value = $1,000 (.38554)
         Present Value = $385.54

8. (1) This is a present value of a single-sum problem.
    (2) n = 10; i = 8%

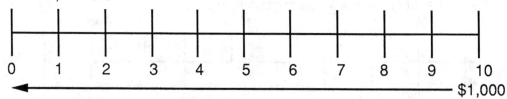

i = 8%
    (3) The interest factor from Table 6-2 is .46319.
    (4) Present Value = Future Value X PV Factor
         Present Value = $1,000 (.46319)
         Present Value = $463.19

9. We would expect the answer to question 8 to be the larger because the smaller the discount rate, the larger the present value. This is the case because the interest amount is smaller. The less the interest, the greater the present value figure.

10. (1) This is a future value of an ordinary annuity problem.
    (2) n = 10; i = 6%

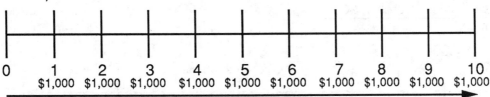

i = 6%

    (3) The interest factor from Table 6-3 is 13.18079.
    (4) Future Value of an Ordinary Annuity = Rent X FVOA Factor
        Future Value of an Ordinary Annuity = $1,000 X 13.18079
        Future Value of an Ordinary Annuity = $13,180.79

11. (1) This is a future value of an annuity due problem.
    (2) n = 10; i = 6%
    (3) The interest factor can be derived as follows:
        Factor for future amount of an ordinary annuity, n = 10   13.18079
        (1 + i)   X   1.06
        Factor for future amount of an annuity due, n = 10   13.97164

    (4) Future Value of an Annuity Due = Rent X FVAD Factor
        Future Value of an Annuity Due = $1,000 X 13.97164
        Future Value of an Annuity Due = $13,971.64

12. We would expect the answer to question 11 to be the larger because there is one more interest period reflected in the annuity due arrangement. The number of rents are the same, the interest rate is the same, but the rents begin earlier in the annuity due setup so there is one more interest period reflected.

EXERCISE 6-3

Purpose: This exercise will exemplify a situation that requires a two-part solution.

Mike Strong borrowed $67,000 on March 1, 1990. This amount plus accrued interest at 12% compounded semiannually is to be repaid March 1, 2000. To retire this debt, Mike plans to contribute to a debt retirement fund five equal amounts starting on March 1, 1995 and continuing for the next four years. The fund is expected to earn 10% per annum.

Instructions
How much must be contributed each year by Mike Strong to provide a fund sufficient to retire the debt on March 1, 2000?

SOLUTION TO EXERCISE 6-3

<u>Amount to be repaid on March 1, 2000:</u>
Time diagram:

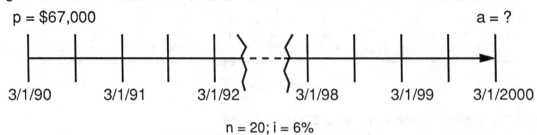

p = present value; a = future value of a single sum.

Future Value = $67,000 (FV Factor)   **OR**   Formula a $= p(a_{\overline{n}|i})$

Future Value = $67,000 (3.20714)   a $= \$67,000\ (a_{\overline{20}|6\%})$

Future Value = $214,878.38   a = $67,000 (3.20714)

                                                  a = $214,878.38

<u>Amount of annual contribution to retirement fund:</u>
Time diagram:

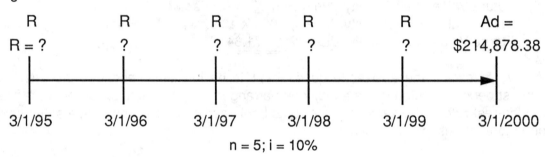

R = rent; Ad = future value of an annuity due.

Future value of ordinary annuity of 1 for 5 periods at 10%   6.10510
1 + i   X   1.1
Future value of an annuity due of 1 for 5 periods at 10%   6.71561
Future value of annuity due = Rent (FVAD Factor)

$214,878.38 = Rent (6.71561)

$$\frac{\$214,878.38}{6.71561} = \text{Rent}$$

$31,996.85 = Rent

<u>Approach:</u> First solve for the future value of a single sum. This future amount is $214,878.38. Then solve for the rent reflected in the future value of an ordinary annuity. The rent is $31,996.85. The solution to the first part establishes the future value of an ordinary annuity for which the rent must be determined in the second part of the problem.

EXERCISE 6-4

Purpose: This exercise will illustrate how to solve present value problems that require the computation of the rent in an annuity or the number of periods or the interest rate.

Instructions

Using the appropriate interest table, provide the solution to each of the following four questions by computing the unknowns.

(a) What is the amount of the payments that Susan Sprague must make at the end of each of eights years to accumulate a fund of $22,000 by the end of the eighth year, if the fund earns 8% interest, compounded annually?

(b) Leslie Oakes is thirty years old today and she wishes to accumulate $350,000 by her fifty-fifth birthday so she can retire to her summer place on Lake Holiday. She wishes to accumulate this amount by making equal deposits on her thirtieth through her fifty-fourth birthdays. What annual deposit must Leslie make if the fund will earn 12% interest compounded annually?

(c) Doug Barney has $10,000 to invest today at 9% to pay a debt of $28,126.70. How many years will it take him to accumulate enough to liquidate the debt?

(d) Jodie Boynton has $13,800 debt that she wishes to repay four years from today; she has $9,090.49 that she intends to invest for the four years. What rate of interest will she need to earn annually in order to accumulate enough to pay the debt?

SOLUTION TO EXERCISE 6-4

(a) Time diagram:

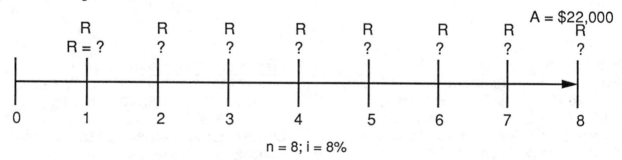

$$n = 8; i = 8\%$$

R = rent; A = future value of an ordinary annuity.

Future Value	= Rent X FVOA Factor	**OR**	Formula A	= $R\left(A_{\overline{n}|i}\right)$ or
$22,000	= Rent (10.63663)		$22,000	= $R\left(A_{\overline{8}|8\%}\right)$
$22,000 ÷ (10.63663)	= Rent		$22,000	= R (10.63663)
$2,068.32	= Rent		R	= $22,000 ÷ 10.63663
			R	= $2,068.32

(b) Time diagram:

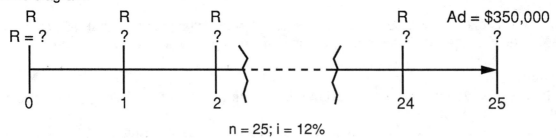

$n = 25; i = 12\%$

R = rent; Ad = future value of an annuity due.

Future value of an ordinary annuity of 1 for 25 periods at 12%	133.33387
Factor 1 + i	X 1.12
Future value of an annuity due of 1 for 25 periods at 12%	149.33393

Future value of annuity due = Rent (FVAD Factor)

$\$350,000$ = Rent (149.33393)

$\$350,000 \div 149.33393$ = Rent

$\$2,343.74$ = Rent

(c)   Time diagram:

p = $10,000.00   a = $28,126.70

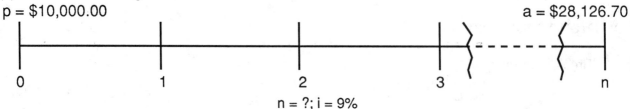

$n = ?; i = 9\%$

Future value approach

Future value = Present Value (FV Factor)

$28,126.70 = $10,000 (FV Factor)

2.81267 = FV Factor for i = 9%, n= ?

By reference to Table 6-1, 2.81267 is the
FV factor for i = 9%, n = 12

n = 12 years

OR Present value approach

Present value = Future value (PV Factor)

$10,000.00 = $28,126.70 (PV Factor)

.35553 = PV Factor for i = 9%, n = ?

By reference to Table 6-2, .35554 is the
PV factor for 1 = 9%, n = 12

n = 12 years

(d) Time diagram:

p = $9,090.49   a = $13,800.00

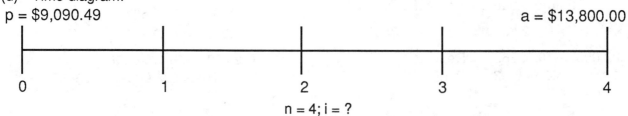

$n = 4; i = ?$

Future value approach

Future value = Present Value (FV Factor)

$13,800.00 = $9,090.49 (FV Factor)

1.51807 = FV Factor for n = 4, i= ?

By reference to Table 6-1, 1.46410 is the
FV factor for n = 4, i = 10% and 1.57352 is

OR Present value approach

Present value = Future value (PV Factor)

$9,090.49 = $13,800.00 (PV Factor)

.65873 = PV Factor for n = 4, i = ?

By reference to Table 6-2, .68301 is the
PV factor for n = 4, i = 10% and .63552 is

6-18

the PV factor for n = 4, i = 12%. 1.51807 is approximately one-half way in between 1.46410 and 1.57352; therefore, i = 11%.

the PV factor for n = 4, i = 12%. .65873 is approximately one-half way in between .68301 and .63552; therefore, i = 11%.

EXERCISE 6-5

Purpose: This exercise will illustrate a situation that involves the present value of an annuity along with the present value of a single sum.

Your client, Warlock, Inc., has acquired Motormount Manufacturing Company in a business combination that is to be accounted for as a purchase transaction (at fair market value). Along with the assets and business of Motormount, Warlock assumed an outstanding debenture bond issue having a principal amount of $7,500,000 with interest payable semiannually at a stated rate of 8%. Motormount received $6,800,000 in proceeds from the issuance five years ago. The bonds are currently 20 years from maturity. Equivalent securities command a 12% rate of interest with interest paid semiannually.

Instructions
Your client requests your advice regarding the amount to record for the acquired bond issue.

SOLUTION TO EXERCISE 6-5

Time diagram:

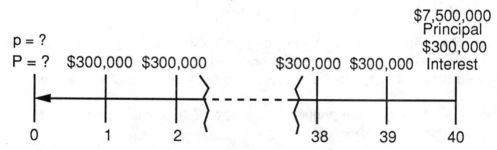

$$i = 6\% \text{ per six months}$$

n = 40 six-month periods; i = 6% per six-month period
P = present value of an ordinary annuity; p = present value of a single sum

Present value of the principal, $a(P_{\overline{40}|6\%}) = \$7,500,000\ (.09722)$	$ 729,150.00
Present value of the interest payments, $R(P_{\overline{40}|6\%}) = \$300,000\ (15.04630)$	4,513,890.00
Total present value of bond liability	$5,243,040.00

Approach: The fair value of the bond liability being acquired by Warlock is determined by discounting all of the future cash flows related to the bond issue back to the present date using the current market rate of interest (6% per six-month interest period). The face amount of the bonds ($7,500,000) is a single sum due in 20 years (40 semiannual periods). The interest payments constitute an ordinary annuity for forty semiannual periods. Each interest payment is computed by multiplying the stated rate (4% per interest period) by the face amount of the bonds.

ANALYSIS OF MULTIPLE-CHOICE TYPE QUESTIONS

Question

1. A grandfather wishes to set up a fund today that will allow his grandson to withdraw $5,000 from the fund at the beginning of each year for four years to pay for college expenses. The first withdrawal is to occur later today. How should grandpa compute the required investment if the fund is to earn 6% interest compounded annually and the fund is to be exhausted by his last witl.drawal?

    a. $5,000 times the factor for the present value of an annuity due of 1 where n = 4, i = 6%.
    b. $5,000 divided by the factor for the present value of an annuity due of 1 where n = 4, i = 6%.
    c. $5,000 times the factor for the amount of an annuity due of 1 where n = 4, i = 6%.
    d. $5,000 divided by the factor for the amount of an annuity due of 1 where n = 4, i = 6%.

Solution = a.

Explanation and Approach: Follow the steps in solving future value and present value problems:

1. This is a present value of an annuity due problem.
2. Time diagram:

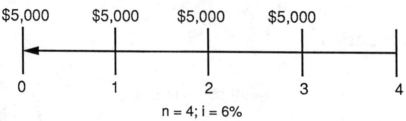

$$n = 4; i = 6\%$$

3. The factor for present value of an annuity due for n = 4, i = 6% would be derived by multiplying the factor for n = 4, i = 6% from the table for present value of an ordinary annuity times 1 + i.
4. Present Value of an Annuity Due = Rent (Present Value of an Annuity Due Factor)

Therefore, the present value of the annuity due equals $5,000 multiplied by the factor for present value of an annuity due for n = 4, i = 6%.

Questions 2 and 3 use the following present value table. Given below are the present value factors for $1.00 discounted at 9% for one to five periods.

Periods	Present value of $1 i = 9%
1	.91743
2	.84168
3	.77218
4	.70843
5	.64993

Question

2.   What amount should be deposited in a bank account today if a balance of $1,000 is desired four years from today?

    a. $1,000 X .91743 X 4.

    b. $1,000 X .70843.

    c. $1,000 ÷ .70843.

    d. $1,000 X (.91743 + .84168 + .77218 + .70843).

Solution = b.

Explanation and Approach: Follow the steps in solving future value and present value problems:

1.   This is a present value of a single-sum problem.

2.   Time diagram:

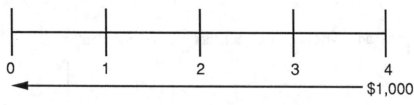

$$n = 4; i = 9\%$$

3.   The present value factor is .70843 for n = 4, i = 9%.

4.   Present Value = Future Value (PV Factor)
    Present Value = $1,000 (.70843)

Question

3.   If $1,000 is deposited today to earn 9% interest compounded annually, how much will be on deposit at the end of three years?

    a. $1,000 X .77218.

    b. $1,000 ÷ .77218.

    c.   ($1,000 ÷ .91743) X 3.

    d.   ($1,000 ÷ .77218) X 3.

Solution = b.

Explanation and Approach:

1.   This is a future value of a single sum problem.

2.   Time diagram:

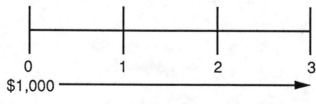

$$n = 3; i = 9\%$$

3.   The future value factor is not given; however, for a single-sum, the future value factor is the inverse of the present value factor. Therefore, one divided by the present value factor for n = 4, i = 9% equals the future value factor for n = 4, i = 9%.

4.   Future Value = Present Value (FV Factor)

     Future Value = $1,000 $\left(\dfrac{1}{.77218}\right)$

     Future Value = $1,000 ÷ .77218

Note: By looking at the time diagram, you can reason out that the amount on deposit at the end of three years should be greater than $1,000 but less than $1,500 (three years of 9% simple interest would give a balance of $1,270 and the compounding process would yield a little higher figure). In looking at the alternative answers, you can see that selection (a) will yield a result that is less than $1,000; selection (b) will give a result close to $1,300; selection (c) will give a result close to $2,700; and selection (d) wiill yield a result that is close to $3,900. Therefore, a reasonableness test would show that answer selection (b) must be the correct choice.

Question

4.   In the time diagram below, which concept is being depicted?

   0          $1 $1 $1 $1

   a.   Present value of an ordinary annuity.
   b.   Present value of an annuity due.
   c.   Future value of an ordinary annuity.
   d.   Future value of an annuity due.

Solution = a.

Explanation: It is an annuity since there is a series of equal periodic payments or receipts. The annuity is an ordinary one because the payments are due at the end (not beginning) of each period. The arrow is drawn so that it is headed back to the present rather than forward to the future. Thus, we have a present value problem.

Question

5.   If the interest rate is 10%, the factor for the future value of an annuity due of 1 for n = 5, i = 10%, is equal to the factor for the future value of an ordinary annuity of 1 for n = 5, i = 10%.
   a.   Plus 1.10.
   b.   Minus 1.10.
   c.   Multiplied by 1.10.
   d.   Divided by 1.10.

Solution = c.

TABLE 6-1   AMOUNT OF 1

Future

$$a_{\overline{n}|} = (1 + i)^n$$

(n) Periods	2%	2½%	3%	4%	5%	6%
1	1.02000	1.02500	1.03000	1.04000	1.05000	1.06000
2	1.04040	1.05063	1.06090	1.08160	1.10250	1.12360
3	1.06121	1.07689	1.09273	1.12486	1.15763	1.19102
4	1.08243	1.10381	1.12551	1.16986	1.21551	1.26248
5	1.10408	1.13141	1.15927	1.21665	1.27628	1.33823
6	1.12616	1.15969	1.19405	1.26532	1.34010	1.41852
7	1.14869	1.18869	1.22987	1.31593	1.40710	1.50363
8	1.17166	1.21840	1.26677	1.36857	1.47746	1.59385
9	1.19509	1.24886	1.30477	1.42331	1.55133	1.68948
10	1.21899	1.28008	1.34392	1.48024	1.62889	1.79085
11	1.24337	1.31209	1.38423	1.53945	1.71034	1.89830
12	1.26824	1.34489	1.42576	1.60103	1.79586	2.01220
13	1.29361	1.37851	1.46853	1.66507	1.88565	2.13293
14	1.31948	1.41297	1.51259	1.73168	1.97993	2.26090
15	1.34587	1.44830	1.55797	1.80094	2.07893	2.39656
16	1.37279	1.48451	1.60471	1.87298	2.18287	2.54035
17	1.40024	1.52162	1.65285	1.94790	2.29202	2.69277
18	1.42825	1.55966	1.70243	2.02582	2.40662	2.85434
19	1.45681	1.59865	1.75351	2.10685	2.52695	3.02560
20	1.48595	1.63862	1.80611	2.19112	2.65330	3.20714
21	1.51567	1.67958	1.86029	2.27877	2.78596	3.39956
22	1.54598	1.72157	1.91610	2.36992	2.92526	3.60354
23	1.57690	1.76461	1.97359	2.46472	3.07152	3.81975
24	1.60844	1.80873	2.03279	2.56330	3.22510	4.04893
25	1.64061	1.85394	2.09378	2.66584	3.38635	4.29187
26	1.67342	1.90029	2.15659	2.77247	3.55567	4.54938
27	1.70689	1.94780	2.22129	2.88337	3.73346	4.82235
28	1.74102	1.99650	2.28793	2.99870	3.92013	5.11169
29	1.77584	2.04641	2.35657	3.11865	4.11614	5.41839
30	1.81136	2.09757	2.42726	3.24340	4.32194	5.74349
31	1.84759	2.15001	2.50008	3.37313	4.53804	6.08810
32	1.88454	2.20376	2.57508	3.50806	4.76494	6.45339
33	1.92223	2.25885	2.65234	3.64838	5.00319	6.84059
34	1.96068	2.31532	2.73191	3.79432	5.25335	7.25103
35	1.99989	2.37321	2.81386	3.94609	5.51602	7.68609
36	2.03989	2.43254	2.89828	4.10393	5.79182	8.14725
37	2.08069	2.49335	2.98523	4.26809	6.08141	8.63609
38	2.12230	2.55568	3.07478	4.43881	6.38548	9.15425
39	2.16474	2.61957	3.16703	4.61637	6.70475	9.70351
40	2.20804	2.68506	3.26204	4.80102	7.03999	10.28572

8%	9%	10%	11%	12%	15%	(n) Periods
1.08000	1.09000	1.10000	1.11000	1.12000	1.15000	1
1.16640	1.18810	1.21000	1.23210	1.25440	1.32250	2
1.25971	1.29503	1.33100	1.36763	1.40493	1.52088	3
1.36049	1.41158	1.46410	1.51807	1.57352	1.74901	4
1.46933	1.53862	1.61051	1.68506	1.76234	2.01136	5
1.58687	1.67710	1.77156	1.87041	1.97382	2.31306	6
1.71382	1.82804	1.94872	2.07616	2.21068	2.66002	7
1.85093	1.99256	2.14359	2.30454	2.47596	3.05902	8
1.99900	2.17189	2.35795	2.55803	2.77308	3.51788	9
2.15892	2.36736	2.59374	2.83942	3.10585	4.04556	10
2.33164	2.58043	2.85312	3.15176	3.47855	4.65239	11
2.51817	2.81267	3.13843	3.49845	3.89598	5.35025	12
2.71962	3.06581	3.45227	3.88328	4.36349	6.15279	13
2.93719	3.34173	3.79750	4.31044	4.88711	7.07571	14
3.17217	3.64248	4.17725	4.78459	5.47357	8.13706	15
3.42594	3.97031	4.59497	5.31089	6.13039	9.35762	16
3.70002	4.32763	5.05447	5.89509	6.86604	10.76126	17
3.99602	4.71712	5.55992	6.54355	7.68997	12.37545	18
4.31570	5.14166	6.11591	7.26334	8.61276	14.23177	19
4.66096	5.60441	6.72750	8.06231	9.64629	16.36654	20
5.03383	6.10881	7.40025	8.94917	10.80385	18.82152	21
5.43654	6.65860	8.14028	9.93357	12.10031	21.64475	22
5.87146	7.25787	8.95430	11.02627	13.55235	24.89146	23
6.34118	7.91108	9.84973	12.23916	15.17863	28.62518	24
6.84847	8.62308	10.83471	13.58546	17.00000	32.91895	25
7.39635	9.39916	11.91818	15.07986	19.04007	37.85680	26
7.98806	10.24508	13.10999	16.73865	21.32488	43.53532	27
8.62711	11.16714	14.42099	18.57990	23.88387	50.06561	28
9.31727	12.17218	15.86309	20.62369	26.74993	57.57545	29
10.06266	13.26768	17.44940	22.89230	29.95992	66.21177	30
10.86767	14.46177	19.19434	25.41045	33.55511	76.14354	31
11.73708	15.76333	21.11378	28.20560	37.58173	87.56507	32
12.67605	17.18203	23.22515	31.30821	42.09153	100.69983	33
13.69013	18.72841	25.54767	34.75212	47.14252	115.80480	34
14.78534	20.41397	28.10244	38.57485	52.79962	133.17552	35
15.96817	22.25123	30.91268	42.81808	59.13557	153.15185	36
17.24563	24.25384	34.00395	47.52807	66.23184	176.12463	37
18.62528	26.43668	37.40434	52.75616	74.17966	202.54332	38
20.11530	28.81598	41.14479	58.55934	83.08122	232.92482	39
21.72452	31.40942	45.25926	65.00087	93.05097	267.86355	40

TABLE 6-2   PRESENT VALUE OF 1

$$p_{\overline{n}|i} = \frac{1}{(1+i)^n} = (1+i)^{-n}$$

(n) Periods	2%	2½%	3%	4%	5%	6%	8%	9%	10%	11%	12%	15%
1	.98039	.97561	.97087	.96154	.95238	.94340	.92593	.91743	.90909	.90090	.89286	.86957
2	.96117	.95181	.94260	.92456	.90703	.89000	.85734	.84168	.82645	.81162	.79719	.75614
3	.94232	.92860	.91514	.88900	.86384	.83962	.79383	.77218	.75132	.73119	.71178	.65752
4	.92385	.90595	.88849	.85480	.82270	.79209	.73503	.70843	.68301	.65873	.63552	.57175
5	.90573	.88385	.86261	.82193	.78353	.74726	.68058	.64993	.62092	.59345	.56743	.49718
6	.88797	.86230	.83748	.79031	.74622	.70496	.63017	.59627	.56447	.53464	.50663	.43233
7	.87056	.84127	.81309	.75992	.71068	.66506	.58349	.54703	.51316	.48166	.45235	.37594
8	.85349	.82075	.78941	.73069	.67684	.62741	.54027	.50187	.46651	.43393	.40388	.32690
9	.83676	.80073	.76642	.70259	.64461	.59190	.50025	.46043	.42410	.39092	.36061	.28426
10	.82035	.78120	.74409	.67556	.61391	.55839	.46319	.42241	.38554	.35218	.32197	.24719
11	.80426	.76214	.72242	.64958	.58468	.52679	.42888	.38753	.35049	.31728	.28748	.21494
12	.78849	.74356	.70138	.62460	.55684	.49697	.39711	.35554	.31863	.28584	.25668	.18691
13	.77303	.72542	.68095	.60057	.53032	.46884	.36770	.32618	.28966	.25751	.22917	.16253
14	.75788	.70773	.66112	.57748	.50507	.44230	.34046	.29925	.26333	.23199	.20462	.14133
15	.74301	.69047	.64186	.55526	.48102	.41727	.31524	.27454	.23939	.20900	.18270	.12289
16	.72845	.67362	.62317	.53391	.45811	.39365	.29189	.25187	.21763	.18829	.16312	.10687
17	.71416	.65720	.60502	.51337	.43630	.37136	.27027	.23107	.19785	.16963	.14564	.09293
18	.70016	.64117	.58739	.49363	.41552	.35034	.25025	.21199	.17986	.15282	.13004	.08081
19	.68643	.62553	.57029	.47464	.39573	.33051	.23171	.19449	.16351	.13768	.11611	.07027
20	.67297	.61027	.55368	.45639	.37689	.31180	.21455	.17843	.14864	.12403	.10367	.06110
21	.65978	.59539	.53755	.43883	.35894	.29416	.19866	.16370	.13513	.11174	.09256	.05313
22	.64684	.58086	.52189	.42196	.34185	.27751	.18394	.15018	.12285	.10067	.08264	.04620
23	.63416	.56670	.50669	.40573	.32557	.26180	.17032	.13778	.11168	.09069	.07379	.04017
24	.62172	.55288	.49193	.39012	.31007	.24698	.15770	.12641	.10153	.08170	.06588	.03493
25	.60953	.53939	.47761	.37512	.29530	.23300	.14602	.11597	.09230	.07361	.05882	.03038
26	.59758	.52623	.46369	.36069	.28124	.21981	.13520	.10639	.08391	.06631	.05252	.02642
27	.58586	.51340	.45019	.34682	.26785	.20737	.12519	.09761	.07628	.05974	.04689	.02297
28	.57437	.50088	.43708	.33348	.25509	.19563	.11591	.08955	.06934	.05382	.04187	.01997
29	.56311	.48866	.42435	.32065	.24295	.18456	.10733	.08216	.06304	.04849	.03738	.01737
30	.55207	.47674	.41199	.30832	.23138	.17411	.09938	.07537	.05731	.04368	.03338	.01510
31	.54125	.46511	.39999	.29646	.22036	.16425	.09202	.06915	.05210	.03935	.02980	.01313
32	.53063	.45377	.38834	.28506	.20987	.15496	.08520	.06344	.04736	.03545	.02661	.01142
33	.52023	.44270	.37703	.27409	.19987	.14619	.07889	.05820	.04306	.03194	.02376	.00993
34	.51003	.43191	.36604	.26355	.19035	.13791	.07305	.05340	.03914	.02878	.02121	.00864
35	.50003	.42137	.35538	.25342	.18129	.13011	.06763	.04899	.03558	.02592	.01894	.00751
36	.49022	.41109	.34503	.24367	.17266	.12274	.06262	.04494	.03235	.02335	.01691	.00653
37	.48061	.40107	.33498	.23430	.16444	.11579	.05799	.04123	.02941	.02104	.01510	.00568
38	.47119	.39128	.32523	.22529	.15661	.10924	.05369	.03783	.02674	.01896	.01348	.00494
39	.46195	.38174	.31575	.21662	.14915	.10306	.04971	.03470	.02430	.01708	.01204	.00429
40	.45289	.37243	.30656	.20829	.14205	.09722	.04603	.03184	.02210	.01538	.01075	.00373

TABLE 6-3 AMOUNT OF AN ORDINARY ANNUITY OF 1

$$A_{\overline{n}|i} = \frac{(1+i)^n - 1}{i}$$

AMOUNT OF AN ORDINARY ANNUITY OF 1 **TABLE 6-3**

(n) Periods	2%	2½%	3%	4%	5%	6%	8%	9%	10%	11%	12%	15%	(n) Periods
1	1.00000	1.00000	1.00000	1.00000	1.00000	1.00000	1.00000	1.00000	1.00000	1.00000	1.00000	1.00000	1
2	2.02000	2.02500	2.03000	2.04000	2.05000	2.06000	2.08000	2.09000	2.10000	2.11000	2.12000	2.15000	2
3	3.06040	3.07563	3.09090	3.12160	3.15250	3.18360	3.24640	3.27810	3.31000	3.34210	3.37440	3.47250	3
4	4.12161	4.15252	4.18363	4.24646	4.31013	4.37462	4.50611	4.57313	4.64100	4.70973	4.77933	4.99338	4
5	5.20404	5.25633	5.30914	5.41632	5.52563	5.63709	5.86660	5.98471	6.10510	6.22780	6.35285	6.74238	5
6	6.30812	6.38774	6.46841	6.63298	6.80191	6.97532	7.33592	7.52334	7.71561	7.91286	8.11519	8.75374	6
7	7.43428	7.54743	7.66246	7.89829	8.14201	8.39384	8.92280	9.20044	9.48717	9.78327	10.08901	11.06680	7
8	8.58297	8.73612	8.89234	9.21423	9.54911	9.89747	10.63663	11.02847	11.43589	11.85943	12.29969	13.72682	8
9	9.75463	9.95452	10.15911	10.58280	11.02656	11.49132	12.48756	13.02104	13.57948	14.16397	14.77566	16.78584	9
10	10.94972	11.20338	11.46338	12.00611	12.57789	13.18079	14.48656	15.19293	15.93743	16.72201	17.54874	20.30372	10
11	12.16872	12.48347	12.80780	13.48635	14.20679	14.97164	16.64549	17.56029	18.53117	19.56143	20.65458	24.34928	11
12	13.41209	13.79555	14.19203	15.02581	15.91713	16.86994	18.97713	20.14072	21.38428	22.71319	24.13313	29.00167	12
13	14.68033	15.14044	15.61779	16.62684	17.71298	18.88214	21.49530	22.95339	24.52271	26.21164	28.02911	34.35192	13
14	15.97394	16.51895	17.08632	18.29191	19.59863	21.01507	24.21492	26.01919	27.97498	30.09492	32.39260	40.50471	14
15	17.29342	17.93193	18.59891	20.02359	21.57856	23.27597	27.15211	29.36092	31.77248	34.40536	37.27972	47.58041	15
16	18.63929	19.38022	20.15688	21.82453	23.65749	25.67253	30.32428	33.00340	35.94973	39.18995	42.75328	55.71747	16
17	20.01207	20.86473	21.76159	23.69751	25.84037	28.21288	33.75023	36.97371	40.54470	44.50084	48.88367	65.07509	17
18	21.41231	22.38635	23.41444	25.64541	28.13238	30.90565	37.45024	41.30134	45.59917	50.39593	55.74972	75.83636	18
19	22.84056	23.94601	25.11687	27.67123	30.53900	33.75999	41.44626	46.01846	51.15909	56.93949	63.43968	88.21181	19
20	24.29737	25.54466	26.87037	29.77808	33.06595	36.78559	45.76196	51.16012	57.27500	64.20283	72.05244	102.44358	20
21	25.78332	27.18327	28.67649	31.96920	35.71925	39.99273	50.42292	56.76453	64.00250	72.26514	81.69874	118.81012	21
22	27.29898	28.86286	30.53678	34.24797	38.50521	43.39229	55.45676	62.87334	71.40275	81.21431	92.50258	137.63164	22
23	28.84496	30.58443	32.45288	36.61789	41.43048	46.99583	60.89330	69.53194	79.54302	91.14788	104.60289	159.27638	23
24	30.42186	32.34904	34.42647	39.08260	44.50200	50.81558	66.76476	76.78981	88.49733	102.17415	118.15524	184.16784	24
25	32.03030	34.15776	36.45926	41.64591	47.72710	54.86451	73.10594	84.70090	98.34706	114.41331	133.33387	212.79302	25
26	33.67091	36.01171	38.55304	44.31174	51.11345	59.15638	79.95442	93.32398	109.18177	127.99877	150.33393	245.71197	26
27	35.34432	37.91200	40.70963	47.08421	54.66913	63.70577	87.35077	102.72314	121.09994	143.07864	169.37401	283.56877	27
28	37.05121	39.85980	42.93092	49.96758	58.40258	68.52811	95.33883	112.96822	134.20994	159.81729	190.69889	327.10408	28
29	38.79223	41.85630	45.21885	52.96629	62.32271	73.63980	103.96594	124.13536	148.63093	178.39719	214.58275	377.16969	29
30	40.56808	43.90270	47.57542	56.08494	66.43885	79.05819	113.28321	136.30754	164.49402	199.02088	241.33268	434.74515	30
31	42.37944	46.00027	50.00268	59.32834	70.76079	84.80168	123.34587	149.57522	181.94343	221.91317	271.29261	500.95692	31
32	44.22703	48.15028	52.50276	62.70147	75.29883	90.88978	134.21354	164.03699	201.13772	247.32362	304.84772	577.10046	32
33	46.11157	50.35403	55.07784	66.20953	80.06377	97.34316	145.95062	179.80032	222.25154	275.52922	342.42945	644.66553	33
34	48.03380	52.61289	57.73018	69.85791	85.06696	104.18376	158.62667	196.98234	245.47670	306.83744	384.52098	765.36535	34
35	49.99448	54.92821	60.46208	73.65222	90.32031	111.43478	172.31680	215.71076	271.02437	341.58955	431.66350	881.17016	35
36	51.99437	57.30141	63.27594	77.59831	95.83632	119.12087	187.10215	236.12472	299.12681	380.16441	484.46312	1014.34568	36
37	54.03425	59.73395	66.17422	81.70225	101.62814	127.26812	203.07032	258.37595	330.03949	422.98249	543.59869	1167.49753	37
38	56.11494	62.22730	69.15945	85.97034	107.70955	135.90421	220.31595	282.62978	364.04343	470.51056	609.83053	1343.62216	38
39	58.23724	64.78298	72.23423	90.40915	114.09502	145.05846	238.94122	309.06646	401.44778	523.26673	684.01020	1546.16549	39
40	60.40198	67.40255	75.40126	95.02552	120.79977	154.76197	259.05652	337.88245	442.59256	581.82607	767.09142	1779.09031	40

TABLE 6–4   PRESENT VALUE OF AN ORDINARY ANNUITY OF 1

PRESENT VALUE OF AN ORDINARY ANNUITY OF 1   **TABLE 6–4**

$$P_{\overline{n}|i} = \frac{1 - \dfrac{1}{(1+i)^n}}{i}$$

(n) Periods	2%	2½%	3%	4%	5%	6%	8%	9%	10%	11%	12%	15%
1	.98039	.97561	.97087	.96154	.95238	.94340	.92593	.91743	.90909	.90090	.89286	.86957
2	1.94156	1.92742	1.91347	1.88609	1.85941	1.83339	1.78326	1.75911	1.73554	1.71252	1.69005	1.62571
3	2.88388	2.85602	2.82861	2.77509	2.72325	2.67301	2.57710	2.53130	2.48685	2.44371	2.40183	2.28323
4	3.80773	3.76197	3.71710	3.62990	3.54595	3.46511	3.31213	3.23972	3.16986	3.10245	3.03735	2.85498
5	4.71346	4.64583	4.57971	4.45182	4.32948	4.21236	3.99271	3.88965	3.79079	3.69590	3.60478	3.35216
6	5.60143	5.50813	5.41719	5.24214	5.07569	4.91732	4.62288	4.48592	4.35526	4.23054	4.11141	3.78448
7	6.47199	6.34939	6.23028	6.00205	5.78637	5.58238	5.20637	5.03295	4.86842	4.71220	4.56376	4.16042
8	7.32548	7.17014	7.01969	6.73274	6.46321	6.20979	5.74664	5.53482	5.33493	5.14612	4.96764	4.48732
9	8.16224	7.97087	7.78611	7.43533	7.10782	6.80169	6.24689	5.99525	5.75902	5.53705	5.32825	4.77158
10	8.98259	8.75206	8.53020	8.11090	7.72173	7.36009	6.71008	6.41766	6.14457	5.88923	5.65022	5.01877
11	9.78685	9.51421	9.25262	8.76048	8.30641	7.88687	7.13896	6.80519	6.49506	6.20652	5.93770	5.23371
12	10.57534	10.25776	9.95400	9.38507	8.86325	8.38384	7.53608	7.16073	6.81369	6.49236	6.19437	5.42062
13	11.34837	10.98319	10.63496	9.98565	9.39357	8.85268	7.90378	7.48690	7.10336	6.74987	6.42355	5.58315
14	12.10625	11.69091	11.29607	10.56312	9.89864	9.29498	8.24424	7.78615	7.36669	6.98187	6.62817	5.72448
15	12.84926	12.38138	11.93794	11.11839	10.37966	9.71225	8.55948	8.06069	7.60608	7.19087	6.81086	5.84737
16	13.57771	13.05500	12.56110	11.65230	10.83777	10.10590	8.85137	8.31256	7.82371	7.37916	6.97399	5.95424
17	14.29187	13.71220	13.16612	12.16567	11.27407	10.47726	9.12164	8.54363	8.02155	7.54879	7.11963	6.04716
18	14.99203	14.35336	13.75351	12.65930	11.68959	10.82760	9.37189	8.75563	8.20141	7.70162	7.24967	6.12797
19	15.67846	14.97889	14.32380	13.13394	12.08532	11.15812	9.60360	8.95012	8.36492	7.83929	7.36578	6.19823
20	16.35143	15.58916	14.87747	13.59033	12.46221	11.46992	9.81815	9.12855	8.51356	7.96333	7.46944	6.25933
21	17.01121	16.18455	15.41502	14.02916	12.82115	11.76408	10.01680	9.29224	8.64869	8.07507	7.56200	6.31246
22	17.65805	16.76541	15.93692	14.45112	13.16300	12.04158	10.20074	9.44243	8.77154	8.17574	7.64465	6.35866
23	18.29220	17.33211	16.44361	14.85684	13.48857	12.30338	10.37106	9.58021	8.88322	8.26643	7.71843	6.39884
24	18.91393	17.88499	16.93554	15.24696	13.79864	12.55036	10.52876	9.70661	8.98474	8.34814	7.78432	6.43377
25	19.52346	18.42438	17.41315	15.62208	14.09394	12.78336	10.67478	9.82258	9.07704	8.42174	7.84314	6.46415
26	20.12104	18.95061	17.87684	15.98277	14.37519	13.00317	10.80998	9.92897	9.16095	8.48806	7.89566	6.49056
27	20.70690	19.46401	18.32703	16.32959	14.64303	13.21053	10.93516	10.02658	9.23722	8.54780	7.94255	6.51353
28	21.28127	19.96489	18.76411	16.66306	14.89813	13.40616	11.05108	10.11613	9.30657	8.60162	7.98442	6.53351
29	21.84438	20.45355	19.18845	16.98371	15.14107	13.59072	11.15841	10.19828	9.36961	8.65011	8.02181	6.55088
30	22.39646	20.93029	19.60044	17.29203	15.37245	13.76483	11.25778	10.27365	9.42691	8.69379	8.05518	6.56598
31	22.93770	21.39541	20.00043	17.58849	15.59281	13.92909	11.34980	10.34280	9.47901	8.73315	8.08499	6.57911
32	23.46833	21.84918	20.38877	17.87355	15.80268	14.08404	11.43500	10.40624	9.52638	8.76860	8.11159	6.59053
33	23.98856	22.29188	20.76579	18.14765	16.00255	14.23023	11.51389	10.46444	9.56943	8.80054	8.13535	6.60046
34	24.49859	22.72379	21.13184	18.41120	16.19290	14.36814	11.58693	10.51784	9.60858	8.82932	8.15656	6.60910
35	24.99862	23.14516	21.48722	18.66461	16.37419	14.49825	11.65457	10.56682	9.64416	8.85524	8.17550	6.61661
36	25.48884	23.55625	21.83225	18.90828	16.54685	14.62099	11.71719	10.61176	9.67651	8.87859	8.19241	6.62314
37	25.96945	23.95732	22.16724	19.14258	16.71129	14.73678	11.77518	10.65299	9.70592	8.89963	8.20751	6.62882
38	26.44064	24.34860	22.49246	19.36786	16.86789	14.84602	11.82887	10.69082	9.73265	8.91859	8.22099	6.63375
39	26.90259	24.73034	22.80822	19.58448	17.01704	14.94907	11.87858	10.72552	9.75697	8.93567	8.23303	6.63805
40	27.35548	25.10278	23.11477	19.79277	17.15909	15.04630	11.92461	10.75736	9.77905	8.95105	8.24378	6.64178

TABLE 6-5   PRESENT VALUE OF AN ANNUITY DUE OF 1

$$PD_{\overline{n}|i} = 1 + \frac{1 - \dfrac{1}{(1+i)^{n-1}}}{i}$$

(n) Periods	2%	2½%	3%	4%	5%	6%	8%	9%	10%	11%	12%	15%	(n) Periods
1	1.00000	1.00000	1.00000	1.00000	1.00000	1.00000	1.00000	1.00000	1.00000	1.00000	1.00000	1.00000	1
2	1.98039	1.97561	1.97087	1.96154	1.95238	1.94340	1.92593	1.91743	1.90909	1.90090	1.89286	1.86957	2
3	2.94156	2.92742	2.91347	2.88609	2.85941	2.83339	2.78326	2.75911	2.73554	2.71252	2.69005	2.62571	3
4	3.88388	3.85602	3.82861	3.77509	3.72325	3.67301	3.57710	3.53130	3.48685	3.44371	3.40183	3.28323	4
5	4.80773	4.76197	4.71710	4.62990	4.54595	4.46511	4.31213	4.23972	4.16986	4.10245	4.03735	3.85498	5
6	5.71346	5.64583	5.57971	5.45182	5.32948	5.21236	4.99271	4.88965	4.79079	4.69590	4.60478	4.35216	6
7	6.60143	6.50813	6.41719	6.24214	6.07569	5.91732	5.62288	5.48592	5.35526	5.23054	5.11141	4.78448	7
8	7.47199	7.34939	7.23028	7.00205	6.78637	6.58238	6.20637	6.03295	5.86842	5.71220	5.56376	5.16042	8
9	8.32548	8.17014	8.01969	7.73274	7.46321	7.20979	6.74664	6.53482	6.33493	6.14612	5.96764	5.48732	9
10	9.16224	8.97087	8.78611	8.43533	8.10782	7.80169	7.24689	6.99525	6.75902	6.53705	6.32825	5.77158	10
11	9.98259	9.75206	9.53020	9.11090	8.72173	8.36009	7.71008	7.41766	7.14457	6.88923	6.65022	6.01877	11
12	10.78685	10.51421	10.25262	9.76048	9.30641	8.88687	8.13896	7.80519	7.49506	7.20652	6.93770	6.23371	12
13	11.57534	11.25776	10.95400	10.38507	9.86325	9.38384	8.53608	8.16073	7.81369	7.49236	7.19437	6.42062	13
14	12.34837	11.98319	11.63496	10.98565	10.39357	9.85268	8.90378	8.48690	8.10336	7.74987	7.42355	6.58315	14
15	13.10625	12.69091	12.29607	11.56312	10.89864	10.29498	9.24424	8.78615	8.36669	7.98187	7.62817	6.72448	15
16	13.84926	13.38138	12.93794	12.11839	11.37966	10.71225	9.55948	9.06069	8.60608	8.19087	7.81086	6.84737	16
17	14.57771	14.05500	13.56110	12.65230	11.83777	11.10590	9.85137	9.31256	8.82371	8.37916	7.97399	6.95424	17
18	15.29187	14.71220	14.16612	13.16567	12.27407	11.47726	10.12164	9.54363	9.02155	8.54879	8.11963	7.04716	18
19	15.99203	15.35336	14.75351	13.65930	12.68959	11.82760	10.37189	9.75563	9.20141	8.70162	8.24967	7.12797	19
20	16.67846	15.97889	15.32380	14.13394	13.08532	12.15812	10.60360	9.95012	9.36492	8.83929	8.36578	7.19823	20
21	17.35143	16.58916	15.87747	14.59033	13.46221	12.46992	10.81815	10.12855	9.51356	8.96333	8.46944	7.25933	21
22	18.01121	17.18455	16.41502	15.02916	13.82115	12.76408	11.01680	10.29224	9.64869	9.07507	8.56200	7.31246	22
23	18.65805	17.76541	16.93692	15.45112	14.16300	13.04158	11.20074	10.44243	9.77154	9.17574	8.64465	7.35866	23
24	19.29220	18.33211	17.44361	15.85684	14.48857	13.30338	11.37106	10.58021	9.88322	9.26643	8.71343	7.39884	24
25	19.91393	18.88499	17.93554	16.24696	14.79864	13.55036	11.52876	10.70661	9.98474	9.34814	8.78432	7.43377	25
26	20.52346	19.42438	18.41315	16.62208	15.09394	13.78336	11.67478	10.82258	10.07704	9.42174	8.84314	7.46415	26
27	21.12104	19.95061	18.87684	16.98277	15.37519	14.00317	11.80998	10.92887	10.16095	9.48806	8.89566	7.49056	27
28	21.70690	20.46401	19.32703	17.32959	15.64303	14.21053	11.93518	11.02658	10.23722	9.54780	8.94255	7.51353	28
29	22.28127	20.96489	19.76411	17.66306	15.89813	14.40616	12.05108	11.11613	10.30657	9.60162	8.98442	7.53351	29
30	22.84438	21.45355	20.18845	17.98371	16.14107	14.59072	12.15841	11.19828	10.36961	9.65011	9.02181	7.55088	30
31	23.39646	21.93029	20.60044	18.29203	16.37245	14.76483	12.25778	11.27365	10.42691	9.69379	9.05518	7.56598	31
32	23.93770	22.39541	21.00043	18.58849	16.59281	14.92909	12.34980	11.34280	10.47901	9.73315	9.08499	7.57911	32
33	24.46833	22.84918	21.38877	18.87355	16.80268	15.08404	12.43500	11.40624	10.52638	9.76860	9.11159	7.59053	33
34	24.98856	23.29188	21.76579	19.14765	17.00255	15.23023	12.51389	11.46444	10.56943	9.80054	9.13535	7.60046	34
35	25.49859	23.72379	22.13184	19.41120	17.19290	15.36814	12.58693	11.51784	10.60858	9.82932	9.15656	7.60910	35
36	25.99862	24.14516	22.48722	19.66461	17.37419	15.49825	12.65457	11.56682	10.64416	9.85524	9.17550	7.61661	36
37	26.48884	24.55625	22.83225	19.90828	17.54685	15.62099	12.71719	11.61176	10.67651	9.87859	9.19241	7.62314	37
38	26.96945	24.95732	23.16724	20.14258	17.71129	15.73678	12.77518	11.65299	10.70592	9.89963	9.20751	7.62882	38
39	27.44064	25.34860	23.49245	20.36786	17.86789	15.84602	12.82887	11.69082	10.73265	9.91859	9.22099	7.63375	39
40	27.90259	25.73034	23.80822	20.58448	18.01704	15.94907	12.87858	11.72552	10.75697	9.93567	9.23303	7.63805	40

CHAPTER 7

CASH AND RECEIVABLES

OVERVIEW

In previous chapters, you learned the basic formats for general purpose financial statements. In this chapter you begin your in-depth study of accounting for items appearing on the balance sheet: (1) what is to be included in an item classification, (2) related internal control procedures, (3) rules for determining the dollar amount to be reported, (4) disclosure requirements, and (5) special accounting procedures which may be required. In this chapter, you will learn what is to be included under the cash caption on the balance sheet and some key internal controls which should be employed for business activities involving cash. Also discussed are the methods of accounting for notes receivable and accounts receivable.

Many businesses grant credit to customers. They know that when making sales "on account," a risk exists because some accounts will never be collected. However, the cost of these bad debts is more than offset by the profit from the extra sales made due to the attraction of granting credit. The collections department may make many attempts to collect an account before "writing-off" a bad debtor. Frequently an account is deemed to be uncollectible a year or more after the date of the credit sale. In this chapter, we will discuss the allowance method of accounting for bad debts. The allowance method permits the accountant to estimate the amount of bad debt expense that should be matched with revenues rather than waiting to book expense at the time of an actual write-off.

TIPS ON CHAPTER TOPICS

TIP: The objective of a bank reconciliation is to explain all reasons why the bank balance differs from the book balance and to identify errors and omissions in the bank's records and in the book's records.

TIP: In the context of a bank reconciliation, "per bank" refers to the records of the bank pertaining to the depositor's account and "per books" refers to the depositor's records of the same bank account.

TIP: Some items in a bank reconciliation will require adjustments either on the depositor's books or in the bank's records while the others will not. When the balance per bank to correct cash balance format is used in preparing a single column bank reconciliation, all of the reconciling items appearing in the lower half of the reconciliation (balance per books to correct cash balance) require adjustment on the depositor's books. All of the reconciling items appearing in the upper half of the reconciliation **except** for deposits in transit and outstanding checks require adjustment on the bank's books.

TIP: Unless otherwise indicated, an NSF check is assumed to be a customer's NSF check; that is, an NSF check from a customer of the depositor rather than a depositor's NSF check.

TIP: A depositor's checking account is a liability on the bank's books, so a bank debit memo decreases the depositor's cash balance and a bank credit memo increases the depositor's cash balance.

TIP: Total receipts per bank for a month include all deposits made by the depositor during the month plus any bank credit memos (such as for interest credited by the bank or a customer's note receivable collected by the bank).

TIP: Total disbursements per bank for a month include all depositor's checks which cleared the banking system during the month plus any bank debit memos originating during the month (such as for bank service charges or a customer's NSF check).

TIP: Beginning cash balance per bank plus total receipts for the month per bank minus total disbursements for the month per bank equals ending cash balance per bank.

TIP: Beginning cash balance per books plus total receipts for the month per books minus total disbursements for the month per books equals ending cash balance per books.

TIP: A four-column bank reconciliation is simply a single column reconciliation of cash balances (bank and books or bank and correct and books and correct) at one date and a single column reconciliation of cash balances at another date plus a reconciliation of total cash receipts and total cash disbursements for the period between those two different dates.

TIP: On a proof of cash (another name for a four-column bank reconciliation), a reconciling item will appear in two of the four columns:
  a. Usually a reconciling item on a proof of cash will appear in one outside column and one inside column. In such instances: If the two columns in which it appears are adjacent, the mathematical signs are opposite of each other; if the two columns in which it appears are nonadjacent, the mathematical signs are the same.
  b. Although it is rare, a reconciling item on a proof of cash may appear in both of the center two columns. In such an instance, the mathematical signs are the same. An example of a reconciling item which appears only in the inside columns and not in either of the outside columns is: A customer's check was deposited during February and recorded as a receipt on the books and by the bank. The check was returned NSF by the bank during February and considered by the bank to be a disbursement; however, this action was not recorded on the depositor's books. The returned check was redeposited during February and therefore considered another deposit per the bank's records but was not considered an additional receipt per books. The check then cleared. Thus, the customer's check appears twice in the receipts per bank and once in the disbursements per bank. This differs from the treatment per books as this same check appears only once in the receipts per books and does not appear at all in the disbursements per books.

TIP: Trade accounts receivable result from the sale of products or services to customers. Non-trade accounts receivable (amounts that are due from nontrade customers who do not buy goods or services in the normal course of the company's main business activity) should be listed separately on the balance sheet from the trade accounts receivable balance.

TIP: In the event that a customer's account has a credit balance on the balance sheet date, it should be classified as a current liability and not offset against other accounts receivable with debit balances.

TIP: The net realizable value of accounts receivable is the amount of the receivables expected to ultimately be converted to cash. (Total accounts receivable - Allowance for doubtful accounts.)

TIP: Whenever you want to analyze the effect of (a) recording bad debt expense, (b) writing off an individual customer's account receivable, and/or (c) the collection of an account receivable that was previously written off, write down the related journal entry(ies) and analyze each debit and credit separately. (See **Illustration 7-2** for examples.)

TIP: The journal entry to record the estimated bad debt expense for a period and to adjust the corresponding allowance for doubtful accounts involves a debit to Bad Debt Expense and a credit to Allowance for Doubtful Accounts.

The entry to write off an individual customer's account (an actual bad debt) involves a debit to Allowance for Doubtful Accounts and a credit to Accounts Receivable.

TIP: Two entries are necessary to record the recovery of an account that was previously written off:
1. An entry to record the reinstatement of the account receivable (debit Accounts Receivable and credit Allowance for Doubtful Accounts.) This is simply a reverse of the write off entry.
2. An entry to record the collection of the receivable (debit Cash and credit Accounts Receivable).

TIP: Allowance for Doubtful Accounts is often called Allowance for Uncollectible Accounts. Bad Debt Expense is often called Uncollectible Accounts Expense **or** Doubtful Accounts Expense.

TIP: The entry to record bad debts reduces current assets and reduces net income. The entry to record the write off of an individual account has **no** net effect on the amount of current assets nor does it affect income. It merely reduces Accounts Receivable and the Allowance for Doubtful Accounts account (which is a contra item) so the entry has no **net** effect on the net realizable value of accounts receivable.

TIP: The normal balance of the Allowance for Doubtful Accounts is a credit. Therefore, a debit balance in this account indicates an abnormal balance. It is not uncommon to have a debit balance in the allowance account before adjusting entries are prepared because individual accounts may be written off at various times during a period and the entry to adjust the allowance account is prepared at the end of the period before financial statements are prepared. After adjustment, the allowance account should have a credit balance.

TIP: When using the allowance method of accounting for bad debts, there are two methods available for determining the amount of the adjusting entry to record bad debts expense and to adjust the allowance account. Each method has adaptations.
1. By estimating bad debt expense
   a. The average percentage relationship between actual debt losses and net credit sales is ascertained. This percentage, adjusted for conditions, is then applied to the actual net credit sales of the period to determine the amount of expense for the period.
   b. Use of the same procedure as in (a) except the percentage of bad debts to total sales is used. This method is not as logical as (a) because cash sales will not result in bad debts, and, if the relationship between cash sales and credit sales shifts, that change will necessitate revision of the percentage being used to estimate bad debts.

2. By estimating the net value of the current receivables
   a. From experience, the average percentage relationship between uncollectible accounts receivable and outstanding accounts receivable is determined. This percentage, adjusted for expected conditions, is applied each period to the ending balance in accounts receivable to determine the desired balance of the allowance account.
   b. Total uncollectible accounts at the end of an accounting period is determined by an aging analysis. The balance in the allowance account is then adjusted so that its balance equals the total amount of the estimated uncollectible accounts. This aging method is preferable to 2(a) because it takes into consideration the age of a receivable. (The older the age, the lower the probability of collection).

Both methods (and their variations) listed above are acceptable. The first method discussed, estimation of bad debt expense based on credit sales, focuses on matching current bad debt expense with revenues of the current period and thus emphasizes the income statement. The second method, estimation of the net value of present receivables, focuses on an evaluation of the net realizable value of all accounts receivable and thus emphasizes the balance sheet. It only incidentally measures bad debt expense; the expense reported may not be related to the credit sales of the current period, thus violating the matching principle. If this method is to be used, the aging technique is preferable to the use of a simple percentage times total accounts receivable.

TIP: When using the allowance method and estimating bad debts expense as a percentage of credit sales for the period, the amount of bad debts expense is simply calculated and recorded; a by-product of this approach is the increasing of the allowance account. When using the allowance method of estimating the net realizable value of accounts receivable (such as by an aging analysis), the amount of bad debts calculated represents the new ending balance of the allowance account. The adjusting entry records the amount necessary to increase (or decrease) the current allowance account balance to equal the newly computed one. A by-product of this approach is the increasing of bad debts expense for the period.

TIP: Very often, an entity may use the percentage-of-sales method to account for bad debts for interim periods and then use the aging method to adjust the allowance account at year-end for annual reporting purposes.

ILLUSTRATION 7-1
TWO FORMATS FOR BANK RECONCILIATIONS

First One:

Balance per bank
- Add positive items per books not on bank's records.
- Deduct negative items per books not on bank's records.
- Add or deduct, whichever is applicable, bank error in recording receipts or disbursements.

Corrected cash balance

Balance per books
- Add positive items per bank not on books.
- Deduct negative items per bank not on books.
- Add or deduct, whichever is applicable, depositor error in recording receipts or disbursements.

Corrected cash balance

Second One:

Balance per bank
- Add positive items per books not on bank's records.
- Deduct negative items per books not on bank's records.
- Add or deduct, whichever is applicable, bank error in recording receipts or disbursements.
- Deduct positive items per bank not on books.
- Add negative items per bank not on books.
- Add or deduct, whichever is applicable, depositor error in recording receipts or disbursements.

Balance per books

Examples of reconciling items:
  Positive item per books not on bank's records:
    Deposit in transit
  Negative item per books not on bank's records:
    Outstanding check
  Positive item per bank not on books:
    Note collected by bank
    Interest paid by bank to depositor on account balance
  Negative item per bank not on books:
    Bank service charge
    Customer's NSF check returned by bank
  Error by bank:
    In recording receipt
    In recording disbursement
  Error by depositor:
    In recording receipt
    In recording disbursement

EXERCISE 7-1

Purpose: This exercise will help you to review situations that give rise to reconciling items on a bank reconciliation and to identify those which require adjusting entries on the depositor's books.

A sketch of the bank reconciliation at July 31, 19xx for the Ace Electric Company appears below.

Instructions
(a) Indicate how each of the 10 items listed below would be handled on the bank reconciliation by placing the proper code letter in the space provided. The applicable code letters appear in the sketch of the bank reconciliation. Use the code "NR" for any item which is not a reconciling item on July 31. The first item is done for you.
(b) Assume that the July 31 balance per bank statement was $4,332. Complete the bank reconciliation using the items given and answer the questions that follow.

Ace Electric Co.
BANK RECONCILIATION
July 31, 19XX

Balance per bank statement, July 31			$X,XXX
A. Add:		$XXX	
		XXX	X,XXX
			$X,XXX
B. Deduct:			X,XXX
Correct cash balance, July 31			$X,XXX
Balance per books, July 31			$X,XXX
C. Add:		$XXX	
		XXX	X,XXX
			$X,XXX
D. Deduct:		$XXX	
		XXX	
		XXX	
		XXX	X,XXX
Correct cash balance, July 31			$X,XXX

(a)   Items

___A___   1.   Deposits of July 30 amounting to $1,482 have not reached the bank as of July 31.

_____   2.   A customer's check for $40 that was deposited on July 20 was returned NSF by the bank; return has not been recorded by Ace.

_____   3.   Bank service charge for July amounts to $3.

_____   4.   Included with the bank statement was check #422 for $702 as payment of an account payable. In comparing the check with the cash disbursement records, it was discovered that the check was incorrectly entered in the cash disbursements journal for $720.

_____   5.   Outstanding checks at July 31 amount to $1,927.

_____ 6. The bank improperly charged a check for $25 of the Ace Plumbing Co. to Ace Electric Co.'s account.

_____ 7. The bank charged $8 during July for printing checks.

_____ 8. During July, the bank collected a customer's note receivable for the Ace Electric Co.; face amount $1,000, interest $20, and the bank charged a $2 collection fee. This transaction has not been recorded by Ace.

_____ 9. A check written by Ace in June for $180 cleared the bank during July.

_____ 10. Deposits of June 30 of $1,200 were recorded by the company on June 30 but were not recorded by the bank until July 2.

(b)   Questions

1. What is the adjusted (correct) cash balance at July 31? $_____

2. What is the balance per books before adjustment at July 31? $_____

3. What reconciling items require an adjusting entry on Ace Electric Company's books? (Identify by

   item numbers.) _____

4. What item(s) requires a special entry on the bank's records to correct an error(s)? _____

   _____

SOLUTION TO EXERCISE 7-1

(a) 1.   A   6.   A
     2.   D   7.   D
     3.   D   8.   C, D
     4.   C   9.   NR
     5.   B   10.   NR

(b) 1. $3,912*
         ($4,332 + $1,482 + $25 - $1,927 = $3,912)

     2. $2,927*
         [X + $18 + $1,020 - $40 - $3 - $8 - $2 = $3,912 (answer to question 1)]
         X = $2,927

     3.   2; 3; 4; 7; 8

     4.   6

*See the completed bank reconciliation on the next page.

Approach: You can compute the correct cash balance by completing the top half of the bank reconciliation (balance per bank to correct cash balance). The correct cash balance can then be entered on the last line of the bottom half of the reconciliation and used along with certain reconciling items to compute the cash balance per books before adjustment.

Ace Electric Co.
BANK RECONCILIATION
July 31, 19XX

Balance per bank statement, July 31			$4,332
Add:	Deposit in transit on July 31	$1,482	
	Check improperly charged by bank	25	1,507
			5,839
Deduct:	Checks outstanding as of July 31		1,927
	Correct cash balance, July 31		$3,912
Balance per books, July 31			$2,927
Add:	Error in recording check #422	$ 18	
	Collection of customer's note receivable and interest by bank	1,020	1,038
			3,965
Deduct:	Customer's NSF check	40	
	Bank service charge for July	3	
	Cost of printing checks	8	
	Bank collection fee	2	53
	Correct cash balance July 31		$3,912

Note: The required adjusting entries would be:

Cash	18	
Accounts Payable		18
Cash	1,020	
Note Receivable		1,000
Interest Revenue		20
Accounts Receivable	40	
Cash		40
Miscellaneous Expense	13	
Cash		13

EXERCISE 7-2

Purpose: This exercise provides an illustration of how to determine the checks outstanding and the deposits in transit at a given date.

Presented below is information related to CBI Industries.

CBI Industries
BANK RECONCILIATION
May 31, 1991

Balance per bank statement		$30,928.46
Less outstanding checks		
No. 6124	$2,125.00	
No. 6138	932.65	
No. 6139	960.57	
No. 6140	1,420.00	5,438.22
		25,490.24
Add deposit in transit		4,710.56
Balance per books (correct balance)		$30,200.80

CHECK REGISTER--JUNE

Date		Payee	No.	V. Pay	Discount	Cash
June	1	Dan Collins Mfg.	6141	$ 237.50		$ 237.50
	1	Geo Bates Mfg.	6142	915.00	$ 9.15	905.85
	8	Office Supply Co., Inc.	6143	122.90	2.45	120.45
	9	Dan Collins Mfg.	6144	306.40		306.40
	10	Petty Cash	6145	89.93		89.93
	17	Allservice Photo	6146	706.00	14.12	691.88
	22	Linda Elbert Publishing	6147	447.50		447.50
	23	Payroll Account	6148	4,130.00		4,130.00
	25	Barnes Tools, Inc.	6149	390.75	3.91	386.84
	28	American Insurance Agency	6150	1,050.00		1,050.00
	28	Riley Construction	6151	2,250.00		2,250.00
	29	R. Petersen, Inc.	6152	750.00		750.00
	30	Lembke Bros.	6153	295.25	5.90	289.35
				$11,691.23	$35.53	$11,655.70

STATEMENT
Carelli First State Bank
General Checking Account of CBI Industries--June 1991

Date		Debits			Credits	Balance
						$30,928.46
June	1	$2,125.00	$ 237.50	$ 905.85	$4,710.56	32,370.67
	12	932.65	120.45		1,507.06	32,824.63
	23	1,420.00	447.50	306.40	1,458.55	32,109.28
	26	4,130.00		11.05 (BSC)		27,968.23
	28	89.93	2,250.00	1,050.00	4,157.48	28,735.78

Cash received June 29 and 30 and deposited in the mail on June 30 for the general checking account at Carelli First State Bank amounted to $4,407.96.

Instructions

From the information above, prepare a bank reconciliation as of June 30, 1991 for CBI Industries. Use the format that reconciles the bank and book balances to the correct cash balance. (Hint: Because the cash account balance at June 30 is not given, it must be calculated from other information in the problem.)

TIP: On the bank statement, debits appear as a result of checks that have cleared during the month or bank debit memos for items such as bank service charges (BSC). Credits on the bank statement represent deposits or bank credit memos.

TIP: The only reason the balance per books at May 31, 1991 was equal to the correct cash balance at that date is that there were no reconciling items requiring adjusting entries on the books at May 31, 1991.

SOLUTION TO EXERCISE 7-2

Preparation of Bank Reconciliation
CBI Industries
BANK RECONCILIATION--General Checking Account
June 30, 1991

Balance per bank statement, June 30, 1991		$28,735.78
Add: Deposit in transit (June receipts not deposited by June 30)		4,407.96
		33,143.74
Deduct: Outstanding checks		
#6139	$960.57	
#6146	691.88	
#6149	386.84	
#6152	750.00	
#6153	289.35	3,078.64
Correct cash balance		$30,065.10
Balance per books, June 30, 1991		$30,076.15[a]
Deduct: Bank charge not yet recorded in books		11.05
Correct cash balance		$30,065.10

[a]

Computation of Cash Balance per Books--General Checking Account		
Cash balance June 1, 1991		$30,200.80
Receipts for June: Deposit of 6/12	$1,507.06	
Deposit of 6/23	1,458.55	
Deposit of 6/28	4,157.48	
Deposit in transit	4,407.96	11,531.05
Cash available		41,731.85
Deduct disbursements per check register		11,655.70
Cash balance June 30, 1991		$30,076.15

Approach: Prepare the format for the bank reconciliation requested (balance per bank to correct and balance per books to correct) as shown in **Illustration 7-1.** Enter the information given (such as balance per bank statement at June 30, 1991, and deposit in transit) where it belongs in the reconciliation. Solve for the other data needed and enter those details into the reconciliation (such as the balance per books and outstanding checks). Outstanding checks at June 30, 1991 are identified by comparing details of the bank statement with the depositor's check register for the month and the reconciliation at the end of the prior month.

EXERCISE 7-3

Purpose: This exercise will allow you to practice preparing a proof of cash under both of the alternative formats.

The following data pertain to the Burghard Company:

1. Per the bank statement for February: January 31 balance, $20,000; February receipts, $22,000; February disbursements, $24,000; February 28 balance, $18,000.

2. Per the books: January 31 unadjusted balance, $16,020; February receipts, $19,410; February disbursements, $21,505, February 28 balance, $13,925.

3. Bank service charge of $20 for January is included in book disbursements for February.

4. Bank service charge of $35 for February is included on the bank statement for February.

5. The first deposit shown on the February bank statement was $5,000 and was included in January's cash receipts per books.

6. $7,000 of checks written in February have not cleared the bank by February 28.

7. A check written for office supplies in February for $970 was incorrectly recorded in the cash disbursements journal and in the check register as $790. This check cleared the bank in February for $970.

8. The bank credited the firm's account in error for $500 in February for another firm's deposit.

9. The bank collected a $1,000 note receivable for the firm in February plus $90 interest. The firm has not yet recorded this transaction.

10. Cash receipts for February 28 of $4,000 did not reach the bank until March 2.

11. All $9,000 of checks outstanding at January 31 cleared the banking system during February.

12. A customer's NSF check in the amount of $300 was returned with the February bank statement. This check was redeposited in March. As of the end of February, Burghard has not yet made an entry for the return of this check by the bank.

Instructions
(a) Prepare a proof of cash using the format balance per bank to balance per books for the Burghard Co. for February.
(b) Prepare a proof of cash using the format that reconciles both the bank and book balances to correct balances.
(c) Prepare any adjusting entry(ies) required for the books.

SOLUTION TO EXERCISE 7-3

(a)

	Balance Jan. 31	February Receipts	February Disbursements	Balance Feb. 28
Per bank	$20,000	$22,000	$24,000	$18,000
Bank service charge--Jan.	20		20	
Bank service charge--Feb.			(35)	35
Deposits in transit--1/31	5,000	(5,000)		
Outstanding checks--2/28			7,000	(7,000)
Company error in recording check			(180)	180
Bank error in recording receipt		(500)		(500)
Collection of note by bank		(1,090)		(1,090)
Deposit in transit--2/28		4,000		4,000
Outstanding checks--1/31	(9,000)		(9,000)	
Customer NSF check			(300)	300
Per books	$16,020	$19,410	$21,505	$13,925

(b)

	Balance Jan. 31	February Receipts	February Disbursements	Balance Feb. 28
Per bank	$20,000	$22,000	$24,000	$18,000
Deposit in transit--1/31	5,000	(5,000)		
Outstanding checks--2/28			7,000	(7,000)
Bank error in recording receipt		(500)		(500)
Deposit in transit--2/28		4,000		4,000
Outstanding checks--1/31	(9,000)		(9,000)	
Correct amounts	$16,000	$20,500	$22,000	$14,500
Per books	$16,020	$19,410	$21,505	$13,925
Bank service charge--Jan.	(20)		(20)	
Bank service charge--Feb.			35	(35)
Company error in recording check			180	(180)
Collection of note by bank		1,090		1,090
Customer NSF check			300	(300)
Correct amounts	$16,000	$20,500	$22,000	$14,500

(c)

Office Expenses--Bank Charges	35	
Cash		35
Office Supplies Expense	180	
Cash		180
Cash	1,090	
Note Receivable		1,000
Interest Revenue		90
Accounts Receivable	300	
Cash		300

ILLUSTRATION 7-2
ENTRIES FOR THE ALLOWANCE METHOD

Journal Entry			Effect on Net Income	Effect on Working Capital	Effect on Allowance Account	Effect on Net Receivables
Entry to record bad debt expense, $1,000						
Bad Debt Expense	1,000		Decrease $1,000	No effect	No effect	No effect
Allowance for Doubtful			No effect	Decrease $1,000	Increase $1,000	Decrease $1,000
Accounts		1,000				
Net effect of entry			Decrease $1,000	Decrease $1,000	Increase $1,000	Decrease $1,000
Entry to write-off a customer's account, $200						
Allowance for Doubtful			No effect	Increase $200	Decrease $200	Increase $200
Accounts	200					
Accounts Receivable		200	No effect	Decrease $200	No effect	Decrease $200
Net effect of entry			No effect	No effect	Decrease $200	No effect
Entries to record collection of account receivable previously written off, $120						
Accounts Receivable	120		No effect	Increase $120	No effect	Increase $120
Allowance for Doubtful						
Accounts		120	No effect	Decrease $120	Increase $120	Decrease $120
Cash	120		No effect	Increase $120	No effect	No effect
Accounts Receivable		120	No effect	Decrease $120	No effect	No effect
Net effect of entries			No effect	No effect	Increase $120	No effect

EXERCISE 7-4

Purpose: This exercise will require you to record: (1) the transfer of accounts receivable with recourse, (2) an assignment of accounts receivable, and (3) the adjusting entry to recognize bad debt expense and adjust the Allowance for Doubtful Accounts account.

The trial balance before adjustment at December 31, 19X4 for the Liz Company shows the following balances:

	Dr.	Cr.
Accounts Receivable	$82,000	
Allowance for Doubtful Accounts	2,120	
Sales (all on credit)		$430,000
Sales Returns and Allowances	7,600	

Instructions

Using the data above, give the journal entries required to record each of the following cases (each situation is independent):

1. To obtain additional cash, Liz factors, without recourse, $24,000 of accounts receivable with Fleetwood Finance. The finance charge is 10% of the amount factored.
2. To obtain a one-year loan of $54,000, Liz assigns $65,000 of specific receivable accounts to Fansteal Financial. The finance charge is 8% of the loan; the cash is received and the accounts are turned over to Fansteal.
3. The company wants to maintain the Allowance for Doubtful Accounts at 4% of gross accounts receivable.
4. The company wishes to increase the allowance by 1 1/2% of net credit sales.
5. Liz performs an aging analysis at December 31, 19X4 which indicates an estimate of $6,000 uncollectible accounts.

SOLUTION TO EXERCISE 7-4

1.	Cash	21,600	
	Loss on Sale of Receivable ($24,000 X 10%)	2,400	
	Accounts Receivable		24,000
2.	Cash	49,680	
	Finance Charge ($54,000 X 8%)	4,320	
	Notes Payable		54,000
	Accounts Receivable Assigned	65,000	
	Accounts Receivable		65,000
3.	Bad Debt Expense	5,400	
	Allowance for Doubtful Accounts ($82,000 X 4%) + $2,120		5,400
4.	Bad Debt Expense	6,336	
	Allowance for Doubtful Accounts [($430,000 - $7,600) X 1.5%]		6,336
5.	Bad Debt Expense	8,120	
	Allowance for Doubtful Accounts		8,120

<u>Explanation:</u>

Item 1: The factoring of accounts receivable without recourse is accounted for as a sale of accounts receivable; hence, the receivables are removed from the accounts, cash is recorded, and a loss is recognized for the excess of the face value of the receivables over the proceeds received.

Item 2: In an assignment of accounts receivable, the owner of the receivables borrows cash from a lender by writing a promissory note that contains a provision designating the accounts receivable as collateral. The accounts receivable are left on Liz's books (but they are put in a separate account Accounts Receivable Assigned). The Note Payable is recorded; the cash received is recorded; and a finance charge is recognized.

Item 3: This entry is to adjust the allowance account. A by-product of the entry is the recognition of uncollectible accounts expense. Because an appropriate balance for the valuation account is determined to be a percentage of the receivable balance at the balance sheet date, the existing balance ($2,120 debit) in the Allowance account must be considered in computing the necessary adjustment.

Item 4: The percentage of net credit sales approach to applying the allowance method of accounting for bad debts focuses on determining an appropriate expense figure. The existing balance in the allowance account is not relevant in the computation.

Item 5: An aging analysis provides the best estimate of the net realizable value of accounts receivable. By using the results of the aging to adjust the allowance account, the amount reported for net receivables on the balance sheet is the net realizable value of accounts receivable. It is important to notice that the balance of the allowance account before adjustment is a determinant in the adjustment required. The following T accounts reflects the facts used to determine the necessary adjustment:

Allowance for Doubtful Accounts

Unadjusted balance	2,120	Adjustment needed	8,120
		Desired balance at 12/31/X4	6,000

EXERCISE 7-5

Purpose: This exercise will help you to compare two possible ways of recording a transfer of accounts receivable with recourse: (1) As a sale, or (2) As a borrowing.

Raytech Corporation factors $90,000 of accounts receivable with NL Financing, Inc. on a with recourse basis. NL Financing will collect the receivables. The receivable records are transferred to NL Financing on August 15, 1992. NL Financing assesses a finance charge of 2% of the amount of accounts receivable and also reserves an amount equal to 4% of accounts receivable to cover probable adjustments.

Instructions
(a)   What conditions must be met for a transfer of receivables with recourse to be accounted for as a sale?
(b)   Assume the conditions from part (a) are met. Prepare the journal entry on August 15, 1992 for Raytech to record the sale of receivables.
(c)   Assume that not all of the conditions from part (a) are met. Prepare the journal entry on August 15, 1992 for Raytech to record the transfer of receivables.

SOLUTION TO EXERCISE 7-5

(a)   Per *SFAS No. 77,* a transfer of receivables with recourse should be accounted for as a sale, recognizing any gain or loss, if **all three** of the following conditions are met:
   1.   The transferor surrenders control of the future economic benefits of the receivables.
   2.   The transferor's obligation under the recourse provisions can be reasonably estimated.
   3.   The transferee cannot require the transferor to repurchase the receivables.

(b)	8/15	Cash	84,600	
		Due from Factor	3,600	
		Loss on Sale of Receivables	1,800	
		Accounts Receivable		90,000
		($90,000 X 2% = $1,800); ($90,000 X 4% = $3,600)		
(c)	8/15	Cash	84,600	
		Due from Factor	3,600	
		Discount on Transferred Accounts Receivable	1,800	
		Liability on Transferred Accounts Receivable		90,000

EXERCISE 7-6

Purpose: This exercise will illustrate the accounting for two situations involving the exchange of a noncash asset or service for a promissory note: (1) the exchange of land for a promissory note where the fair value of the land is known, and (2) the exchange of services for a note where the fair value of the services are not known.

General Host's annual accounting period ends on December 31. Reversing entries are used when appropriate. On July 1, 1992, General Host Company made two sales:
1. It sold land having a fair market value of $700,000 in exchange for a four-year noninterest-bearing promissory note in the face amount of $1,101,460. The land is carried on General Host Company's books at a cost of $620,000.
2. It rendered services in exchange for a 3%, 8-year promissory note having a face value of $300,000 with interest payable annually. General Host Company recently had to pay 8% interest for money that it borrowed from Arizona National Bank. The customer in this transaction has a credit rating that requires them to borrow money at 12% interest.

Instructions
(a) Prepare the two journal entries that should be recorded by General Host Company for the sales transactions above.
(b) Prepare the amortization schedule for the note receivable accepted in the first transaction [Note (1)].
(c) Prepare the amortization schedule for the note receivable accepted in the second transaction [Note (2)].
(d) Prepare the necessary journal entries at December 31, 1992 and December 31, 1993 that relate to the first transaction.
(e) Prepare the necessary journal entries at December 31, 1992, June 30, 1993, and December 31, 1993 that relate to the second transaction. Assume the customer makes the scheduled interest payments on time.

SOLUTION TO EXERCISE 7-6

(a) 7/1/92 Notes Receivable 1,101,460
                Discount on Notes Receivable 401,46
                Land .... 620,0(
                Gain on Sale of Land ($700,000 - $620,000).... 80,0

The exchange price is equal to the fair market value of the property (which is $700,000). interest rate implicit in this price is therefore calculated by:
    $700,000 = $1,101,460 (PV Factor)
    $700,000 divided by $1,101,460 = .63552
    By reference to Table 6-2 (Present Value of 1 Table), .63552 is the PV factor for n =
    i = 12%.

7/1/92 Notes Receivable 300,000.00
                Discount on Notes Receivable .... 134,?
                Service Revenue 165,

Use the market rate of interest to compute the present value of the note which is then establish the exchange price in the transaction. The market rate of interest should be the borrower normally would have to pay to borrow money for similar activities.

Computation of the present value of the note:
Maturity value

Present value of $300,000 due in 8 years at 12%--$300,000 X .40388		$300,000.00
Present value of $9,000 payable annually for 8 years at 12%--$9,000 X 4.96764	$121,164.00	
Present value of the note and interest	44,708.76	
Discount		165,872.76
		$134,127.24

(b)

AMORTIZATION SCHEDULE FOR NOTE (1)

Date	12% Effective Interest	Amortization of Discount	P.V. Balance
7/1/92			
6/30/93	$ 84,000.00	$ 84,000.00	$ 700,000.00
6/30/94	94,080.00	94,080.00	784,000.00
6/30/95	105,369.60	105,369.60	878,080.00
6/30/96	118,010.40[1]	118,010.40	983,449.60
Totals	$401,460.00	$401,460.00	1,101,460.00

[1]Includes rounding error of $3.55.

(c)

AMORTIZATION SCHEDULE FOR NOTE (2)

Date	3% Stated Interest	12% Effective Interest	Amortization of Discount	P.V. Balance
7/1/92				$165,872.76
6/30/93	$9,000.00	$ 19,904.73	$ 10,904.73	176,777.49
6/30/94	9,000.00	21,213.30	12,213.30	188,990.79
6/30/95	9,000.00	22,678.89	13,678.89	202,669.68
6/30/96	9,000.00	24,320.36	15,320.36	217,990.04
6/30/97	9,000.00	26,158.80	17,158.80	235,148.84
6/30/98	9,000.00	28,217.86	19,217.86	254,366.70
6/30/99	9,000.00	30,524.00	21,524.00	275,890.70
6/30/00	9,000.00	33,109.30[2]	24,109.30	300,000.00
Totals	$72,000.00	$206,127.24	$134,127.24	

[2]Includes rounding error of $2.42.

(d) 12/31/92 Discount on Notes Receivable 42,000
        Interest Revenue   42,000
        (1/2 X $84,000 = $42,000)

| 12/31/93 | Discount on Notes Receivable .... | 89,040 | |
| | Interest Revenue .... | | 89,040 |

(1/2 X $84,000 = $42,000; 1/2 X $94,080 = $47,040; $42,000 + $47,040 = $89,040)

(e)

12/31/92	Interest Receivable	4,500.00	
	Discount on Notes Receivable	5,452.37	
	Interest Revenue		9,952.37

(1/2 X $9,000 = $4,500;
1/2 X $19,904.73 = $9,952.37)

| 1/1/93 | Interest Revenue .... | 4,500.00 | |
| | Interest Receivable .... | | 4,500.00 |

(To reverse last period's accrual)

| 6/30/93 | Cash .... | 9,000.00 | |
| | Interest Revenue .... | | 9,000.00 |

12/31/93	Interest Receivable	4,500.00	
	Discount on Notes Receivable	11,559.01	
	Interest Revenue		16,059.01

(1/2 X $9,000.00 = $4,500.00
1/2 X $19,904.73 = $9,952.36
1/2 x $21,213.30 = $10,606.65
$9,952.36 + $10,606.65 = $20,559.01
$20,559.01 - $4,500.00 = $16,059.01)

ILLUSTRATION 7-3
DISCOUNTING OF NOTES RECEIVABLE

Steps in Discounting a Note:
1. Compute the **maturity value** of the note (face value plus interest to maturity).
2. Compute the **discount** (the bank's discount rate multiplied by the maturity value multiplied by the time to maturity).
3. Compute the **proceeds** (maturity value minus the bank's discount).
4. Compute the **book carrying value** of the note (face value plus interest accrued to date of discounting).
5. Compute the **gain or loss** if a sale, or the **interest revenue or expense** if a borrowing (proceeds minus the book carrying value).
6. Record the journal entry.

The journal entries may be recorded as follows:

Discounting Without Recourse--Treated as a Sale

Accounts	Amount to Debit	Amount to Credit
Interest Receivable	Interest accrued to date of discounting.	
Interest Revenue		Interest accrued to date of discounting.
Cash	Proceeds.	
Loss or	Plug.	
Gain		Plug.
Notes Receivable		Face value of note.
Interest Receivable		Interest accrued to date of discounting.

No contingent liability is disclosed.

Discounting With Recourse--When Treated as a Sale--Alternative 1

Accounts	Amount to Debit	Amount to Credit
Interest Receivable	Interest accrued to date of discounting.	
Interest Revenue		Interest accrued to date of discounting.
Cash	Proceeds.	
Loss or	Plug.	
Gain		Plug.
Notes Receivable		Face value of note.
Interest Receivable		Interest accrued to date of discounting.

A contingent liability is to be disclosed in the notes to the financial statements.

Discounting With Recourse--When Treated as a Sale--Alternative 2

Accounts	Amount to Debit	Amount to Credit
Interest Receivable	Interest accrued to date of discounting.	
Interest Revenue		Interest accrued to date of discounting.
Cash	Proceeds.	
Loss or	Plug.	
Gain		Plug.
Notes Rec. Discounted		Face value of note.
Interest Receivable		Interest accrued to date of discounting.

The contra-asset account Notes Receivable Discounted serves to disclose the contingent liability on the note.

Discounting With Recourse--When Treated as a Borrowing

Accounts	Amount to Debit	Amount to Credit
Interest Receivable	Interest accrued to date of discounting.	
Interest Revenue		Interest accrued to date of discounting.
Cash	Proceeds.	
Interest Expense or	Plug.	
Interest Revenue		Plug.
Liability on Discounted		
Notes Receivable		Face value of note.
Interest Receivable		Interest accrued to date of discounting.

The Liability account serves to disclose the contingent liability on the note.

TIP: The **book carrying value** of the note is often called the **carrying value** or **carrying amount** or **book value** of the note.

EXERCISE 7-7

Purpose: This exercise will illustrate the computations and entries involved in accounting for the discounting of a note receivable that is treated as a borrowing transaction.

Presented below is information related to Gould Co. and Henry, Inc.

May 1 Gould Co. gave Henry, Inc. a $7,200.00, 60-day, 10% note in payment of its account of the same amount.
     16 Henry, Inc. discounted the note at the bank at a 12% discount rate.
June 30 On the maturity date of the note, Gould Co. paid the amount due.

Instructions
(a) Record the transactions above on both the books of Gould Co. and the books of Henry, Inc. (Assume it is a borrowing transaction.)
(b) Assume that Gould Co. dishonored its note and the bank notified Henry, Inc., that it had charged the maturity value plus a protest fee of $25 to the Henry, Inc. bank account. What entry(ies) should Henry, Inc. make upon receiving this notification.

SOLUTION TO EXERCISE 7-7

(a)

Gould Co.

5/1	Accounts Payable	7,200.00	
	Notes Payable		7,200.00
5/16	No entry.		
6/30	Notes Payable	7,200.00	
	Interest Expense ($7,200 X 1/6 X 10%)	120.00	
	Cash		7,320.00

Henry, Inc.

5/1	Notes Receivable	7,200.00	
	Accounts Receivable		7,200.00
5/16	Interest Receivable	30.00	
	Interest Revenue ($7,200 X 15/360 x 10%)		30.00
5/16	Cash	7,210.20	
	Interest Expense	19.80[a]	
	Liability on Discounted Notes Receivable		7,200.00
	Interest Receivable		30.00

[a]

Face value of note	$7,200.00
Interest at 10% for 60 days	120.00
Maturity value	7,320.00
Discount on $7,320 for 45 days at 12%	109.80
	7,210.20
Book carrying value ($7,200 + $30)	7,230.00
Interest expense	$ 19.80

7-22

6/30	Liability on Discounted Notes Receivable	7,200.00	
	Notes Receivable		7,200.00

(b)

Henry, Inc.

Notes Receivable Past Due ($7,200 + $120 + $25)	7,345.00*	
Cash		7,345.00
Liability on Discounted Notes Receivable	7,200.00	
Notes Receivable		7,200.00

*That portion of this amount relating to interest and the bank protest fees ($145) might alternatively be charged to Accounts Receivable. In practice, sometimes the entire debit is made to Accounts Receivable.

ANALYSIS OF MULTIPLE-CHOICE TYPE QUESTIONS

Question

1. The following information pertains to Cruiser Co. at December 31, 1992:

Bank statement balance	$20,000
Checkbook balance	28,200
Deposit in transit	10,000
Outstanding checks	2,000
Bank service charges for December	200

    In Cruiser's balance sheet at December 31, 1992, cash should be reported as
    a. $18,000.
    b. $20,000.
    c. $28,000.
    d. $30,000.

Solution = c.

Explanation and Approach: When a question relates to data used in a bank reconciliation, you should sketch out the format for a bank reconciliation, put in the information given, and solve for the unknown piece.

Balance per bank statement	$20,000
Deposit in transit	10,000
Outstanding checks	(2,000)
Correct cash balance	$28,000
Balance per books	$28,200
Bank service charges	(200)
Correct cash balance	$28,000

In this particular question, the completion of either the top half or the bottom half of the reconciliation using the bank-to-correct balance method would be enough to solve for the answer requested.

Question

2.   The following information pertains to Tommy-Jer Corporation at December 31, 1992:

Balance per bank	$10,000
Deposit in transit	3,000
Outstanding checks	8,000
Bank service charges for December	200
Bank erroneously charged Tommy-Jer's account for Sonny-Ber's check written for $700. As of December 31, the bank had not corrected this error.	700

Tommy-Jer's cash balance per ledger (books) before adjustment at December 31, 1992 is
a. $14,100.
b. $5,900.
c. $5,500.
d. $4,100.

Solution = b.

Explanation and Approach: The balance per books (before adjustment) can easily be computed by putting the data into the format for a bank reconciliation. Either format (balance per bank to balance per books or balance per bank to correct balance) can be used. Each approach is illustrated below:

Balance per bank statement	$10,000
Deposit in transit	3,000
Outstanding checks	(8,000)
Bank service charges	200
Bank error in charge for check	700
Balance per ledger	$ 5,900

Balance per bank statement	$10,000
Deposit in transit	3,000
Outstanding checks	(8,000)
Bank error in charge for check	700
Correct cash balance	$ 5,700

Balance per books	$ X
Bank service charge	(200)
Correct cash balance	$5,700

X = $5,900

Question

3.   Gatorland recorded uncollectible accounts expense of $30,000 and wrote off accounts receivable of $25,000 during year 5. The net effect of these two transactions on working capital was a decrease of
a. $55,000.
b. $30,000.
c. $25,000.
d. $5,000.

Solution = b.

Explanation and Approach: Reconstruct both entries referred to in the question. Then analyze each debit and each credit separately as to its effect on working capital (total current assets minus total current liabilities).

			Effect on Working Capital
Uncollectible Accounts Expense	30,000		None
Allowance for Doubtful Accounts		30,000	Decrease 30,000
Allowance for Doubtful Accounts	25,000		Increase 25,000
Accounts Receivable		25,000	Decrease 25,000
Net Effect			Decrease 30,000

Question

4.   Chelser Corporation performed an analysis and an aging of its accounts receivable at December 31, 19X8 which disclosed the following:

Accounts receivable balance	$100,000
Allowance for uncollectible accounts balance	5,000
Accounts deemed uncollectible	7,400

The net realizable value of the accounts receivable at December 31 should be
a. $87,600.
b. $92,600.
c. $95,000.
d. $97,600.

Solution = b.

Explanation and Approach: Read the last sentence of the question: "The net realizable value of the accounts receivable at December 31 should be." Underline net realizable value of accounts receivable. Write down the definition of net realizable value of accounts receivable--amount of accounts receivable ultimately expected to be converted into cash. Read the details of the question. If an aging shows $7,400 of the $100,000 accounts are deemed uncollectible, then the remaining $92,600 are expected to be converted into cash. (Because the balance of the allowance account does not agree with the amount of uncollectibles per the aging, the allowance for uncollectible accounts balance must be the unadjusted balance.

Question

5.   Seminole Corporation sold to a bank with recourse a 90-day, 12% interest-bearing note receivable 60 days after the note was received from a customer. The proceeds were computed using a 15% discount rate. The amount to be credited to Note Receivable at the date of the discounting transaction would be the
a.   amount of cash proceeds.
b.   face value of the note.
c.   maturity value of the note.
d.   face value of the note less the amount of the discount.

Solution = b.

Explanation and Approach: You should sketch the journal entry and examine the amount credited to the Note Receivable account. Placing an amount into your example for the face value of the note may help. For example, assuming the face of the note is $10,000, the entry at the date of discounting would be:

Cash	10,171.25	
Loss on Sale of Note	28.75	
Note Receivable		10,000.00
Interest Receivable ($300 X 2/3)		200.00

$10,000.00 X 12% X 90/360 = $300.00 interest for 90 days
$10,000.00 + $300.00 = $10,300.00 maturity value
$10,300.00 X 15% x 30/360 = $128.75 discount
$10,300.00 - $128.75 = $10,171.25 cash proceeds

As you can see from the entry, the amount to be credited to the Note Receivable account will always be the amount in that account, which is the face value of the note.

CHAPTER 8

VALUATION OF INVENTORIES:
A COST BASIS APPROACH

OVERVIEW

In accounting, the term inventory refers to a stock of goods held for sale in the ordinary course of business or goods that will be used or consumed in the production of goods to be sold. There are a number of questions regarding inventory addressed in this chapter. Some of these are: (1) What goods should be included in inventory? (2) How does a periodic system differ from a perpetual system? (3) How will the selection of a particular cost flow assumption affect the income statement and balance sheet? (4) How do inventory errors affect the financial statements? (5) How do you compute the various layers of inventory when the dollar-value LIFO method is used?

TIPS ON CHAPTER TOPICS

TIP: The cost of an inventory item includes all costs necessary to acquire the item and bring it to the location and condition for its intended purpose. This cost would include the item's purchase price, transportation-in, and any special handling charges. However, transportation-out is not included in the cost of inventory; it is classified as a selling expense on the income statement for the period in which the expense was incurred.

TIP: FOB terms designate the time that title passes. FOB shipping point or seller means the title passes to the buyer when it leaves the seller's dock. FOB destination or buyer means the title passes to the buyer when it arrives at the buyer's dock.

TIP: Assuming that Palmer Company in Bay Hill, Florida sells to Payne Stewart in Orlando, Florida, the following shows synonymous terms:

FOB shipping point	FOB destination
or FOB seller	or FOB buyer
or FOB Bay Hill, Florida	or FOB Orlando, Florida

TIP: FIFO (first-in, first-out) means the cost of the first items put into inventory are used to price the first items out to cost of goods sold. Thus, the earliest acquisition prices are used to price cost of goods sold for the period, and the latest (most current) acquisition prices are used to price items in the ending inventory. LIFO (last-in, first-out) uses the most recent costs to price the units sold during the period, and it uses the oldest prices to cost the items in the ending inventory. Thus, in a period of rising prices, the method that will yield the lowest net income on the income statement and the lowest ending inventory on the balance sheet is the LIFO method.

TIP: The cost of the ending inventory determined by using the weighted-average method is between the amount of the ending inventory determined by using the LIFO method and the amount of the ending inventory determined by using the FIFO method.

TIP: When working a problem which requires the computation of either ending inventory or cost of goods sold, remember that the total of the ending inventory and the cost of goods sold should equal the total cost of goods available for sale during the period (beginning inventory plus the net cost of purchases).

TIP: When using the weighted-average method and a perpetual system, a new average unit cost must be computed only after each new purchase; a sale will not affect the average unit cost.

TIP: The ending inventory for year 1 is the beginning inventory for year 2. Thus, when the ending inventory for year 1 is overstated, it will cause an overstatement in the net income for year 1 and an understatement in net income for year 2. This error will cause retained earnings at the end of year 1 to be overstated because net income for year 1 (which is overstated) is closed into retained earnings. The balance of retained earnings at the end of year 2 will be unaffected by this error because the net income for year 2 (which is understated by the same amount as the overstatement in retained earnings at the end of year 1) is closed into retained earnings; the error at this point counterbalances. Working capital at the end of year 1 is overstated (because inventory is a current asset), but working capital at the end of year 2 is unaffected because the inventory figure at the end of year 2 is determined by a physical inventory counting and pricing procedure. No new error in this process is assumed unless otherwise indicated.

TIP: An understatement in ending inventory of year 1 will cause an understatement in net income for year 1 and an overstatement in net income for year 2. Thus, retained earnings and working capital at the end of year 1 are understated. However, assuming no more errors are committed at the end of year 2, retained earnings and working capital are not affected at the end of year 2.

TIP: When using the dollar-value LIFO method, you must determine the layers of inventory in terms of base prices. Then each of those layers must be priced in terms of the price level of the period in which each particular layer was added.

TIP: When performing the computations for the dollar-value LIFO method, watch that the results are what you would expect them to be. For instance, most companies experience a trend of increasing prices. Therefore, in converting the ending inventory at current cost to base prices, you would expect the ending inventory at base prices to be an amount that is less than the ending inventory at current cost.

TIP: When using the dollar-value LIFO cost method, a current price index may be given, or you may have to solve for it. For instance, if prices increased over the current year by 8%, the current index would be 108. Using another example, if ending inventory is given as $128,800 at current cost and $115,000 at base prices, the current index is 112 ($128,800 ÷ $115,000 = 1.12 which is 112 percent).

EXERCISE 8-1

Purpose: This exercise will enable you to practice identifying the effects of inventory errors on the financial statements.

The net income per books of Sharon Dietz Company was determined without knowledge of the errors indicated.

Year	Net Income Per Books	Error in Ending Inventory	
1987	$50,000	Overstated	$ 3,000
1988	52,000	Overstated	7,000
1989	54,000	Understated	11,000
1990	56,000	No error	
1991	58,000	Understated	4,000
1992	60,000	Overstated	8,000

Instructions

Prepare a work sheet to show the adjusted net income figure for each of the six years after taking into account the inventory errors.

SOLUTION TO EXERCISE 8-1

Errors in Inventories

Year	Net Income Per Books	Add Overstate- ment Jan. 1	Deduct Understate- ment Jan. 1	Deduct Overstate- ment Dec. 31	Add Understate- ment Dec. 31	Corrected Net Income
1987	$50,000			$3,000		$47,000
1988	52,000	$3,000		7,000		48,000
1989	54,000	7,000			$11,000	72,000
1990	56,000		$11,000			45,000
1991	58,000				4,000	62,000
1992	60,000		4,000	8,000		48,000

Explanation and Approach: When more than one error affects a given year (such as in 1988), analyze each error separately then combine the effects of each analysis to get the net impact of the errors. The beginning inventory for 1988 (ending inventory for 1987) was overstated by $3,000. Therefore, cost of goods sold was overstated by $3,000, and net income for 1988 was understated by $3,000. The ending inventory for 1988 was overstated by $7,000. Therefore, cost of goods sold was understated, and net income for 1988 was overstated by $7,000. An understatement in net income of $3,000 and an overstatement of $7,000 in 1988 net to an overstatement of $4,000 for the net income figure reported for 1988. This overstatement of $4,000 combined with the $52,000 amount reported yields a corrected net income figure of $48,000 for 1988.

EXERCISE 8-2

<u>Purpose:</u>   This exercise reviews the characteristics and the effects of using various pricing methods to determine inventory costs.

Instructions
Answer each of the following questions by inserting one of these abbreviations in the space provided:

SI   (specific identification)
WA   (weighted-average)
FIFO   (first-in-first-out)
LIFO   (last-in-first-out)

_____   1.   Which inventory cost method **best** matches current costs with current revenues on the income statement?

_____   2.   Which inventory cost method yields the most realistic amount for inventory, compared to replacement cost, on the balance sheet?

_____   3.   Which method results in the most exact ending inventory valuation when inventory items of the same type are **not** homogeneous?

_____   4.   Which method is based on the assumption that inventory flow is "mixed" and therefore "mixes" all acquisition prices?

During a period of **rising prices,** which method yields the:

_____   5.   lowest net income figure?

_____   6.   lowest amount for inventory on the balance sheet?

_____   7.   lowest cost of goods sold figure?

_____   8.   lowest owners' equity figure?

During a period of **declining prices,** which method yields the:

_____   9.   lowest net income figure?

_____   10.   lowest amount for inventory on the balance sheet?

_____   11.   lowest cost of goods sold figure?

_____   12.   lowest owners' equity figure?

SOLUTION TO EXERCISE 8-2

1.	LIFO	7.	FIFO
2.	FIFO	8.	LIFO
3.	SI	9.	FIFO
4.	WA	10.	FIFO
5.	LIFO	11.	LIFO
6.	LIFO	12.	FIFO

EXERCISE 8-3

Purpose: This exercise will allow you to practice performing calculations to determine inventory cost under each of three costing (pricing) methods, using both the modified perpetual and the perpetual systems.

Def Leppard Company's record of transactions concerning Part WD40 for the month of April was as follows:

Purchases		Sales	
Apr. 1 (balance on hand)	100 @ $5.00	Apr. 5	300
Apr. 4	400 @ 5.10	Apr. 12	200
Apr. 11	300 @ 5.20	Apr. 27	800
Apr. 18	200 @ 5.35	Apr. 28	100
Apr. 26	500 @ 5.60		
Apr. 30	200 @ 5.80		

Instructions

(a) Compute the inventory at April 30 on each of the following bases. Assume that perpetual inventory records are kept in units only. Carry unit costs to the nearest cent.
   1. First-in, first-out (FIFO).
   2. Last-in, first-out (LIFO).
   3. Average cost.

(b) If the perpetual inventory record is kept in dollars, and costs are computed at the time of each withdrawal, what amount would be shown as ending inventory in 1, 2, and 3 above? Carry average unit costs to four decimal places.

SOLUTION TO EXERCISE 8-3

(a)

Purchases--Total Units		Sales--Total Units	
April 1 (balance on hand)	100	April 5	300
April 4	400	April 12	200
April 11	300	April 27	800
April 18	200	April 28	100
April 26	500	Total units	1,400
April 30	200		
Total units available for sale	1,700		
Total units sold	1,400		
Total units in ending inventory	300		

Assuming costs are not computed for each withdrawal:

1. First-in, first-out.

Date of Invoice	No. Units	Unit Cost	Total Cost
April 30	200	$5.80	$1,160
April 26	100	5.60	560
Ending Inventory			$1,720

2. Last-in, first-out.

Date of Invoice	No. Units	Unit Cost	Total Cost
April 1	100	$5.00	$ 500
April 4	200	5.10	1,020
Ending Inventory			$1,520

8-5

3. Average cost. Cost of Part WD40 available:

Date of Invoice	No. Units	Unit Cost	Total Cost
April 1	100	$5.00	$ 500
April 4	400	5.10	2,040
April 11	300	5.20	1,560
April 18	200	5.35	1,070
April 26	500	5.60	2,800
April 30	200	5.80	1,160
Total Available	1,700		$9,130

Average cost per unit = $9,130 ÷ 1,700 = $5.37.
Inventory, April 30 = 300 X $5.37 = $1,611.

(b) Assuming costs are computed for each withdrawal:
  1. First-in, first-out.
     The inventory would be the same in amount as in part (a), $1,720.
  2. Last-in, first-out.

Date	Purchased No. of Units	Purchased Unit Cost	Sold No. of Units	Sold Unit Cost	Balance* No. of Units	Balance* Unit Cost	Amount
April 1	100	$5.00			100	$5.00	$ 500
" 4	400	5.10			400	5.10	
					+ 100	5.00	2,540
" 5			300	$5.10	100	5.10	
					+ 100	5.00	1,010
" 11	300	5.20			300	5.20	
					+ 100	5.10	
					+ 100	5.00	2,570
" 12			200	5.20	100	5.20	
					+ 100	5.10	
					+ 100	5.00	1,530
" 18	200	5.35			200	5.35	
					+ 100	5.20	
					+ 100	5.10	
					+ 100	5.00	2,600
" 26	500	5.60			500	5.60	
					+ 200	5.35	
					+ 100	5.20	
					+ 100	5.10	
					+ 100	5.00	5,400
" 27			800	500 @ 5.60 200 @ 5.35 100 @ 5.20	100	5.10	
					+ 100	5.00	1,010
" 28			100	5.10	100	5.00	500
" 30	200	5.80			200	5.80	
					+ 100	5.00	1,660

Inventory April 30 is $1,660.
*The balance on hand is listed in detail after each transaction.

3. Average cost.

	Purchased		Sold		Balance		
Date	No. of Units	Unit Cost	No. of Units	Unit Cost	No. of Units	Unit Cost*	Amount
April 1	100	$5.00			100	$5.0000	$ 500
" 4	400	5.10			500	5.0800[a]	2,540
" 5			300	$5.0800	200	5.0800	1,016
" 11	300	5.20			500	5.1520[b]	2,576
" 12			200	5.1520	300	5.1520	1,546
" 18	200	5.35			500	5.2320	2,616
" 26	500	5.60			1,000	5.4160	5,416
" 27			800	5.4160	200	5.4160	1,083
" 28			100	5.4160	100	5.4160	542
" 30	200	5.80			300	5.6733	1,702

Inventory April 30 is $1,702.

*Four decimal places are used to minimize rounding errors.

[a][(100 units X $5) + (400 units X $5.10)]/500 = $5.08 per unit.

[b][(200 units X $5.08) (300 units X $5.20)]/500 = $5.1520 per unit.

EXERCISE 8-4

Purpose: This exercise will enable you to practice determining how to handle goods in transit and other items necessary for proper inventory valuation.

Jennifer Chudoba Company, a manufacturer of small tools, provided the following information from its accounting records for the year ended December 31, 1992.

Inventory at December 31, 1992 (at cost, based on physical count of goods in Chudoba's plant at cost on December 31, 1992)	$1,520,000
Accounts payable at December 31, 1992	1,200,000
Net sales (sales less sales returns)	8,150,000

Additional information is as follows:

1. Included in the physical count were tools billed to a customer f.o.b. shipping point on December 31, 1992. These tools had a cost of $31,000 and were billed at $40,000. The shipment was on Chudoba's loading dock waiting to be picked up by the common carrier.

2. Goods were in transit from a vendor to Chudoba on December 31, 1992. The invoice cost was $65,000, and the goods were shipped f.o.b. shipping point on December 29, 1992.

3. Work-in-process inventory costing $30,000 was sent to an outside processor for plating on December 30, 1992.

4. Tools returned by customers and held pending inspection in the returned goods area on December 31, 1992 were not included in the physical count. On January 8, 1993, the tools costing $32,000 were inspected and returned to inventory. Credit memos totaling $43,000 were issued to the customers on the same date.

5. Tools shipped to a customer f.o.b. destination on December 26, 1992, were in transit at December 31, 1992, and had a cost of $21,000. Upon notification of receipt by the customer on January 2, 1993, Chudoba issued a sales invoice for $42,000.

6. Goods, with an invoice cost of $27,000, received from a vendor at 5:00 p.m. on December 31, 1992, were recorded on a receiving report dated January 2, 1993. The goods were not included in the physical count, but the invoice was included in accounts payable at December 31, 1992.

7. Goods received from a vendor on December 26, 1992, were included in the physical count. However, the related $56,000 vendor invoice was not included in accounts payable at December 31, 1992, because the accounts payable copy of the receiving report was lost.

8. On January 3, 1993, a monthly freight bill in the amount of $6,000 was received. The bill specifically related to merchandise purchased in December 1992, one-half of which was still in the inventory at December 31, 1992. The freight charges were not included in either the inventory or in the accounts payable balance at December 31, 1992.

Instructions
Using the format shown below, prepare a schedule of adjustments as of December 31, 1992, to the initial amounts per Chudoba's accounting records. Show separately the effect, if any, of each of the eight transactions on the December 31, 1992 amounts. If the transactions would have no effect on the initial amount shown, state NONE.

	Inventory	Accounts Payable	Net Sales
Initial amounts	$1,520,000	$1,200,000	$8,150,000
Adjustments--increase (decrease)			
1.			
2.			
3.			
4.			
5.			
6.			
7.			
8.			
Total adjustments			
Adjusted amounts			

(AICPA adapted)

SOLUTION TO EXERCISE 8-4

Jennifer Chudoba Company
Schedule of Adjustments
December 31, 1992

	Inventory	Accounts Payable	Net Sales
Initial amounts	$1,520,000	$1,200,000	$8,150,000
Adjustments:			
1.	NONE	NONE	(40,000)
2.	65,000	65,000	NONE
3.	30,000	NONE	NONE
4.	32,000	NONE	(43,000)
5.	21,000	NONE	NONE
6.	27,000	NONE	NONE
7.	NONE	56,000	NONE
8.	3,000	6,000	NONE
Total adjustments	178,000	127,000	(83,000)
Adjusted amounts	$1,698,000	$1,327,000	$8,067,000

Explanation:

1. The $31,000 of tools on the loading dock were properly included in the physical count. The sale should not be recorded until the goods are picked up by the common carrier. Therefore, no adjustment is made to inventory, but sales must be reduced by the $40,000 billing price.

2. The $65,000 of goods in transit from a vendor to Chudoba were shipped f.o.b. shipping point on 12/29/92. Title passes to the buyer as soon as goods are delivered to the common carrier when sold f.o.b. shipping point. Therefore, these goods are properly includable in Chudoba's inventory and accounts payable at 12/31/92. Both inventory and accounts payable must be increased by $65,000.

3. The work-in-process inventory sent to an outside processor is Chudoba's property and should be included in ending inventory. Since this inventory was not in the plant at the time of the physical count, the inventory column must be increased by $30,000.

4. The tools costing $32,000 were recorded as sales ($43,000) in 1992. However, these items were returned by customers on December 31, so 1992 net sales should be reduced by the $43,000 return. Also, $32,000 has to be added to the inventory column since these goods were not included in the physical count.

5. The $21,000 of tools shipped to a customer f.o.b. destination are still owned by Chudoba while in transit because title does not pass on these goods until they are received by the buyer. Therefore, $21,000 must be added to the inventory column. No adjustment is necessary in the sales column because the sale was properly recorded in 1993 when the customer received the goods.

6. The goods received from a vendor at 5:00 p.m. on 12/31/92 should be included in ending inventory, but were not included in the physical count. Therefore, $27,000 must be added to the inventory column. No adjustment is made to accounts payable, since the invoice was included in 12/31/92 accounts payable.

7. The $56,000 of goods received on 12/26/92 were properly included in the physical count of inventory; $56,000 must be added to accounts payable since the invoice was not included in the 12/31/92 accounts payable balance.

8. Since one-half of the freight-in cost ($6,000) pertains to merchandise properly included in inventory as of 12/31/92, $3,000 should be added to the inventory column. The remaining $3,000 debit should be reflected in cost of goods sold. The full $6,000 must be added to accounts payable since the liability was not recorded.

EXERCISE 8-5

Purpose: This exercise will illustrate the effect on net income when the LIFO cost method rather than the FIFO cost method is used in a period of rising prices. It also requires you to examine the effect of both the beginning inventory and the ending inventory on the net income computation.

Using the FIFO cost method, Worrell Company had a beginning inventory of $24,000, ending inventory of $30,000, and net income of $80,000. If Worrell had used the LIFO cost method, the beginning inventory would have been $20,000 and the ending inventory would have been $23,000.

Instructions
Compute what net income would have been if the LIFO cost method had been used.

SOLUTION TO EXERCISE 8-5

Using LIFO:
> Beginning inventory would have been less by $4,000; therefore,
>> Cost of goods sold would have been less by $4,000 and
>> Net income would have been more by $4,000, and
> Ending inventory would have been less by $7,000; therefore,
>> Cost of goods sold would have been more by $7,000 and
>> Net income would have been less by $7,000, therefore:

Net income using FIFO	$80,000
Decrease in beginning inventory using LIFO	4,000
Decrease in ending inventory using LIFO	(7,000)
Net income using LIFO	$77,000

EXERCISE 8-6

Purpose: This exercise illustrates the use of the dollar-value LIFO method. It shows how a decrease in the ending inventory in terms of base prices from one year to the next affects the calculations and then what happens when an increase in the ending inventory at base prices occurs.

Presented below is information related to Stacy Lattisaw Company.

Date	Ending Inventory (End of Year Prices)	Price Index (Percentage)
December 31, 1989	$ 80,000	100
December 31, 1990	115,500	105
December 31, 1991	108,000	120
December 31, 1992	123,500	130
December 31, 1993	154,000	140
December 31, 1994	174,000	145

Instructions
Compute the ending inventory for Stacy Lattisaw Company for 1989 through 1994 using the dollar-value LIFO method.

SOLUTION TO EXERCISE 8-6

	Current $	÷	Price Index (Percentage)	=	Base Year $	Change
1989	$ 80,000		100		$ 80,000	--
1990	115,500		105		110,000	$+30,000
1991	108,000		120		90,000	(20,000)
1992	123,500		130		95,000	+5,000
1993	154,000		140		110,000	+15,000
1994	174,000		145		120,000	+10,000

Ending Inventory--Dollar Value LIFO.

1989 $80,000

1990 $80,000 @ 100 = $ 80,000
        30,000 @ 105 =   31,500
                          $111,500

1991 $80,000 @ 100 = $ 80,000
        10,000 @ 105 =   10,500
                          $ 90,500

1992 $80,000 @ 100 = $ 80,000
        10,000 @ 105 =   10,500
         5,000 @ 130 =   6,500
                          $ 97,000

1993 $80,000 @ 100 = $ 80,000
        10,000 @ 105 =   10,500
         5,000 @ 130 =   6,500
        15,000 @ 140 =   21,000
                          $118,000

1994 $80,000 @ 100 = $ 80,000
        10,000 @ 105 =   10,500
         5,000 @ 130 =   6,500
        15,000 @ 140 =   21,000
        10,000 @ 145 =   14,500
                          $132,500

Explanation and Approach: (1) The ending inventory must first be converted from current dollars to base-period dollars. This is done by dividing the ending inventory at current prices by the current price index. (2) Next, the ending inventory at base prices is apportioned into layers, according to individual years in which the inventory was acquired. (3) Each layer is then priced using the index of the year in which it was acquired in order to obtain the inventory at dollar-value LIFO cost.

TIP: Whenever a layer or a portion thereof, is eliminated (such as the case in 1991), it is gone forever and cannot be restored. Notice how in 1992, when there is again an increase in inventory, the newly added layer for 1992 is priced at the index of the year in which that layer was added (1992) and **not** at the index of the portion of the 1990 layer that was eliminated in 1991. This process is consistent with the last costs into inventory being the first costs out (LIFO); thus, inventory is valued at the earliest purchase prices.

ANALYSIS OF MULTIPLE-CHOICE TYPE QUESTIONS

Question

1. At December 31, 1992, a physical count of merchandise inventory belonging to Rhoda Corp. showed $1,000,000 to be on hand. The $1,000,000 was calculated before any potential necessary adjustments related to the following:

    • Excluded from the $1,000,000 was $80,000 of goods shipped f.o.b. shipping point by a vendor to Rhoda on December 30, 1992 and received on January 3, 1993.

    • Excluded from the $1,000,000 was $72,000 of goods shipped f.o.b. destination to Rhoda on December 30, 1992 and received on January 3, 1993.

    • Excluded from the $1,000,000 was $95,000 of goods shipped f.o.b. destination by Rhoda to a customer on December 28, 1991. The customer received the goods on January 4, 1993.

    The correct amount to report for inventory on Rhoda's balance sheet at December 31, 1992, is
    a. $1,072,000.
    b. $1,095,000.
    c. $1,175,000.
    d. $1,247,000.

Solution = c.

Explanation: (1) The $80,000 should be added to the $1,000,000 because f.o.b. shipping point means the title transferred when the goods left the seller's dock on December 30, 1992.

(2) The $72,000 is properly excluded from the ending inventory because title did not pass to Rhoda until Rhoda received the goods on January 3, 1993.

(3) The $95,000 should be added to the $1,000,000 because the goods belong to Rhoda until they are received by the customer (in 1993).

$1,000,000
+ 80,000
+ 95,000
$1,175,000 Amount to report for ending inventory at December 31, 1992.

Question

2.   If beginning inventory is understated by $7,000, and ending inventory is overstated by $3,000, net income for the period will be
   a.   overstated by $10,000.
   b.   overstated by $4,000.
   c.   understated by $4,000.
   d.   understated by $10,000.

Solution = a.

Explanation and Approach: Each error's effect on net income should be determined separately. The effect on net income is dependent on the effect on the computation of cost of goods sold (which is an expense affecting net income). The effects are then combined to compute the **total** effect on net income for the period.

	First Error		Second Error		Total Effect	
Beginning Inventory	Understated	$7,000			Understated	$7,000
+ Purchases						
Goods Available	Understated	$7,000			Understated	$7,000
< Ending Inventory >			Overstated	$3,000	Overstated	$3,000
Cost of Goods Sold	Understated	$7,000	Understated	$3,000	Understated	$10,000
Net Income	Overstated	$7,000	Overstated	$3,000	Overstated	$10,000

Question

3.   Which inventory costing method most closely approximates current cost for each of the following?

	Ending Inventory	Cost of Goods Sold
a.	FIFO	FIFO
b.	FIFO	LIFO
c.	LIFO	FIFO
d..	LIFO	LIFO

Solution = b.

Explanation and Approach: Write down which inventory method (LIFO or FIFO) reports current cost for ending inventory and which uses current cost to price cost of goods sold and then look for your answer combination. FIFO uses the first cost in as the first cost out, so the last (most current) costs are used to price the ending inventory. Therefore, FIFO is the answer for the first column. In contrast, LIFO uses the last cost in (current cost) as the first cost out (to cost of goods sold), so LIFO reflects current costs in cost of goods sold. Therefore, LIFO is the answer for the second column. Answer (b) is the determined combination.

Question

4.   For 1992, Selma Co. had beginning inventory of $75,000, ending inventory of $90,000 and net income of $120,000 using the LIFO inventory method. If the FIFO method had been used, beginning inventory would have been $85,000, ending inventory would have been $105,000 and net income would have been
   a. $125,000.
   b. $115,000.
   c. $145,000.
   d. $95,000.

Solution = a.

Explanation and Approach: Develop the answer by analyzing the effects on the cost of goods sold computation and resulting effects on net income.

	LIFO	FIFO	Effect on Cost of Goods Sold		Effect on Net Income	
Beginning Inventory	$ 75,000	$ 85,000	Increase	$10,000	Decrease	$10,000
+ Purchases						
Goods Available						
< Ending Inventory >	90,000	105,000	Decrease	15,000	Increase	15,000
Cost of Goods Sold						
Net Income	120,000	?	Decrease	5,000	Increase	5,000

Net income using LIFO	$120,000
Increase in net income	5,000
Net income using FIFO	$125,000

Question

5.   McGraty Corp. uses dollar-value LIFO. Its inventory was $500,000 in terms of base prices at December 31, 1992. At December 31, 1993, McGraty's inventory was $600,000 at base prices and $660,000 at current cost. McGraty's inventory at December 31, 1993, using dollar-value LIFO is
a. $660,000.
b. $610,000.
c. $600,000.
d. $550,000.

Solution = b.

Explanation and Approach: Set up the problem as you normally would a dollar-value LIFO problem even though the data given is not what you might expect.

Date	Ending Inventory at Current Costs	÷ Price Index (Percentage)	= Ending Inventory at Base Prices	Dollar-Value LIFO Cost
12/31/92			$500,000	
12/31/93	$660,000	?	600,000	?

Normally you are told the index and are then able to divide the inventory at current cost by the index to get the inventory at base prices. Here, you need to solve for the index by dividing $660,000 by $600,000 which gives you 1.10 so the index, in percentage terms, is 110. The ending inventory at dollar value LIFO therefore is:

$500,000 X 100 =	$500,000
$100,000 X 110 =	110,000
	$610,000

CHAPTER 9

INVENTORIES: ADDITIONAL VALUATION PROBLEMS

OVERVIEW

page 5-15 Balance sheet.

Sometimes a business is faced with the situation where impairments in the value of its inventory are so great relative to selling prices that items cannot be sold at a normal profit. In compliance with conservatism, any impairments in value should be recognized in the current period and the inventory should be valued at the lower-of-cost-or-market (LCM) value for the balance sheet. By following the LCM rule, the impairment is recognized in the period in which it occurs, rather in the later period of disposal of the merchandise. Accounting for declines in inventory value is discussed in this chapter.

Sometimes a business may need to estimate the value of inventory on hand at a certain date. Two estimation techniques--the gross profit and the retail method of inventory estimation--are discussed in this chapter. Although the conventional retail method yields results which are to approximate a lower-of-average-cost-or-market valuation for the inventory, the retail method also can be used to approximate FIFO cost, lower of FIFO cost or market, weighted-average cost, LIFO cost, etc. The conventional retail method and a few variations are discussed in this chapter.

TIPS ON CHAPTER TOPICS

TIP: As used in the phrase lower of cost or market, the term market refers to the market in which the entity buys (not the market in which it sells). Thus, market means current replacement cost (by purchase or by reproduction) except that: (1) market should not exceed the net realizable value (ceiling) and (2) market should not be less than net realizable value reduced by an allowance for an approximately normal profit margin (floor).

TIP: The net realizable value of inventory is the net amount of cash expected to ultimately be received from the sale of the inventory. Thus, the net realizable value of inventory is the estimated selling price in the ordinary course of business less reasonably predictable costs of completion and disposal.

TIP: There are two simple steps to follow in order to apply the lower of cost or market rule to an inventory item. Be sure and follow them in order:

Step 1: Find market:
List the replacement cost, net realizable value (ceiling), and the net realizable value less a normal profit margin (floor) and choose the middle value of these three amounts. Thus:
  (a) market is replacement cost **if** the replacement cost falls in the range between the "ceiling" value and the "floor" value.
  (b) market is the "ceiling" value if the replacement cost falls above the ceiling.
  (c) market is the "floor" value if the replacement cost falls below the floor.
Step 2: Compare market (as determined in Step 1) with cost and choose the lower of the two. This choice is the amount to be reported on the balance sheet.

TIP: If the utility of an inventory item declines prior to the period of sale (disposal), that loss of utility should be recognized in the period of decline rather than the period of disposal. Thus, if an inventory item has become obsolete, the excess of the item's original cost over its net realizable value should be recognized as a loss in the period of the decline in utility.

TIP: Gross profit is synonymous with gross margin.

TIP: The gross profit percentage (expressed as a percentage of selling price) and the cost of goods sold percentage (also expressed as a percentage of selling price) are complements; that is, they sum to 100%. When the gross profit method of inventory estimation is used and the gross margin is expressed in terms of cost, the gross margin must first be expressed in terms of selling price before you can proceed with the computations. One method of conversion is to memorize and use the following formula:

$$\text{Gross margin on selling price} = \frac{\text{Percentage markup on cost}}{100\% + \text{Percentage markup on cost}}$$

Another approach to deriving this formula is shown here by example. It uses the familiar formula: Sales (S) - Cost of Goods Sold (CGS) = GP.
   Example: If GP = 25% of cost, then cost of goods sold is 100%.
   Putting this much information into our formula above: S - 100% = 25%.
   Therefore S = 125%.
   Expressing GP as a percentage of S we get: 25%/125% = 20%.
   Thus, gross profit = 20% of sales.

TIP: The conventional retail method is used to approximate a lower-of-average-cost-or-market figure for inventory valuation. There are other versions of the retail method. In each application, an amount of inventory expressed in terms of retail prices is converted to a cost or to a lower-of-cost-or-market amount by multiplying the retail figure by a ratio. The components of the ratio vary depending on which version of the retail method is desired.

TIP: The conventional retail method includes net markups (often called net additional markups) but excludes net markdowns from the ratio computation. The reason for this is that a lower-of-cost-or-market valuation is desired when the conventional retail method is used. (Net markdowns would also be included in the ratio if a straight average cost value rather than a lower-of-average-cost-or-market valuation were desired.) The omission of the net markdowns from the ratio computation results in a higher denominator and therefore a lower resulting ratio than what would be derived if the net markdowns were to be included in the ratio computation. When there have been markdowns, any related writedowns in inventory should be reflected in the current income statement (from a conservative point of view). This is accomplished by reporting the inventory at a lower value which means more of the cost of goods available for sale goes to the income statement as cost of goods sold expense.

TIP: In using the conventional retail method, the net markdowns are omitted from the ratio computation, but they must be included in determining the estimated ending inventory at retail.

TIP: The retail inventory method can be used only if sufficient information is accumulated and maintained. Purchases are recorded in the accounts at cost. Although not recorded in the accounts, the retail value of purchases and the changes in that value (markups, markup cancellations, markdowns, and markdown cancellations) must be recorded in supplemental records for use in inventory calculations utilizing the retail inventory method.

EXERCISE 9-1

Purpose: This exercise reviews the steps involved in the determination of the lower-of-cost-or-market (LCM) valuation for inventory.

The Richard G. Long Company handles ten different inventory items. The normal profit on each item is 25% of the selling price.

Instructions

From the information below, complete the blanks to calculate the value to be used for the inventory figure for financial statements if the LCM rule is applied to individual items.

				Per Unit						
Item	Number of Units on Hand	Cost	Replacement Cost	Expected Selling Price	Expected Cost to Sell	Ceiling	Floor	Market	LCM	Item Total
1	100	$ 7.00	$ 7.50	$10.00	$1.00	9	6.50	7.50	7.00	
2	10	7.00	6.25	10.00	1.00					
3	50	7.00	9.25	10.00	1.00					
4	10	9.50	9.25	10.00	1.00					
5	20	5.00	6.25	10.00	1.00					
6	100	8.00	7.25	10.00	1.00					
7	30	12.00	11.50	16.00	1.00					
8	10	16.00	15.50	16.00	1.00					
9	20	14.00	11.00	20.00	2.00					
10	10	17.00	16.00	20.00	2.00					

Grand Total

SOLUTION TO EXERCISE 9-1

	Per Unit				
Item	Ceiling	Floor	Market	LCM	Item Total
1	$ 9.00	$ 6.50	$ 7.50	$ 7.00	$ 700.00
2	9.00	6.50	6.50	6.50	65.00
3	9.00	6.50	9.00	7.00	350.00
4	9.00	6.50	9.00	9.00	90.00
5	9.00	6.50	6.50	5.00	100.00
6	9.00	6.50	7.25	7.25	725.00
7	15.00	11.00	11.50	11.50	345.00
8	15.00	11.00	15.00	15.00	150.00
9	18.00	13.00	13.00	13.00	260.00
10	18.00	13.00	16.00	16.00	160.00
	Grand Total				$2,945.00

Approach: Write down the two steps involved in determining the lower of cost or market and perform the steps in order for each of the items:

Step 1: Find market. Market is the middle value of replacement cost, ceiling, and floor. For example:

	Item 1	Item 2	Item 3	Item 4
Estimated selling price	$10.00	$10.00	$10.00	$10.00
- Cost to complete and dispose	1.00	1.00	1.00	1.00
Net realizable value (ceiling)	9.00	9.00	9.00	9.00
- Normal profit margin	2.50*	2.50	2.50	2.50
Floor	$ 6.50	$ 6.50	$ 6.50	$ 6.50

*$10.00 X 25% = $2.50.

Ceiling	$9.00	$9.00	$9.00	$9.00
Floor	6.50	6.50	6.50	6.50
Replacement cost	7.50	6.25	9.25	9.25
Middle of these three values	7.50	6.50	9.00	9.00

Step 2: Compare cost with market and choose the lower.

Cost	$7.00	$7.00	$7.00	$9.50
Market (from Step 1)	7.50	6.50	9.00	9.00
Lower of cost or market	7.00	6.50	7.00	9.00

EXERCISE 9-2

Purpose: This exercise will illustrate the effects of the failure to properly apply the LCM rule.

Bava uses the lower-of-cost-or market rule to value its inventory. At December 31, 1992, the following facts pertain to Product X-17:

Original cost	$420
Replacement cost	365
Expected selling price	400
Estimated selling expenses	50
Normal profit	25% of selling price
Quantity	100

The accountant for Bava used the replacement cost value ($365) to value Product X-17 at December 31, 1992.

Instructions
Answer the following questions:
1. Is $365 the correct unit value for Product X-17 for balance sheet reporting at December 31, 1992? Explain.
2. If $365 is not the correct value, explain the effect of the misstatement on the following: (a) income statement for the year ending December 31, 1992, (b) balance sheet at December 31, 1992, (c) income statement for the year ending December 31, 1993, and (d) balance sheet at December 31, 1993. Assume that all of Product X-17 on hand at December 31, 1992 was sold during 1993.

9-4

SOLUTION TO EXERCISE 9-2

1. $365 is **not** the correct value for Product X-17 at December 31, 1992. The ceiling value of $350 should have been used for the market figure (replacement cost of $365 exceeds the ceiling value of $350) and the ceiling is lower than original cost ($420); hence, $350 is the correct unit value for ending inventory at December 31, 1992.

Computations:

Expected selling price	$400
Estimated selling expenses	(50)
Ceiling	350
Normal profit ($400 X 25%)	(100)
Floor	$250
Ceiling	$350
Floor	250
Replacement cost	365
Middle of these three values	350
Cost	420
Market	350
Lower of cost or market	$350

2. (a) Net income for 1992 is overstated by $1,500.
   (b) Assets are overstated by $1,500. Owners' equity is overstated by $1,500.
   (c) Net income for 1993 is understated by $1,500.
   (d) No effect on the balance sheet at December 31, 1993.

Explanation to part 2:
   (a) $365 - $350 = $15
       $15 X 100 = $1,500
       The error will cause an overstatement of ending inventory which results in an understatement of cost of goods sold expense which causes an overstatement in net income for 1992 in the amount of $1,500.
   (b) Ending inventory is overstated by $1,500, so assets at December 31, 1992 are overstated by $1,500. Owners' equity at December 31, 1992 is also overstated by $1,500 because net income for 1992 (which is overstated by $1,500) is closed into owners' equity at the end of the accounting period.
       HINT: Visualize the basic accounting equation. This error will maintain balance in the basic accounting equation. If assets are overstated, then something else in the equation must be effected to keep the equation in balance. In this case, it is an overstatement of owners' equity because the error affects income (and that effect flows into owners' equity).
   (c) The inventory is all sold in 1993. Bava's accountant is using $365 as the carrying value for each of the 100 units when the correct unit value should be $350. This will cause net income for the year ending December 31, 1993 to be understated by $1,500 because cost of goods sold will be overstated by $1,500.
   (d) The inventory in question is no longer on hand at December 31, 1993, so there is no effect on assets at that date. The $1,500 understatement in income for 1993 is closed into owners' equity which has a balance that is overstated by $1,500 at the beginning of 1993; thus, the owners' equity balance at December 31, 1993 is correct.

CASE 9-1

Purpose: This case addresses three inventory topics: (1) inventoriable costs, (2) the LCM rule, and (3) the retail method.

Palmer Corporation, a retailer and wholesaler of national brand-name household lighting fixtures, purchases its inventories from various suppliers.

Instructions

(a) 1. What criteria should be used to determine which of Palmer's costs are inventoriable?
   2. Are Palmer's administrative costs inventoriable? Defend your answer.

(b) 1. Palmer uses the lower of cost or market rule for its wholesale inventories. What are the theoretical arguments for that rule?
   2. The replacement cost of the inventories is below the net realizable value less a normal profit margin, which, in turn, is below the original cost. What amount should be used to value the inventories? Why?

(c) Palmer calculates the estimated cost of its ending inventories held for sale at retail using the conventional retail inventory method. How would Palmer treat the beginning inventories and net markdowns in calculating the cost ratio used to determine its ending inventories? Why?

(AICPA adapted)

SOLUTION TO CASE 9-1

(a) 1. Palmer's inventoriable costs should include all costs incurred to get the lighting fixtures ready for sale to the customer. It includes not only the purchase price of the fixtures but also the other associated costs incurred on the fixtures up to the time they are ready for sale to the customer, for example, transportation-in.
   2. No, administration costs are assumed to expire with the passage of time and not to attach to the product. Furthermore, administrative costs do not relate directly to inventories, but are incurred for the benefit of all functions of the business.

(b) 1. The lower of cost or market rule is used for valuing inventories because of the concept of balance sheet conservatism and because the decline in the utility of the inventories below its cost should be recognized as a loss in the current period.
   2. The net realizable value less a normal profit margin should be used to value the inventories because market should not be less than net realizable value less a normal profit margin. To carry the inventories at net realizable value less a normal profit margin provides a means of measuring residual usefulness of an inventory expenditure. It makes no sense to price inventory below net realizable value less a normal profit margin because this minimum amount (floor) measures what the company can receive for the inventory and still earn a normal profit in the period of sale.

(c) Palmer's beginning inventories at cost and at retail would be included in the calculation of the cost ratio.

Net markdowns would be excluded from the calculation of the cost ratio. This procedure reduces the cost ratio because there is a larger denominator for the cost ratio calculation. Thus the concept of balance sheet conservatism is being followed and a lower of cost or market valuation is approximated.

EXERCISE 9-3

Purpose: This exercise will illustrate the use of the gross profit method of inventory estimation when: (1) gross margin is expressed as a percentage of cost, and (2) gross margin is expressed as a percentage of selling price.

Tim McInnes requires an estimate of the cost of goods lost by fire on March 9. Merchandise on hand on January 1 was $38,000. Purchases since January 1 were $72,000; freight-in, $3,400; purchase returns and allowances, $2,400. Sales totaled $100,000 to March 9. Goods costing $7,700 were left undamaged by the fire; the remaining goods were destroyed.

Instructions
(a)   Compute the cost of goods destroyed, assuming that the gross profit is 33 1/3% of cost.
(b)   Compute the cost of goods destroyed, assuming that the gross profit is 33 1/3% of sales.

SOLUTION TO EXERCISE 9-3

(a)

Merchandise on hand, January 1		$ 38,000
Purchases	$72,000	
Purchase returns and allowances	(2,400)	
Net purchases	69,600	
Freight-in	3,400	73,000
Total merchandise available for sale		111,000
*Estimated cost of goods sold		(75,000)
Estimated ending inventory on March 9		36,000
Undamaged goods		(7,700)
Estimated fire loss		$ 28,300

$$\text{*Gross profit} = \frac{33\ 1/3\%}{100\% + 33\ 1/3\%} = 25\%\ \text{of sales.}$$

Therefore, cost of goods sold = 75% of sales of $100,000 = $75,000.

(b)   Gross profit is 33 1/3% of sales.
        Therefore, cost of goods sold = 66 2/3% of sales of $100,000 = $66,667.

Total merchandise available for sale (as computed above)	$111,000
Estimated cost of goods sold	(66,667)
Estimated ending inventory at March 9	44,333
Undamaged goods	(7,700)
Estimated fire loss	$ 36,633

TIP: It is important to understand that Inventory is accounted for in terms of the **cost** of goods acquired, and the Sales account reflects the **selling prices** of goods that have been sold during the period. Therefore, the profit element must be removed from the sales amount to arrive at the cost of the goods sold.

Approach: Use these steps to perform the calculations:

(1) **Compute the cost of goods available for sale** for the period January 1 through March 9. This is done by combining the cost of inventory on hand at the beginning of the year (January 1) and the net cost of purchases during the period (net purchases plus freight-in).

(2) **Determine the estimated cost of goods sold** during the period. This is done by multiplying the sales figure for the period by the cost of goods sold percentage. The cost of goods sold percentage is 100% minus the gross margin percentage. **Caution:** The gross margin percentage used here must be stated in terms of selling price. In part (b) of this exercise, gross profit is given in terms of sales. In part (a), however, you must convert the "33 1/3% of cost" to "25% of sales" before the cost of goods sold percentage of 75% can be applied to the sales amount.

(3) **Compute the estimated inventory on hand at the end of the period** (March 9, date of fire) by subtracting the estimated cost of goods sold (Step 2) from the cost of goods available for sale (Step 1).

(4) **Determine the estimated loss** from fire by deducting the cost of the undamaged goods from the estimated cost of inventory on hand at March 9 (Step 3).

EXERCISE 9-4

Purpose: This exercise illustrates four variations of the retail inventory method. It will provide an opportunity to compare and contrast these four approaches.

The records of Nancy Castle's Boutique report the following data for the month of April.

Sales	$79,000
Sales returns	1,000
Markups	10,000
Markup cancellations	1,500
Markdowns	9,300
Markdown cancellations	2,800
Freight on purchases	2,400
Purchases (at cost)	48,000
Purchases (at sales price)	88,000
Purchase returns (at cost)	2,000
Purchase returns (at sales price)	3,000
Beginning inventory (at cost)	30,000
Beginning inventory (at sales price)	46,500

Instructions
(a) Compute the ending inventory by the conventional retail inventory method.
(b) Compute the ending inventory using the retail method to approximate an average cost amount.
(c) Compute the ending inventory using the retail method to approximate a LIFO cost figure (assuming stable prices).
(d) Compute the ending inventory using the retail method to approximate a FIFO cost figure.

SOLUTION TO EXERCISE 9-4

	Cost		Retail
Beginning inventory	$30,000		$ 46,500
Purchases	48,000		88,000
Purchase returns	(2,000)		(3,000)
Freight on purchases	2,400		
Goods available for sale	78,400		131,500
Net markups:			
Markups		$10,000	
Markup cancellations		(1,500)	8,500
	78,400		140,000
Net markdowns:			
Markdowns		9,300	
Markdown cancellations		(2,800)	(6,500)
	$78,400		133,500
Net sales ($79,000 - $1,000)			(78,000)
Ending inventory, at retail			$ 55,500

(handwritten: (78,000))

(a) Cost-to-retail ratio = $\frac{\$78,400}{\$140,000}$ = 56%

Ending inventory at lower of average cost or market = 56% X $55,500 = $31,080.

(b) Cost-to-retail ratio = $\frac{\$78,400}{\$133,500}$ = 58.73%

Ending inventory at average cost = 58.73% X $55,500 = $32,595.

(c) Cost-to-retail ratio = $\frac{\$48,400a}{87,000 \text{ b}}$ = 55.63%

	Retail		LIFO Cost
Beginning inventory layer	$46,500	X 64.516[c]	$30,000
Layer added in April	9,000[d]	X 55.630	5,007
Ending inventory	$55,500		$35,007

(d) Cost-to-retail ratio = $\frac{\$48,400a}{87,000 \text{ b}}$ = 55.63%

Ending inventory at FIFO cost = 55.63% X $55,500 = $30,875.

[a]$78,400 - $30,000 = $48,400   Net cost of purchases.

[b]$133,500 - $46,500 = $87,000   Retail value of purchases plus net markups less net markdowns.

[c]$30,000 ÷ $46,500 = 64.516%   Ratio for beginning inventory.

[d]$55,500 - $46,500 = $9,000   Excess of ending inventory at retail over beginning inventory at retail.

Explanation and Approach:

(a) Step 1:   **Compute the ending inventory at retail.** This is done by determining the retail value of goods available for sale, adjusting that figure for net markups and net markdowns, and deducting the retail value of goods no longer on hand (sales, estimated theft, etc.).

Step 2:   **Compute the cost-to-retail ratio.** The conventional retail method approximates an average cost amount so both beginning inventory and net purchases information is used in the ratio. The conventional retail method is to approximate a lower-of-cost-or-market value so the net markups are included but the net markdowns are excluded from the ratio computation.

Step 3:   **Determine the ending inventory at an approximate lower-of-average-cost-or-market value.** Apply the appropriate cost-to-retail ratio (Step 2) to the total ending inventory at retail (Step 1).

(b) Step 1:   **Compute the ending inventory at retail.** This is done the same way as Step 1 in Part (a) above.

Step 2:   **Compute the cost-to-retail ratio.** Average cost is a mixture of all costs experienced so both beginning inventory and net purchases information is used in the ratio. Because a cost figure (rather than a lower-of-cost-or-market) value is desired, both the net markups and the net markdowns are reflected in the ratio computation.

Step 3:   **Determine the ending inventory at an approximate average cost.** Apply the appropriate cost-to-retail ratio (Step 2) to the total ending inventory at retail (Step 1).

(c) Step 1:   **Compute the ending inventory at retail.** This is done the same way as Step 1 in Part (a) above.

Step 2:   **Compute the cost-to-retail ratio.** When the LIFO method is used, ending inventory is priced in layers. If the ending inventory at retail is higher than the beginning inventory at retail, a new inventory layer was added during the period (Part (c) assumes stable prices). Therefore, two ratios are needed: the ratio for the beginning inventory (beginning inventory at cost divided by the beginning inventory at retail) and the ratio for the layer which was added during the current period. Because the layer added came from purchases of the current period, beginning inventory information is **not** included in this ratio. Because LIFO cost rather than a lower-of-cost-or-market valuation is desired, both the net markups and net markdowns are reflected in the ratio computation.

Step 3:   **Determine the ending inventory at an approximate LIFO cost (assuming stable prices).** Use the appropriate ratio for each layer in the ending inventory. Because a new layer was added in April, the beginning inventory layer is in tact at the end of the period. The ratio for the beginning inventory is used to determine the LIFO cost of that layer (64.516% as determined in Step 2). The ratio for the added layer (55.63% as determined in Step 2) is used to price the $9,000 increase in inventory during the period at retail prices.

TIP: If the ending inventory at retail had been equal to or less than the beginning inventory at retail figure ($46,500), then only one ratio would be needed. That ratio would be the first one discussed in Step 2 above (the ratio which expresses the relationship of the cost of the beginning inventory to the retail value of the beginning inventory). The ending inventory at retail would have been multiplied by that ratio (64.516%) to determine the LIFO cost of the ending inventory.

TIP: If prices had not been stable, additional procedures would have been required to eliminate the effects of price-level changes in order to measure the real increase in inventory, not the dollar increase.

(d) Step 1: **Compute the ending inventory at retail.** This is done the same way as Step 1 in Part (a) above.

Step 2: **Compute the cost-to-retail ratio.** FIFO cost means the first prices in are the first to be used for pricing the cost of goods sold, so the ending inventory is priced using the latest acquisition costs. The latest acquisition prices come from purchases of the current period. Therefore, the beginning inventory information should **not** be used to determine this ratio. Because the FIFO cost is a cost basis rather than a lower-of-cost-or-market valuation, both the net markups and the net markdowns are reflected in the ratio computation.

Step 3: **Determine the ending inventory at an approximate FIFO cost figure.** Apply the appropriate cost-to-retail ratio (Step 2) to the total ending inventory at retail (Step 1).

TIP: Compare the steps for each variation of the retail method utilized in this exercise. Notice that **Step 1** is the **same** for each of the four scenarios and, therefore, yields the same results ($55,500 ending inventory at retail). Notice that Step 3 always applies a ratio to this $55,500 (and in the LIFO case, two ratios were used). The differences among these four scenarios then stem from the appropriate ratio (Step 2) to be applied in each case. Look at each scenario and think through the logic of the ratio calculation as explained in this solution. This process should make it easier to recall how to handle similar situations as you encounter them. **Illustration 9-1** will help to summarize and compare these variations on the use of the retail method.

ILLUSTRATION 9-1
HOW TO COMPUTE AND APPLY THE COST/RETAIL RATIO
FOR THE RETAIL METHOD

Method (Basis)	Ratio	How To Compute Ending Inventory
All	Cost/Retail	Selected retail figure X ratio
1. Conventional (Lower of Average Cost or Market).	Beginning inventory at cost + net cost of purchases divided by beginning inventory at retail + net purchases at retail + net markups.	Ending inventory at retail X ratio.
2. LIFO Cost (ignoring change in price level).		
a. If ending inventory at retail is higher than beginning inventory at retail (added layer).	Purchases at cost divided by purchases at retail + net markups - net markdowns.	Beginning inventory at cost plus added layer at retail X ratio.
b. If ending inventory at retail is less than beginning inventory at retail.	Beginning inventory at cost divided by beginning inventory at retail.	Ending inventory at retail X ratio.
3. Average Cost.	Beginning inventory at cost + net cost of purchases divided by beginning inventory at retail + net purchases at retail + net markups - net markdowns	Ending inventory at retail X ratio.
4. a. FIFO Cost.	Purchases at cost divided by purchases at retail + net markups - net markdowns.	Ending inventory at retail X ratio.
b. FIFO LCM.	Purchases at cost divided by purchases at retail + net markups.	Ending inventory at retail X ratio.

EXERCISE 9-5

Purpose: This exercise will illustrate the use of the dollar-value LIFO method when there is: (a) a decrease in inventory and (b) an increase in inventory.

You assemble the following information for Henrietta's Department Store, which computes its inventory under the dollar-value LIFO method.

	Cost	Retail
Inventory on January 1, 1992	$227,200	$320,000
Purchases	340,400	460,000
Increase in price level for year		8%

Instructions
(a) Compute the cost of the inventory on December 31, 1992, assuming that the inventory at retail is $286,200.
(b) Compute the cost of the inventory on December 31, 1992, assuming that the inventory at retail is $351,000.

SOLUTION TO EXERCISE 9-5

(a) Ending inventory at current retail prices $286,200
Ending inventory at base retail prices ($286,200 ÷ 1.08) 265,000

Since inspection reveals that the inventory quantity has declined below the beginning level (compare $265,000 with $320,000), the ending inventory is merely a portion of the beginning inventory. Therefore, the cost-to-retail ratio reflected in the beginning inventory layer is used to price the ending inventory.

$$\frac{\$227,200}{\$320,000} = 71\% \text{ Cost-to-retail ratio for beginning inventory}$$

$265,000 \times 71\% = \underline{\$188,150}$

(b) Ending inventory at current retail prices $351,000

Ending inventory at base retail prices ($351,000 ÷ 1.08)	325,000
Beginning inventory at base retail prices	320,000
Layer added - at base prices	5,000

Ending inventory:	Retail at Base Price	Dollar-Value LIFO
Beginning inventory	$320,000	$227,200
Additional layer	5,000	3,996*
Ending inventory	$325,000	$231,196

*The $5,000 layer at base prices must be restored to the price level of the period in which it was added: $5,000 X 1.08 = $5,400 and then the cost-to-retail ratio for items purchased during the current year must be applied to that $5,400: $5,400 X 74%** = $3,996.

**The cost-to-retail ratio for items purchased during 1992 is computed as follows: $\frac{\$340,400}{460,000} = 74\%$.

Explanation and Approach: Part (a):

Step 1: **Deflate the $286,200 ending inventory at current retail prices to base retail prices of $265,000.** The ending inventory at current retail prices is reduced to base retail prices by dividing the $286,200 by the ending price level index (108%). The price level increased 8% during the year so assigning an index of 100 (base) to the beginning of the year would mean the index at the end of the year would be 108% (8% higher than 100).

Step 2: **Determine whether a real increase or a decrease has occurred in inventory.** This is done by comparing the ending inventory at base retail prices ($265,000) with the beginning inventory at base retail prices ($320,000).

Step 3: **Determine the ending inventory at dollar-value LIFO.** The ending inventory is merely a portion of the beginning inventory layer. The ending inventory at base retail prices is then converted to a cost figure by using the appropriate cost-to-retail ratio which is the ratio reflected in the beginning inventory.

Explanation and Approach: Part (b):

Step 1: **Deflate the $351,000 ending inventory at current retail prices to base retail prices of $325,000.** This is done by dividing the $351,000 by 108%.

Step 2: **Determine whether a real increase or a decrease has occurred in inventory.** This is done by comparing the ending inventory at base retail prices ($325,000) with the beginning inventory at base retail prices ($320,000). A real increase of $5,000 in terms of base retail prices has occurred.

Step 3: **Determine the ending inventory at dollar-value LIFO.** The ending inventory is composed of two layers--the beginning inventory layer and a layer added during 1992. The cost of the beginning inventory layer is carried over from last period. The added layer must first be priced in terms of current retail prices (multiply $5,000 X 1.08) because the layer was added in 1992 and then that result ($5,400) is converted to a cost figure by multiplying it by the appropriate cost-to-retail ratio (74%). The appropriate cost-to-retail ratio is the relationship of cost to retail of the purchases of 1992.

EXERCISE 9-6

Purpose: This exercise illustrates the procedures involved when switching from the conventional retail method to the LIFO retail method in a period of rising prices.

Go West Stores has just experienced a large fire loss to its inventories. Fortunately, the records for the years 1990-1992 have been salvaged. The conventional retail method was in use during 1990. The corporation switched to the LIFO retail method for the year ending December 31, 1991. You have been hired to reconstruct the divisional financial statements for the years 1990-1992 and are currently engaged in recomputing the final inventory figures as originally stated in the financial statements of the respective years. The following data are available for your examination.

	1990	1991	1992
Beginning inventory @ retail	$200,000	$300,000	$378,000
Ending inventory @ retail	300,000	378,000	358,400
Ending inventory @ cost (Conventional)	?	249,480	240,128
Ending inventory @ cost (LIFO)	?	?	?
Price index	100	108	112
Cost ratio--conventional retail	65	66	67
Cost ratio--LIFO retail	70	72	75

Instructions

(a) Compute the ending inventory under the (1) conventional retail method for 1990, and (2) the LIFO retail method for the years 1991 and 1992. Round to the nearest dollar.

(b) Prepare the entry that was necessary when the change was made from the conventional retail to the LIFO retail method.

SOLUTION TO EXERCISE 9-6

		Cost	Retail
(a) (1) **1990**			
12/31/90 inventory			$300,000
Cost ratio (conventional retail) = 65%			
12/31/90 inventory at cost (conventional retail)			
($300,000 X 65%)		$195,000	
(2) **1991**			
12/31/90 inventory at retail			$300,000
Cost ratio (LIFO retail) = 70%			
12/31/90 inventory at cost (LIFO retail)			
($300 X 70%)		$210,000	
To compute ending inventory:			
12/31/91 inventory at current prices			$378,000
Price index = 1.08			
12/31/91 inventory at base prices ($378,000 ÷ 1.08)			$350,000
Less 12/31/90 inventory at base prices			300,000
Increase at base prices			50,000
Increase at current prices ($50,000 X 1.08)			54,000
Cost ratio (LIFO retail) = 72%			
Increase at cost ($54,000 X 72%)		38,880	
12/31/91 inventory at cost (LIFO retail)		$248,880	
1992			
12/31/92 inventory at current prices			$358,400
Price index = 1.12			
12/31/92 inventory at base prices ($358,400 ÷ 1.12)			$320,000
12/31/91 inventory at base prices			350,000
(There has been a decrease, and part of the layer added in 1991 has been removed.)			
To compute ending inventory:			
12/31/90 inventory (base prices)		$210,000	$300,000
Layer at base prices ($320,000 - $300,000)			20,000
Price index (1991) = 1.08			
Layer at 1991 prices ($20,000 X 1.08)			21,600
Cost ratio (1991 - LIFO retail) = 72%			
Layer at cost ($21,600 X 72%)		15,552	
12/31/92 inventory at cost (LIFO retail)		$225,552	

(b) Inventory (beginning) 15,000

   Adjustment to Record Inventory at Cost*
   [$300,000 X (70% - 65%)].. 15,000

*Note: This account is an income statement account showing the effect of changing from a lower of cost or market approach to a straight cost basis. The amount of $15,000 is the difference between the $195,000 inventory at 12/31/90 at cost using the conventional retail method and the $210,000 that would have resulted at 12/31/90 using LIFO cost.

ANALYSIS OF MULTIPLE-CHOICE TYPE QUESTIONS

Question

1. Crosby Co. is just beginning its first year of operations. Crosby intends to use either the perpetual moving average method or the periodic weighted average method, and to apply the lower of cost or market rule either to individual items or to the total inventory. Prices of most inventory items are expected to increase throughout 1991, although the prices of a few items are expected to decrease. What inventory system should Crosby Co. select if it wants to minimize the inventory carrying amount at the end of the first year?

	Inventory Method	Cost or Market Application
a.	Perpetual	Individual items
b.	Perpetual	Total inventory
c.	Periodic	Individual items
d.	Periodic	Total inventory

Solution = c.

Explanation and Approach: Think about the results of using the perpetual moving average method versus the results of using the periodic weighted average method. In a period of rising prices, the periodic weighted average method will yield the lower ending inventory figure (the ending weighted average unit cost for the perpetual system will be higher than the weighted average unit cost for the period for the periodic system). Then think about the results of applying the lower-of-cost-or-market rule to individual items versus the results of applying it to the total inventory. The individual item approach gives the most conservative valuation for balance sheet purposes. Combine the results of these analyses to get the final answer.

Question

2. Peachy Products has an item in inventory with a cost of $85. Current replacement cost is $75. The expected selling price is $100, estimated selling costs are $18, and the normal profit is $5. Using the lower-of-cost-or-market rule, the item should be included in the inventory at:
   a. $75.
   b. $77.
   c. $82.
   d. $85.

Solution = b.

Explanation and Approach: Write down the two steps in determining LCM and follow them:
   (1) Find market: Three possibilities:
   Ceiling ($100 - $18) = $82
   Floor ($82 - $5) = $77
   Replacement cost = $75
   Choose the middle value of these three: $77 = market

   (2) Compare market with cost and choose the lower.
   Market of $77 versus cost of $85. Lower = $77

Question
3.

The following information pertains to the Godfrey Company for the six months ended June 30 of the current year:

Merchandise inventory, January 1	$ 700,000
Purchases	5,000,000
Freight-in	400,000
Sales	6,000,000

Gross profit is normally 25% of sales. What is the estimated amount of inventory on hand at June 30?

a. $100,000.
b. $1,600,000.
c. $2,100,000.
d. $4,600,000.

Solution = b.

Explanation and Approach: Use the following steps to solve a gross profit inventory method question:

(1) Compute the cost of goods available for sale during the period:

Beginning inventory	$ 700,000
Purchases	5,000,000
Freight-in	400,000
Cost of goods available for sale	$6,100,000

(2) Determine the estimated cost of goods sold during the period:

Sales	$6,000,000
Cost of goods sold percentage (100% - 25%)	75%
Estimated cost of goods sold	$4,500,000

Note: This problem was simple because the gross profit percentage given in the problem is stated in terms of sales. When the gross margin percentage is expressed in terms of cost, that percentage must first be converted to the equivalent percentage of selling price before the other computations can be performed.

(3) Compute the estimated inventory on hand at the end of the period:

Cost of goods available for sale	$6,100,000
Estimated cost of goods sold	4,500,000
Estimated ending inventory	$1,600,000

Question
4.

A company uses the retail method to estimate ending inventory for interim reporting purposes. If the retail method is used to approximate a lower-of-average-cost-or-market valuation, which of the following describes the proper treatment of net additional markups and net markdowns in the cost-to-retail ratio calculation?

	Net Additional Markups	Net Markdowns
a.	Include	Include
b.	Include	Exclude
c.	Exclude	Include
d.	Exclude	Exclude

9-17

Solution = b.

Explanation and Approach: First notice that the lower-of-average-cost-or-market approach to the retail method is often referred to as the conventional retail method. Recall that using a lower-of-cost-or-market figure is an application of the principle of conservatism. Also recall that the retail method involves multiplying the ending inventory at retail by a ratio. The lower the ratio, the lower the computed inventory value. Including the net additional markups (increases in retail prices) but excluding the net markdowns (decreases in retail prices) gives the highest denominator possible for the ratio calculation which yields the lowest ratio possible. (Note: Net additional markups are often simply called net markups.)

Question

5. The Billy Dial Department Store uses a calendar year and the LIFO retail inventory method (assuming stable prices). The following information is available at December 31, 1992:

	Cost	Retail
Beginning inventory	$37,200	$ 60,000
Purchases	200,000	290,000
Freight-in	4,000	
Net markups		30,000
Net markdowns		20,000
Sales		285,000

What is the ending inventory at LIFO cost?
a. $46,763.
b. $47,400.
c. $47,603.
d. $50,250.

Solution = b.

Computations:	Cost	Retail
Beginning inventory	$ 37,200	$ 60,000
Purchases	200,000	290,000
Freight-in	4,000	
Goods available for sale	241,200	350,000
Net additional markups		30,000
Subtotals	$241,200	380,000
Net markdowns		(20,000)
Sales		(285,000)
Ending inventory at retail		$ 75,000

Ending inventory:	Retail	Ratio	Cost
Beginning layer	$60,000	62%*	$37,200
Added layer	15,000	68%**	10,200
Ending inventory	$75,000		$47,400

$* \dfrac{\$37,200}{\$60,000} = 62\%$ $** \dfrac{\$204,000}{\$300,000^a} = 68\%$

^{a}($300,000 = $290,000 Purchases + $30,000 Markups - $20,000 Markdowns)

Explanation and Approach: Think about how LIFO works. If the ending inventory is greater than the beginning inventory, the ending inventory is comprised of the beginning inventory plus a new layer; if the ending inventory is less than the beginning inventory, the ending inventory is comprised of a remaining portion of the beginning inventory layer. Think about how the retail method of inventory estimation works. An estimate of the ending inventory at retail is made by deducting sales from the retail value of goods available for sale and the ending inventory at retail is converted to a cost or to a lower-of-cost-or-market value by applying an appropriate ratio which is an expression of the relationship between inventory cost and its retail value. Apply the following steps to compute the amount required:

Step 1: **Compute the ending inventory at retail.** Arrive at $75,000.

Step 2: **Compute the cost-to-retail ratio.** Comparing ending inventory at retail ($75,000) with beginning inventory at retail ($60,000) indicates a layer was added during 1992. Therefore, two ratios are needed: the ratio for the beginning inventory layer and the ratio for the layer which was added during 1992. The ratio for the new layer should exclude the beginning inventory but include both net additional markups and net markdowns.

Step 3: **Determine the ending inventory at an approximate LIFO cost.** Apply the beginning inventory ratio (62%) to the beginning inventory at retail ($60,000) and apply the purchases ratio (68%) to the added layer at retail ($15,000).

CHAPTER 10

ACQUISITION AND DISPOSITION OF PROPERTY, PLANT, AND EQUIPMENT

OVERVIEW

Assets that have physical existence and that are expected to be used in revenue-generating operations for more than one year or operating cycle, whichever is longer, are classified as long-term tangible assets. Some problems may arise in determining the acquisition cost of a fixed asset such as: the initial acquisition may be the result of several expenditures, one fixed asset may be exchanged for another fixed asset, a plant asset may be obtained on a deferred payment plan, and additional expenditures may be involved subsequent to acquisition. These and other issues and their related accounting procedures are examined in this chapter.

TIPS ON CHAPTER TOPICS

TIP: Property, plant, and equipment is a classification that is often referred to as fixed assets. Included in this section should be long-lived tangible assets that are currently being used in operations (to generate goods and services for customers). Two exceptions to this guideline are: (1) Construction of Plant in Process, and (2) Deposits on Machinery. In each of these cases, the asset is not yet being used in operations but an expenditure has been made which is to be classified in the property, plant, and equipment section of the balance sheet.

TIP: In determining the cost of a plant asset, keep in mind the same guideline we had for inventory. The cost includes all costs necessary to get the item to the condition and location for its intended use.

TIP: In determining the cost of a plant asset, keep in mind the historical cost principle. **Cost** is measured by the cash or the fair market value of the noncash consideration given or the fair market value of the consideration received, whichever is the more objectively determinable. Fair market value refers to cash equivalent value. When cash is given to acquire an asset, it is a relatively simple matter to determine the asset's cost. However, when a noncash asset is given in exchange or when a deferred payment plan is involved, more thought is required to determine the asset's cost. Pay close attention to these areas as they are often the subjects from which discriminating exam questions are derived.

TIP: "Boot" is a term used to describe monetary consideration given or received in an exchange of similar assets. When boot is involved part of the exchanged asset is considered sold, therefore, part of the earning process is considered complete and a partial gain is recognized by the party receiving the boot.

TIP: When one noncash asset is exchanged for another noncash asset, it is important to determine if it is a dissimilar or similar asset exchange. If it is a similar asset exchange **and** if a gain is experienced on the disposal of the old asset, then we are to depart from the historical cost principle in determining the cost of the new asset; the whole gain or a portion of the gain (depending on whether boot is given or received) is to be deferred. This is because the earnings process is not complete.

TIP: When a deferred payment plan is involved in the acquisition of a noncash asset, pay careful attention to whether a fair rate of interest is stated in the agreement. When an unreasonably low stated interest rate is present, interest must be imputed so that the effective amount of interest reported reflects the market rate of interest.

TIP: In the context of accounting for property, plant, and equipment, the term "capitalize" means to record and carryforward into one or more periods expenditures from which benefits or proceeds will be realized; thus, a balance sheet account is debited.

TIP: There may be many expenditures related to the acquisition and operation of property, plant, and equipment. The accountant must determine whether to record these individual expenditures by a debit to the income statement or by a debit to the balance sheet. In making this determination, keep in mind that expenditures benefiting the company for more than the current accounting period should be capitalized in order to properly match expenses with revenues over successive accounting periods; expenditures for items that do not yield benefits beyond the current accounting period should be expensed.

TIP: As used in this chapter, the term **capital expenditure** refers to one which is expected to benefit more than one period; hence, it is initially accounted for as an asset and should be expensed over the periods benefited. A **revenue expenditure** is one which is expected **not** to be of benefit to any period beyond the current period; hence, it is recorded by a debit to either an expense account or to a loss account in the period incurred.

TIP: A plant asset often requires expenditures subsequent to acquisition. If the expenditure benefits the future, it should be capitalized by a charge to an asset account or to an accumulated depreciation account. Such an expenditure is of benefit to the future if it provides new asset services or enhances the quality of existing services or increases the life of existing assets.

TIP: In the context of the topic of property, plant, and equipment, the term **carrying value** refers to the amount derived by deducting the balance in the accumulated depreciation account from the balance in the related asset account. Synonymous terms are: **book value,** net asset value, undepreciated value, and carrying amount. Book value may be very different from fair value. Fair value is often referred to as fair market value.

TIP: The cost of tearing down an old building should be charged (debited) to the Land account if the building was someone else's old building and recently acquired along with the land as a site to be used for another structure. (The cost is charged to Land because it was necessary to get the land in the condition for its intended purpose--to provide space upon which to erect a new building.) The cost of tearing down an old building should be charged to Loss on Disposal of Building if the building has been used in the entity's operations and is now demolished to make way for another building or an alternative use of the land. Therefore, the cost of tearing down an old building is **never** charged to the Building account.

TIP: There are several areas in accounting which utilize the formula to allocate a single sum between two or more items based on the relative fair market values of the items involved. That formula is as follows:

$$\frac{\text{Market Value of One Item in Group}}{\text{Market Value of All Items in Group}} \times \text{Amount to be Allocated} = \begin{array}{c} \text{Amount to be Assigned to} \\ \text{Item Designed in the} \\ \text{Numerator} \end{array}$$

This formula is used in Chapter 10 to allocate one lump-sum amount of cost to the individual assets acquired in a lump sum purchase (often called a basket purchase of fixed assets). The formula will also be used in volume two of this book in Chapter 15 to allocate the proceeds from the issuance of several classes of securities, in Chapter 17 to allocate the proceeds from the issuance of bonds with detachable warrants and in Chapter 18 to allocate the cost of an investment. The formula is also useful in the managerial accounting arena such as in the case where there are joint costs to be computed.

TIP: A nonreciprocal transfer of a nonmonetary asset is to be recorded at the fair market value of the asset at the date of transfer. Property donated to an organization is an example of this type of transaction and results in a credit to Additional Paid-in Capital.

CASE 10-1

Purpose: This case will review the costs to be capitalized for property, plant, and equipment.

Property, plant, and equipment generally represents a large portion of the total assets of a company. Accounting for the acquisition and usage of such assets is, therefore, an important part of the financial reporting process.

Instructions
(a) Distinguish between a revenue expenditure and a capital expenditure. Explain why its distinction is important.
(b) Identify at least six costs that should be capitalized as the cost of land. Assume that land with an existing building is acquired for cash and that the existing building is to be removed immediately in order to provide space for a new building on that site.
(c) Identify at least five costs that should be capitalized as the cost of a building.
(d) Identify at least six costs that should be capitalized when equipment is acquired for cash.
(e) Describe the factors that determine whether expenditures relating to property, plant, and equipment already in use should be capitalized.

(AICPA Adapted)

SOLUTION TO CASE 10-1

(a) A capital expenditure is expected to yield benefits either in all future accounting periods (acquisition of land) or in a limited number of accounting periods. Capital expenditures are capitalized, that is, recorded as assets, and if related to assets of limited life, amortized over the periods which will be benefited. A revenue expenditure is an expenditure for which the benefits are **not** expected to extend beyond the current period. Hence, they benefit only the current period (recorded as an expense) or they benefit no period at all (recorded as a loss).

The distinction between capital and revenue expenditures is of significance because it involves the timing of the recognition of expense and, consequently, the determination of periodic earnings. This distinction also affects the costs reflected in the asset accounts which will be recovered from future periods' revenues.

If a revenue expenditure is improperly capitalized, net income of the current period is overstated, assets are overstated, and future earnings are understated for all the periods to which the improperly capitalized cost is amortized. If the cost is not amortized, future earnings will not be affected but assets and retained earnings will continue to be overstated for as long as the cost remains on the books. If a nonamortizable capital expenditure is improperly expensed, current earnings are understated and assets and retained earnings are understated for all foreseeable periods in the future. If an amortizable capital expenditure is improperly expensed, net income of the current period is understated, assets and retained earnings are understated, and net income is overstated for all future periods to which the cost should have been amortized.

(b)   The cost of land may include:
    (1)   purchase price.
    (2)   survey fees.
    (3)   title search fees.
    (4)   escrow fees.
    (5)   delinquent property taxes assumed by buyer.
    (6)   broker's commission.
    (7)   legal fees.
    (8)   recording fee.
    (9)   unpaid interest assumed by buyer.
  (10)   cost of clearing, grading, landscaping and subdividing (less salvage).
  (11)   cost of removing old building (less salvage).
  (12)   special assessments such as lighting or sewers if they are permanent in nature.
  (13)   landscaping of permanent nature.
  (14)   any other cost necessary to acquire the land and get it in the condition necessary for its intended purpose.

TIP: Typically, the cost of land includes cost of elements that occur prior to excavation for a new building. Costs related to the foundation of the building are elements of building cost.

(c)   The cost of a building may include:
    (1)   construction costs (including an allocation of overhead if self-constructed).
    (2)   excavation fees.
    (3)   architectural fees.
    (4)   building permit fee.
    (5)   cost of insurance during construction (if paid by property owner).
    (6)   property taxes during construction.
    (7)   interest during construction (only interest actually incurred).
    (8)   cost of temporary buildings.
    (9)   any other cost necessary to acquire the building and get it in the location and condition for its intended purpose.

(d)   The cost of equipment may include:
    (1)   purchase price (less discounts allowed).
    (2)   sales tax.

(3) installation charges.
(4) freight charges during transit.
(5) insurance during transit.
(6) cost of labor and materials for test runs.
(7) cost of special platforms.
(8) ownership search.
(9) ownership registration.
(10) breaking-in costs.
(11) other costs necessary to acquire the equipment and get it to the location and condition for its intended use.

(e) The factors that determine whether expenditures relating to property, plant, and equipment already in use should be capitalized are as follows:
(1) Expenditures are material.
(2) They are nonrecurring in nature.
(3) They benefit future periods by doing one of the following:
   a. They extend the useful life of a plant asset.
   b. They enhance the quality of existing services.
   c. They add new asset services.

(AICPA Adapted)

Approach:
1. Scan all requirements before you begin on the first question. Sometimes the latter requirements will help you to see more clearly what is really being requested in the earlier requirements. Sometimes the solution to one requirement appears to overlap with the solution to another part of the question.
2. Prepare a key word outline before you begin writing detailed answers. This outline should very briefly list the concepts you want to cover in your paragraph(s). This outline will help you to organize your thoughts before you begin writing sentences.

EXERCISE 10-1

Purpose: This exercise will help you identify which expenditures should be capitalized and which should be expensed.

TIP: Remember that expenditures which benefit the company for more than the current accounting period should be capitalized in order to properly match expenses with revenues over successive accounting periods. Expenditures for items that do not yield benefits beyond the current accounting period should be expensed.

Instructions
Assume all amounts are material. For each of the following independent items, indicate by use of the appropriate letter if it should be:

C. Capitalized
or
E. Expensed

_____ 1. Invoice price of drill press. C

_____ 2. Sales tax on computer. E

10-5

_____ 3. Costs of permanent partitions constructed in old office building.

_____ 4. Installation charges for new conveyer system.

_____ 5. Costs of trees and shrubs planted in front of office building.

_____ 6. Costs of surveying new land site.

_____ 7. Costs of major overhaul of delivery truck.

_____ 8. Costs of building new counters for show room.

_____ 9. Costs of powders, soaps, and wax for office floors.

_____ 10. Cost of janitorial services for office and show room.

_____ 11. Costs of carpet strips and rubber welcome mats.

_____ 12. Costs of annual termite inspection of warehouse.

_____ 13. Insurance charged for new equipment while in transit.

_____ 14. Property taxes on land used for parking lot.

_____ 15. Cost of a fan installed to help cool old factory machine.

_____ 16. Cost of exterminator's services.

_____ 17. Costs of major redecorating of executives' offices.

_____ 18. Cost of fertilizers for shrubs and trees.

_____ 19. Cost of labor services for self-constructed machine.

_____ 20. Costs of materials used and labor services expended during trial runs of new machine.

SOLUTION TO EXERCISE 10-1

1.	C	6.	C	11.	C	16.	E
2.	C	7.	C	12.	E	17.	C
3.	C	8.	C	13.	C	18.	E*
4.	C	9.	E*	14.	E	19.	C
5.	C	10.	E	15.	C	20.	C

*This answer assumes the products were consumed during the current period. Material amounts of unused supplies on hand at the balance sheet date should be reported as a prepaid expense.

EXERCISE 10-2

Purpose: This exercise will give you practice in identifying capital versus revenue expenditures.

Hughes Supply Company, a newly formed corporation, incurred the following expenditures related to Land, to Buildings, and to Machinery and Equipment.

Abstract company's fee for title search L		$ 520
Architect's fees		2,800 B
Cash paid for land and dilapidated building thereon L		100,000 L
Removal of old building	$20,000	
Less salvage	5,500	14,500
Surveying before construction L		370 B
Interest on short-term loans during construction		7,400 B
Excavation before construction for basement L		19,000
Machinery purchased (subject to 3% cash discount, which was not taken)		55,000
Freight on machinery purchased		1,340
Storage charges on machinery, necessitated by noncompletion of building when machinery was delivered		2,180
New building constructed (building construction took 6 months from date of purchase of land and old building)		500,000
Assessment by city for drainage project		1,600 L
Hauling charges for delivery of machinery from storage to new building		620
Installation of machinery		2,000
Trees, shrubs, and other landscaping after completion of building (permanent in nature)		5,400 L

Instructions

(a) Identify the amounts that should be debited to Land.

(b) Identify the amounts that should be debited to Buildings. Assume the benefits of capitalizing interest during construction exceed the cost of implementation.

(c) Identify the amounts that should be charged to Machinery and Equipment.

(d) Indicate how the costs above not debited to Land, Buildings, or Machinery and Equipment should be recorded.

SOLUTION TO EXERCISE 10-2

	(a) Land	(b) Bldgs.	(c) M & E	(d) Other	
Abstract fees	$ 520				
Architect's fees		$ 2,800			
Cash paid for land & old building	100,000				
Removal of old building ($20,000 - $5,500)	14,500				
Surveying before construction		370			
Interest on loans during construction		7,400			
Excavation before construction		19,000			
Machinery purchased			$53,350	$1,650	Misc. Expense (Discount Lost)
Freight on machinery			1,340		
Storage charges caused by non-completion of building				2,180	Misc. Exp. (Loss)
New building		500,000			
Assessment by city	1,600				
Hauling charges--machinery				620	Misc. Exp. (Loss)
Installation--machinery			2,000		
Landscaping	5,400				
Totals	$122,020	$529,570	$56,690	$4,450	

CASE 10-2

Purpose: This case will review the rules for determining a plant asset's cost when the asset is acquired on a deferred payment plan or in a nonmonetary exchange.

A company often acquires property, plant, and equipment by means other than immediate cash payment.

Instructions
(a) Explain how to determine a plant asset's cost if it is acquired on a deferred payment plan.
(b) Explain how to determine a plant asset's cost if it is acquired in exchange for a dissimilar nonmonetary asset.
(c) Explain how to determine a machine's cost if it is acquired in exchange for a similar machine and a small cash payment is also made.
(d) Explain how to determine a machine's cost if it is acquired in exchange for a similar machine and a small amount of cash is received.

SOLUTION TO CASE 10-2
(a) A plant asset acquired on a deferred-payment plan should be recorded at an equivalent cash price excluding interest. If interest is not stated in the sales contract, an imputed interest rate should be determined. The asset should then be recorded at the contract's present value, which is computed by discounting the payments at the stated or imputed interest rate. The interest portion (stated or imputed) of the contract price should be charged to interest expense over the life of the contract.

(b)   A plant asset acquired in exchange for a dissimilar nonmonetary asset should be recorded at the fair value (cash equivalent value) of the consideration given or the fair value of the consideration received, whichever is more clearly determinable. This is an application of the historical cost principle. Any gain or loss on the exchange should be recognized because the earning process is considered complete.

(c)   When exchanging an old machine and paying cash for a new machine, the new machine should be recorded at the amount of monetary consideration (cash) paid plus the undepreciated cost of the nonmonetary asset (old machine) surrendered if there is no indicated loss. If there is an indicated loss, it should be recognized. This would reduce the recorded amount of the new machine. An experienced loss is indicated when the old asset's market value is less than its carrying value at the date of exchange; a gain is indicated if the asset's market value exceeds its carrying value. No experienced gain, however, should be recognized by the party paying monetary consideration.

Therefore, in the case of paying cash when a loss is experienced on the old machine, the historical principle is followed in determining the cost of the new asset and the loss on the old asset is recognized in total. In the case of paying cash when a gain is experienced on the old machine (in a similar asset exchange), there is a departure from the historical cost principle in determining the cost of the new asset and the gain is **not** recognized. The gain is deferred because the earnings process has not been culminated.

(d)   If a loss is experienced on the old asset, the cost of a machine acquired in exchange for a similar machine plus some boot is equal to the carrying value of the old asset minus the boot received minus the loss recognized on the old asset. If a gain is experienced on the old asset, the cost of a machine acquired in exchange for a similar machine plus some boot is equal to the carrying value of the old machine minus the boot received plus the portion of the gain that is recognized. The portion of the gain to be recognized is determined by the ratio of monetary assets to the total consideration received.

EXERCISE 10-3

Purpose: This exercise will provide an example of the capitalization of interest during construction.

On July 31, 1991, Masco Company engaged Intel Tooling Company to construct a special-purpose piece of factory machinery. Construction was begun immediately and was completed on November 1, 1991. To help finance construction, on July 31, Masco issued a $300,000, 3-year, 12% note payable at Hudson National Bank, on which interest is payable each July 31. $100,000 of the proceeds of the note was paid to Intel on July 31. The remainder of the proceeds was temporarily invested in short-term marketable securities at 10% until November 1. On November 1, Masco made a final $200,000 payment to Intel. Other than the note to Hudson, Masco's only outstanding liability at December 31, 1991 is a $30,000, 8%, 6-year note payable, dated January 1, 1988, on which interest is payable each December 31.

Instructions
(a)   Calculate the weighted-average accumulated expenditures, interest revenue, avoidable interest, total interest incurred, and interest cost to be capitalized during 1991. Round all computations to the nearest dollar.

(b) Prepare the journal entries needed on the books of Masco Company at each of the following dates: July 31, 1991; November 1, 1991; and December 31, 1991.

SOLUTION TO EXERCISE 10-3

(a) Computation of Weighted-Average Accumulated Expenditures

	Expenditures		Capitalization		Weighted-Average
Date	Amount	X	Period	=	Accumulated Expenditures
July 31	$100,000		3/12		$25,000
November 1	200,000		0		0
					$25,000

Interest revenue: $200,000 X 10% X 3/12 = $5,000

Avoidable interest:	Weighted-Average				
	Accumulated Expenditures	X	Interest Rate	=	Avoidable Interest
	$25,000		12%		$3,000

Total interest incurred:	$300,000 X 12% X 5/12 =	$15,000
	$30,000 X 8% =	2,400
		$17,400

Interest to be capitalized:	$3,000

(b)

7/31	Cash	300,000	
	Note Payable		300,000
	Machine	100,000	
	Temporary Investment	200,000	
	Cash		300,000
11/1	Cash	205,000	
	Interest Revenue ($200,000 X 10% X 3/12)		5,000
	Temporary Investment		200,000
	Machine	200,000	
	Cash		200,000
12/31	Machine	3,000	
	Interest Expense ($17,400 - $3,000)	14,400	
	Cash ($30,000 X 8%)		2,400
	Interest Payable ($300,000 X 12% X 5/12)		15,000

Explanation: Paragraphs 6 and 7 of *SFAS No. 34* state:

"The historical cost of acquiring an asset includes the costs necessarily incurred to bring it to the condition and location necessary for its intended use. If an asset requires a period of time in which to carry out the activities necessary to bring it to that condition and location, the interest cost incurred during that period as a result of expenditures for the asset is a part of the historical cost of acquiring the asset. The objectives of capitalizing interest are (a) to obtain a measure of acquisition cost that more closely reflects the enterprise's total investment in the asset and (b) to charge a cost that relates to the acquisition of a resource that will benefit future periods against the revenues of the periods benefited."

Examples of assets that qualify for interest capitalization are: (1) assets that an enterprise constructs for its own use (such as facilities), and (2) assets intended for sale or lease that are constructed as discrete projects (such as ships or real estate projects). Interest cannot be capitalized for inventories that are routinely manufactured or otherwise produced in large quantities on a repetitive basis. Masco's machine is a qualifying asset.

The amount to be capitalized is that portion of the interest cost incurred during the assets' acquisition periods that theoretically could have been avoided (for example, by avoiding additional borrowings or by using the funds expended for the assets to repay existing borrowings) if expenditures for the assets had not been made.

Avoidable interest is determined by applying an appropriate interest rate(s) to the weighted-average amount of accumulated expenditures for the asset during the period. The appropriate rate is that rate associated with a specific new borrowing, if any. If average accumulated expenditures for the asset exceed the amount of a specific new borrowing associated with the asset, the capitalization rate to be applied to such excess shall be a weighted average of the rates applicable to other borrowings of the enterprise.

The weighted-average amount of accumulated expenditures for the asset represents the average investment tied up in the qualifying asset during the period. For Masco, a $100,000 balance in Machine for the three-month capitalization period (date of expenditures to the date the asset is ready for use) means an equivalent (average) investment of $25,000 on an annual basis. Masco uses only the 12% rate applicable to the specific new borrowing to compute the avoidable interest because the specific borrowing ($300,000) exceeds the weighted-average accumulated expenditures.

The amount of interest to be capitalized is not to exceed the actual interest costs incurred. Thus, Masco compares its avoidable interest of $3,000 and its actual interest incurred of $17,400 and chooses the lower amount to capitalize. Any interest amounts earned on funds borrowed which are temporarily in excess of the company's needs are to be reported as interest revenue rather than be used to offset the amount of interest to be capitalized. Thus, Masco will report $5,000 as interest revenue and that $5,000 will not affect the amount of interest to be capitalized.

EXERCISE 10-4

Purpose: This exercise will give you practice in dealing with a deferred payment plan for an acquisition of a plant asset.

James Worthy, Inc. purchased a computer on December 31, 1990, for $90,000, paying $15,000 down and agreeing to pay the balance in five equal installments of $15,000 payable each December 31 beginning in 1991. An assumed interest of 10% is implicit in the purchase price.

Instructions (Round to the nearest cent.)
(a) Prepare the journal entry(ies) at the date of purchase.
(b) Prepare an amortization schedule for the installment agreement.
(c) Prepare the journal entry(ies) at December 31, 1991, to record the payment and interest

(assume the effective interest method is employed).

(d) Prepare the journal entry(ies) at December 31, 1992, to record the payment and interest (assume the effective interest method is employed).

SOLUTION TO EXERCISE 10-4

(a)

Equipment	71,681.85*	
Discount on Notes Payable	18,318.15	
Cash		15,000.00
Notes Payable...		75,000.00

*PV of a $15,000 ordinary annuity @ 10% for 5 years

($15,000 X 3.79079)	$56,861.85
Down payment	15,000.00
Capitalized value of equipment	$71,861.85

(b)

Date	Cash Payment	10% Interest Expense	Reduction of Principal	Liability Balance
12/31/90				$56,861.85
12/31/91	$15,000.00	$5,686.19	$ 9,313.81	47,548.04
12/31/92	15,000.00	4,754.80	10,245.20	37,302.84
12/31/93	15,000.00	3,730.28	11,269.72	26,033.12
12/31/94	15,000.00	2,603.31	12,396.69	13,636.43
12/31/95	15,000.00	1,363.57**	13,636.43	-0-
Totals	$75,000.00	$18,138.15	$56,861.85	

**This is a plug figure which includes a rounding error of $.07.

(c)

Notes Payable	15,000.00	
Interest Expense (see schedule)	5,686.19	
Cash		15,000.00
Discount on Notes Payable		5,686.19

(d)

Notes Payable	15,000.00	
Interest Expense	4,754.80	
Cash		15,000.00
Discount on Notes Payable		4,754.80

Note: For each entry in (c) and (d), two entries could replace the one compound entry.

EXERCISE 10-5

Purpose: This exercise will (1) illustrate several different ways in which you may dispose of property, and (2) discuss the appropriate accounting procedures for each.

Presented below is a schedule of property dispositions for Don Pagach Co.

SCHEDULE OF PROPERTY DISPOSITIONS

	Cost	Accumulated Depreciation	Cash Proceeds	Fair Market Value	Nature of Disposition
Land	$40,000	--	$32,000	$32,000	Condemnation
Building	15,000	--	3,600	--	Demolition
Warehouse	65,000	$11,000	74,000	74,000	Destruction by fire
Machine	8,000	3,200	1,800	7,200	Trade-in
Furniture	10,000	7,850	--	2,800	Contribution
Automobile	8,000	3,460	2,960	2,960	Sale

The following additional information is available:

Land. On February 15, a condemnation award was received as consideration for unimproved land held primarily as an investment, and on March 31, another parcel of unimproved land to be held as an investment was purchased at a cost of $35,000.

Building. On April 2, land and building were purchased at a total cost of $75,000, of which 20% was allocated to the building on the corporate books. The real estate was acquired with the intention of demolishing the building, and this was accomplished during the month of November. Cash proceeds received in November represent the net proceeds from demolition of the building.

Warehouse. On June 30, the warehouse was destroyed by fire. The warehouse was purchased January 2, 1978, and had been depreciated $11,000. On December 27, part of the insurance proceeds was used to purchase a replacement warehouse at a cost of $65,000.

Machine. On December 26, the machine was exchanged for another machine having a fair market value of $5,400 and cash of $1,800 was received. (Round to nearest dollar.)

Furniture. On August 15, furniture was contributed to a qualified charitable organization. No other contributions were made or pledged during the year.

Automobile. On November 3, the automobile was sold to Dee Pentice, a stockholder.

Instructions--Indicate how these items would be reported on the income statement of Don Pagach Co.

(AICPA adapted)

SOLUTION TO EXERCISE 10-5

The following accounting treatment appears appropriate for these items:

Land. The loss on the condemnation of the land of $8,000 ($40,000 - $32,000) should be reported as an extraordinary item on the income statement. A condemnation comes about from a governmental unit exercising its right of eminent domain. Eminent domain is defined as "expropriation of assets by a government." Expropriation of assets is given as an example of an extraordinary item in *APB Opinion 30.* The $35,000 land purchase has no income statement effect.

Building. There is no recognized gain or loss on the demolition of the building. The entire purchase cost ($15,000), decreased by the demolition proceeds ($3,600), is allocated to land.

Warehouse. The gain on the destruction of the warehouse should be reported in the "other revenues and gains" section of the income statement. A fire can happen in any environment; therefore, it is not an extraordinary item. The gain is computed as follows:

Insurance proceeds		$74,000
Cost	$65,000	
Accumulated depreciation	(11,000)	(54,000)
Realized gain		$20,000

Some contend that a portion of this gain should be deferred because the proceeds are reinvested in similar assets. Deferral of the gain in this situation is not permitted under GAAP.

Machine. The recognized gain on the transaction would be computed as follows:

Fair market value of old machine		$7,200
Cost	$ 8,000	
Accumulated depreciation	(3,200)	(4,800)
Total gain experienced		$2,400

$$\text{Total gain recognized} = \$2,400 \times \frac{\$1,800}{\$1,800 + \$5,400} = \$600$$

This gain would probably be reported in the "other revenues and gains" section. It might be considered an unusual item, but it would usually not be infrequent. The cost of the new machine would be capitalized at $3,600:

Fair market value of new machine		$5,400		Carrying value of old asset	
Gain experienced	$2,400		**OR**	($8,000 - $3,200)	$4,800
Gain recognized	(600)				
Gain deferred		1,800		Boot received	(1,800)
Cost of new machine		$3,600		Gain recognized	600
				Cost of new machine	$3,600

Furniture. The contribution of the furniture would be reported as a contribution expense of $2,800 with a related gain on disposition of furniture of $650: $2,800 - ($10,000 - $7,850).

Automobile. The loss on sale of the automobile of $1,580 [$2,960 - ($8,000 - $3,460)] should probably be reported in the "other expenses and losses" section. This is a related party transactions; such transactions require special disclosure.

TIP: The receipt of the condemnation award (February 15) represents an involuntary conversion of nonmonetary assets to monetary assets. Any gain or loss related to the transaction shall be recognized even though the enterprise reinvests or is obligated to reinvest the monetary assets in replacement nonmonetary assets. The receipt of insurance proceeds due to the destruction of the warehouse is also an involuntary conversion of nonmonetary assets to monetary assets.

TIP: The sale of property, plant, and equipment for cash should be accounted for as follows:

    (1)   The carrying value at the date of the sale (cost of the property, plant, and equipment less the accumulated depreciation) should be removed from the accounts.

    (2)   The excess of cash from the sale over the carrying value removed is accounted for as a gain on the sale, while the excess of carrying value removed over cash from the sale is accounted for as a loss on the sale.

ILLUSTRATION 10-1
SUMMARY OF REQUIREMENTS FOR RECOGNIZING
GAINS AND LOSSES ON EXCHANGES OF NONMONETARY ASSETS

1.   Compute the total gain or loss experienced on the transaction, which is equal to the difference between the fair value of the asset given up and the book value of the asset given up. An excess of fair value over book value indicates a gain; an excess of book value over fair value indicates a loss.

2.   If a loss is computed in 1, always recognize the entire loss.

3.   If a gain is computed in 1,

    (a)   and the earnings process is considered completed, the entire gain is recognized (dissimilar assets).

    (b)   and the earnings process is not considered completed (similar assets),

        (1)   and no cash is involved, no gain is recognized.

        (2)   and some cash is given, no gain is recognized.

        (3)   and some cash is received, the following portion of the gain is recognized:

$$\frac{\text{Cash Received (Boot)}}{\text{Cash Received (Boot)} + \text{Fair Value of Other Assets Received}} \times \text{Total Gain Experienced}$$

EXERCISE 10-6

<u>Purpose</u>: This exercise will allow you to practice recording the exchange of similar productive assets.

Soon Yoon Company exchanged equipment used in its manufacturing operations plus $5,000 in cash for similar equipment used in the operations of Peggy Gunshanan Company. The following information pertains to the exchange:

	Soon Yoon Co.	Peggy Gunshanan Co.
Equipment (cost)	$28,000	$28,000
Accumulated depreciation	22,000	10,000
Fair value of equipment	10,500	15,500
Cash given up	5,000	

BV 6000

Instructions

(a)   Prepare the journal entries to record the exchange on the books of both companies.

(b)   Prepare the journal entries to record the exchange on the books of both companies assuming the fair value of Soon Yoon Co.'s old asset is $5,500 (rather than $10,500) and the fair value of Peggy Gunshanan's old equipment is $10,500 (rather than $15,500).

(c) Prepare the journal entries to record the exchange on the books of both companies assuming the fair value of Soon Yoon Co.'s old asset is $15,500 (rather than $10,500) and the fair value of Peggy Gunshanan's old equipment is $20,500 (rather than $15,500).

SOLUTION TO EXERCISE 10-6

(a) Soon Yoon Company:

Equipment (New)	11,000	
Accumulated Depreciation	22,000	
Equipment (Old)		28,000
Cash		5,000

Computation of book value:

Cost of old asset	$28,000
Accumulated depreciation	(22,000)
Book value of old asset	$ 6,000

Computation of gain:

Fair value of equipment given	$10,500
Book value of equipment given	(6,000)
Gain experienced on old asset	$ 4,500

Valuation of new equipment:

Book value of equipment given	$ 6,000	Fair value of equip. received	$15,500
Fair value of boot given	5,000	**OR** Gain deferred	(4,500)
Cost of new equipment	$11,000	Cost of new equipment	$11,000

Peggy Gunshanan Company:

Cash	5,000	
Equipment (New)	10,500	
Accumulated Depreciation	10,000	
Loss on Disposal of Plant Asset	2,500	
Equipment (Old)		28,000

Computation of book value:

Cost of old asset	$28,000
Accumulated depreciation	(10,000)
Book value of old asset	$18,000

Computation of loss:

Fair value of old asset	$15,500
Book value of old asset	(18,000)
Loss experienced on old asset	$ (2,500)

Valuation of new equipment:

Book value of equipment given	$18,000
Loss recognized on disposal	(2,500)
Fair value of equipment given	15,500
Boot received	(5,000)
Cost of new equipment	$10,500

Explanation and Approach: Refer to **Illustration 10-1** which summarizes the rules for recognizing gains and losses on exchanges of nonmonetary assets.

Soon Yoon has experienced a gain of $4,500 on the old asset. It is an exchange of similar productive assets; hence, the earnings process is not considered complete. Boot is given; therefore, the gain is not recognized. Rather than crediting a gain, the gain is reflected in the cost of the new asset by reducing what otherwise would have been recorded as the new asset's cost. Thus, the gain is deferred and there is a departure from the cost principle in determining the cost of the new asset.

Peggy Gunshanan has experienced a loss. A loss is always recognized regardless of whether the exchange is of dissimilar or similar assets and regardless of whether boot is given or received. (Think about the principle of conservatism here to help you to remember this.) The cost principle is followed in determining the amount to record for the equipment received.

TIP: The parties will bargain so that the total fair value given equals the total fair value received. Therefore, since Peggy Gunshanan is giving up equipment worth $15,500 but Soon Yoon's equipment is only worth $10,500, Soon Yoon is also giving $5,000 cash to Peggy Gunshanan.

(b) Soon Yoon Company:

Equipment (New)	10,500	
Accumulated Depreciation	22,000	
Loss on Disposal of Plant Asset	500	
Equipment (Old)		28,000
Cash		5,000

Computation of loss:

Fair value of equipment given	$5,500
Book value of equipment given	6,000
Loss on disposal	$ (500)

Valuation of new equipment:

Book value of equipment given	$ 6,000
Loss recognized on old asset	(500)
Fair value of boot given	5,000
Cost of new equipment	$10,500

OR

Fair value of equipment given	$ 5,500
Fair value of boot given	5,000
Cost of new equipment	$10,500

Peggy Gunshanan Company:

Cash	5,000	
Equipment (New)	5,500	
Accumulated Depreciation	10,000	
Loss on Disposal of Plant Asset	7,500	
Equipment (Old)		28,000

Computation of loss:

Fair value of equipment given	$10,500
Book value of equipment given	(18,000)
Loss on disposal of equipment	$ (7,500)

Valuation of new equipment:

Book value of equipment given	$18,000
Loss recognized	(7,500)
Fair value of equipment given	10,500
Boot received	(5,000)
Cost of new equipment	$ 5,500

Explanation: Both Soon Yoon and Peggy Gunshanan experienced losses on the disposal of their old plant assets. A loss is always to be recognized (because of conservatism). The cost principle is followed in determining the cost of the new plant asset.

(c)   Soon Yoon Company:

Equipment (New)	11,000	
Accumulated Depreciation	22,000	
Equipment (Old)		28,000
Cash		5,000

Computation of gain:

Fair value of equipment given	$15,500
Book value of equipment given	(6,000)
Gain experienced on old asset	$ 9,500

Valuation of new equipment:

Book value of equipment given	$ 6,000
Fair value of boot given	5,000
Cost of new equipment	$11,000

OR

Fair value of equipment given	$15,500
Gain deferred	(9,500)
Fair value of boot given	5,000
Cost of new equipment	$11,000

Peggy Gunshanan Company:

Cash	5,000	
Equipment (New)	13,610	
Accumulated Depreciation	10,000	
Equipment (Old)		28,000
Gain on Disposal of Plant Asset		610

Computation of gain experienced:

Fair value of equipment given	$20,500
Book value of equipment given	18,000
Gain experienced on old asset	$ 2,500

Computation of gain recognized:

$$\frac{\$5,000}{\$5,000 + \$15,500} \times \$2,500 = \underline{\$609.76}$$

Valuation of new equipment:

Book value of equipment given	$18,000
Fair value of boot received	(5,000)
Gain recognized	610
Cost of new equipment	$13,610

OR

Fair value of equipment given	$20,500
Boot received	(5,000)
Gain deferred ($2,500 - $610)	(1,890)
Cost of new equipment	$13,610

Explanation: Soon's gain is deferred (**not** recognized currently) because Soon is giving boot in an exchange of similar productive assets. The reasoning for the restriction on recognition is that the earnings process is not yet complete. The "gain" serves to reduce the recorded value of the new asset.

Peggy Gunshanan's gain is partially recognized because boot is being received in an exchange of similar productive assets. The portion of the gain recognized is determined by a ratio of the boot received to the total consideration received. The portion of the gain experienced but not recognized reduces what otherwise would have been recorded as the cost of the new equipment.

CASE 10-3

Purpose: This case will provide a few examples of the accounting for costs subsequent to the acquisition of fixed assets.

Hardent Resources Group has been in its plant facility for fifteen years. Although the plant is quite functional, numerous repair costs are incurred to maintain it in sound working order. The company's plant asset book value is currently $800,000, as indicated below:

Original cost	$1,200,000
Accumulated depreciation	400,000
Book value	$ 800,000

During the current year, the following expenditures were made involving the plant facility:
(a) Because of increased demands for its product, the company increased its plant capacity by building a new addition at a cost of $210,000.
(b) The entire plant was repainted at a cost of $18,000.
(c) The roof was an asbestos cement slate; for safety purposes it was removed and replaced with a wood shingle roof at a cost of $58,000. Book value of the old roof was $39,000.
(d) The electrical system was completely updated at a cost of $21,000. The cost of the old electrical system was not known. It is estimated that the useful life of the building will not change as a result of this updating.
(e) A series of major repairs were made at a cost of $45,000, because parts of the wood structure were rotting. The cost of the old wood structure was not known. These extensive repairs are estimated to increase the useful life of the building.

Instructions
Indicate how each of these transactions would be recorded in the accounting records.

SOLUTION TO CASE 10-3

(a) Any addition to plant assets is capitalized because a new asset has been created. This addition increases the service potential of the plant.

(b) Expenditures that do not increase the service benefits of the asset are expensed. Painting costs are considered ordinary repairs because they maintain the existing condition of the asset or restore it to normal operating efficiency.

(c) The approach to follow is remove the old book value of the roof and substitute the cost of the new roof. It is assumed that the expenditure increases the future service potential of the asset.

(d) Conceptually the book value of the old electrical system should be removed. However, practically it is often difficult if not impossible to determine this amount. In this case, one of two approaches is followed. One approach is to capitalize the replacement on the theory that sufficient depreciation was taken on the item to reduce the carrying amount to almost zero. A second approach is to debit accumulated depreciation on the theory that the replacement extends the useful life of the asset and thereby recaptures some or all of the past depreciation. In our present situation, the problem specifically states that the useful life is not extended and therefore debiting accumulated depreciation is inappropriate. Thus, this expenditure should be added to the cost of the plant facility.

(e)   See discussion in (d) above. In this case, because the useful life of the asset has increased, a debit to accumulated depreciation would appear to be the most appropriate.

EXERCISE 10-7

Purpose: This assignment is designed to give you additional practice in analyzing changes in property, plant, and equipment accounts during a period. Problems of this type frequently appear on professional exams.

At December 31, 1992, certain accounts included in the property, plant, and equipment section of the Busch Company's balance sheet had the following balances:

Land	$100,000
Buildings	800,000
Leasehold improvements	500,000
Machinery and equipment	700,000

During 1993 the following transactions occurred:

- Land site number 52 was acquired for $1,000,000. Additionally, to acquire the land Busch paid a $60,000 commission to a real estate agent. Costs of $15,000 were incurred to clear the land. During the course of clearing the land, timber and gravel were recovered and sold for $5,000.

- A second tract of land (site number 53) with a building was acquired for $300,000. The closing statement indicated that the land value was $200,000 and the building value was $100,000. Shortly after acquisition, the building was demolished at a cost of $30,000. A new building was constructed for $150,000 plus the following costs:

Excavation fees	$11,000
Architectural design fees	8,000
Building permit fee	1,000
Imputed interest on equity funds used during construction	6,000

  The building was completed and occupied on September 30, 1993.

- A third tract of land (site number 54) was acquired for $600,000 and was put on the market for resale.

- Extensive work was done to a building occupied by Busch under a lease agreement that expires on December 31, 2002. The total cost of the work was $125,000, which consisted of the following:

Painting of ceilings	$ 10,000	estimated useful life is one year
Electrical work	35,000	estimated useful life is ten years
Construction of extension to current working area	80,000	estimated useful life is thirty years
	$125,000	

  The lessor paid one-half of the costs incurred in connection with the extension to the current working area.

- During December 1993 costs of $65,000 were incurred to improve leased office space. The related lease will terminate on December 31, 1995, and is not expected to be renewed.

10-21

- A group of new machines was purchased under a royalty agreement which provides for payment of royalties based on units of production for the machines. The invoice price of the machines was $75,000, freight costs were $2,000, unloading charges were $1,500, and royalty payments for 1993 were $13,000.

Instructions

1. Prepare a detailed analysis of the changes in each of the following balance sheet accounts for 1993:

> Land
> Buildings
> Leasehold improvements
> Machinery and equipment

Disregard the related accumulated depreciation accounts.

2. List the items in the fact situation which were not used to determine the answer to 1. above, and indicate **where, or if,** these items should be included in Busch's financial statements.

(AICPA Adapted)

SOLUTION TO EXERCISE 10-7

1.

Busch Company
ANALYSIS OF LAND ACCOUNT
for 1993

Balance at January 1, 1993			$ 100,000
Land site number 52			
Acquisition cost		$1,000,000	
Commission to real estate agent		60,000	
Clearing costs	$15,000		
Less amounts recovered	5,000	10,000	
Total land site number 52			1,070,000
Land site number 53			
Land value		200,000	
Building value		100,000	
Demolition cost		30,000	
Total land site number 53			330,000
Balance at December 31, 1993			$1,500,000

Busch Company
ANALYSIS OF BUILDINGS ACCOUNT
for 1993

Balance at January 1, 1993		$800,000
Cost of new building constructed on land site number 53		
Construction costs	$150,000	
Excavation fees	11,000	
Architectural design fees	8,000	
Building permit fee	1,000	170,000
Balance at December 31, 1993		$970,000

Busch Company
ANALYSIS OF LEASEHOLD IMPROVEMENTS ACCOUNT
for 1993

Balance at January 1, 1993	$500,000
Electrical work	35,000
Construction of extension to current work area ($80,000 X 1/2)	40,000
Office space	65,000
Balance at December 31, 1993	$640,000

Busch Company
ANALYSIS OF MACHINERY AND EQUIPMENT ACCOUNT
for 1993

Balance at January 1, 1993		$700,000
Cost of new machines acquired		
Invoice price	$75,000	
Freight costs	2,000	
Unloading charges	1,500	78,500
Balance at December 31, 1993		$778,500

2. Items in the fact situation which were not used to determine the answer to 1. above.

- Imputed interest of $6,000 on equity funds used during construction should not be included anywhere in Busch's financial statements. Only interest actually incurred should be capitalized during construction.

- Land site number 54, which was acquired for $600,000 and held for resale, should be included in Busch's balance sheet in the investment classification.

- Painting of ceilings for $10,000 should be included as a normal operating expense in Busch's income statement.

- Royalty payments of $13,000 should be included as a normal operating expense in Busch's income statement.

ANALYSIS OF MULTIPLE-CHOICE TYPE QUESTIONS

Question

1. Jacobson Manufacturing Company purchased a machine for $65,000 on January 2, 1992. At the date of purchase, Jacobson incurred the following additional costs:

Loss on sale of old machine	$2,000
Freight-in	900
Installation cost	1,500
Breaking-in costs	650

The amount to record for the acquisition cost of the new machine is
   a. $65,000.
   b. $67,400.
   c. $68,050.
   d. $69,400.

Solution = c.

Explanation and Approach: Apply the guideline: The cost of a plant asset includes all costs required to get the item to the location and condition for its intended purpose.

Purchase price	$65,000
Freight-in	900
Installation cost	1,500
Breaking-in costs	650
Total acquisition cost	$68,050

The loss on sale of an old machine should be charged to an income statement account (and reported on the income statement) so it will not impact the asset value.

Question

2. Herndon Inc. has a fiscal year ending October 31. On November 1, 1992, Herndon borrowed $20,000,000 at 15% to finance construction of a new plant. Repayments of the loan are to commence the month following completion of the plant. During the year ended October 31, 1993, expenditures for the partially completed structure totaled $12,000,000. These expenditures were incurred evenly through the year. Interest earned on the unexpended portion of the loan amounted to $800,000 for the year. What amount of interest should be capitalized as of October 31, 1993?

 a. $0.
 b. $100,000.
 c. $900,000.
 d. $2,200,000.

Solution = c.

Explanation: The situation is one which qualifies for the capitalization of interest. The following steps should help to compute the amount:

(1) **Find the weighted-average accumulated expenditures** for the period:

Total expenditures at beginning of the period	$ -0-
Total expenditures at end of the period	12,000,000
Sum	$12,000,000

÷ 2 = average of $6,000,000

(2) **Determine the interest rate to use.** Because the amount of a specific borrowing ($20,000,000) exceeds the weighted-average accumulated expenditures ($6,000,000), use the interest rate for that specific borrowing (15%).

(3) **Compute the avoidable interest** by multiplying the appropriate interest rate (15% from Step 2) by the weighted-average accumulated expenditures ($6,000,000 from Step 1).

 $6,000,000 X 15% = $900,000 Avoidable interest

(4) **Determine the amount of interest to capitalize** by selecting the lower of the actual interest incurred (15% X $20,000,000 = $3,000,000) or the amount of avoidable interest ($900,000 from Step 3). The lower in this case is the $900,000 avoidable interest.

Note: The interest earned ($800,000) is to be reported as revenue on the income statement and should not be used to offset the interest to be capitalized.

10-24

Question

3. In January 1992, Barbie Company entered into a contract to acquire a new machine for its factory. The machine which had a cash price of $300,000 was acquired in exchange for the following:

Down payment	$ 30,000
Note payable in 24 equal monthly installments	240,000
500 shares of Barbie common stock	
with an agreed value of $100 per share	50,000
Total	$320,000

Prior to the machine's use, installation costs of $8,000 were incurred. The amount to record for the acquisition cost of the machine is
a. $300,000.
b. $308,000.
c. $320,000.
d. $328,000.

Solution = b.

Explanation and Approach: Anytime you have a question regarding the acquisition cost of a plant asset, write down (or mentally review) the two rules regarding asset cost: (1) Cost is measured by the fair market value (cash equivalent) of the consideration given or the fair market value of the consideration received, whichever is the more objectively determinable; and (2) An asset's cost includes all costs necessary to get it to the location and condition for its intended purpose. Then apply the rules to the situation given.

The cash equivalent of the machine acquired is $300,000 (cash price). The cash equivalent of the consideration given is the cash down payment of $15,000 plus the fair value of the stock ($50,000) plus the present value of the note payable (something less than $240,000). Because no information is given about the market value of the note or the appropriate interest rate for the note but the cash equivalent price is given for the asset received, the more objectively determinable figure is the $300,000. The installation cost must be added to get the total acquisition cost.

Question

4. Two home builders agree to exchange tracts of land that each holds for purposes of development. An appraiser was hired and the following information is available.

	Batson	Beamer
Book value of land	$50,000	$ 72,000
Fair value of land	80,000	100,000
Cash paid	20,000	

In recording this exchange should a gain be recognized by Batson, Beamer, or both parties?

	Batson	Beamer
a.	Yes	Yes
b.	Yes	No
c.	No	Yes
d.	No	No

Solution = c.

Explanation and Approach:
(1) **Determine if it is an exchange of similar or dissimilar assets.** One tract of land for another to use for the same purpose is an exchange of similar assets.
(2) **Determine if a gain or loss is experienced.** Fair value exceeds book value for both parties so both have experienced a gain.
(3) **Determine if boot is given or received.** Batson is giving boot; Beamer is receiving boot.
(4) **Write down the rules for recognition of gain in a similar asset exchange.** The party giving boot (Batson) is not to recognize any gain. The party receiving boot is to recognize a portion of the gain experienced. In this case, the receipt of cash by Beamer represents a partial sale of the land, thus completing a portion of the earning process.

Question

5. Refer to the facts of Question 4. The amount to be recorded by Batson for the acquisition cost of the new tract of land is
   a. $50,000.
   b. $70,000.
   c. $72,000.
   d. $80,000.
   e. $100,000.

Solution = b.

Explanation and Approach: When boot is given in a similar asset exchange, no gain is to be recognized. The cost of the new asset is equal to the recorded value (book value) of the old, reduced for any impairment (minus any loss recognized), plus the boot given. ($50,000 + $20,000 = $70,000). A journal entry approach can also be used (the debit to the new asset account is a plug figure):

Land (New)	70,000	**Plug last.**
Land (Old)	50,000	**Do second.**
Cash	20,000	**Do first.**

CHAPTER 11

DEPRECIATION AND DEPLETION

OVERVIEW

Expenses arise from the cost of goods or services that are consumed in the process of generating revenue. When a long-term tangible asset is acquired, a bundle of future asset services have really been acquired at a total cost equal to the acquisition cost of the asset **minus** the expected estimated market value at the end of the asset's useful life. As a productive asset is used, services (benefits) are consumed; therefore, a portion of the original asset cost should be charged to expense. The process of allocating (expensing) the cost of long-term tangible assets over the accounting periods during which the asset is used is called depreciation. The process of allocating the costs of natural resources to inventory (and later to cost of goods sold) is called depletion. Depreciation and depletion are discussed in this chapter.

TIPS ON CHAPTER TOPICS

TIP: Salvage value is often referred to as residual value, and sometimes it is called estimated scrap value.

TIP: Salvage value is used in the computation of depreciation for the early years of life of an asset whenever the straight-line method or the sum-of-the-years'-digits method or an activity method is used. Salvage value is **not** a factor in determining depreciation for the early years of life if a declining balance method is used; however, salvage value can effect the amount computed for depreciation in the last year(s) of an asset's life. An asset should **not** be depreciated below its salvage value.

TIP: The activity method is often called the variable charge approach or the units of output or the units of production method.

TIP: The double-declining balance method is sometimes called the 200% declining-balance method. The rate used to compute depreciation is twice the straight-line rate when using this method. Another declining balance method is the 150% declining balance method; it uses a rate that is one and one-half times the straight-line rate.

TIP: **Book value (carrying value)** is determined by deducting the balance of accumulated depreciation from the balance of the related asset account. The balance in the related asset account is generally the asset's original cost. Thus, the estimated salvage value does not directly affect the book value computation.

TIP: Depreciable cost or depreciation base is a term that refers to the total amount to be depreciated over the life of the asset. It is determined by deducting the estimated salvage value from the cost of the asset.

TIP: When an asset being depreciated by a group or composite depreciation method is disposed of, no gain or loss is recorded; the difference between the original cost of the asset and the proceeds from disposal is charged to Accumulated Depreciation.

CASE 11-1

Purpose: This case examines the process of matching the cost of fixed assets with the revenues which the assets generate.

Plant assets provide services over two or more periods. There is a cost to the services consumed; this cost should be matched with the periods benefited.

Instructions
(a) Briefly define depreciation as used in accounting.
(b) Identify the factors that are relevant in determining the annual depreciation and explain whether these factors are determined objectively or whether they are based on judgment.

(AICPA Adapted)

SOLUTION TO CASE 11-1

(a) Depreciation is the accounting process of allocating an asset's historical cost (recorded amount) to the accounting periods benefited by the use of the asset. It is a process of cost allocation, not valuation. Depreciation is not intended to provide funds for an asset's replacement; it is merely an application of the matching principle.

(b) The factors relevant in determining the annual depreciation for a depreciable asset are the initial recorded amount (acquisition cost), estimated salvage value, estimated useful life, and depreciation method.

Assets are typically recorded at their acquisition cost, which is in most cases objectively determinable. But cost assignments in other cases--"basket purchases" and selection of an implicit interest rate in asset acquisition under deferred-payment plans--may be quite subjective and involve considerable judgment.

The salvage value is an estimate of an amount potentially realizable when the asset is retired from service. It is initially a judgment factor and is affected by the length of its useful life to the enterprise.

The useful life is also a judgment factor. It involves selecting the "unit" of measure of service life and estimating the number of such units embodied in the asset. Such units may be measured in terms of time periods or in terms of activity (for example, years or machine hours). When selecting the life, one should select the lower (shorter) of the physical life or the economic life to this user. Physical life involves wear and tear and casualties; economic life involves such things as technological obsolescence and inadequacy.

Selecting the depreciation method is generally a judgment decision; but, a method may be inherent in the definition adopted for the units of service life, as discussed earlier. For example, if such units are machine hours, the method is a function of the number of machine hours used during each period. A method should be selected that will best measure the portion of services expiring each period. Once a method is selected, it may be objectively applied by using a predetermined, objectively derived formula.

EXERCISE 11-1

Purpose: This exercise will give you practice in computing depreciation for three successive periods for three commonly used methods.

Hudspeth Company purchases equipment on January 1, Year 1, at a cost of $430,000. The asset is expected to have a service life of 12 years and a salvage value of $40,000.

Instructions
(a) Compute the amount of depreciation for each of Years 1 through 3 using the straight-line depreciation method.
(b) Compute the amount of depreciation for each of Years 1 through 3 using the sum-of-the-years'- digits method.
(c) Compute the amount of depreciation for each of Years 1 through 3 using the double-declining balance method. (In performing your calculations, round the constant percentage to the nearest one-hundredth of a point and round final answers to the nearest dollar.)

SOLUTION TO EXERCISE 11-1

(a) $\dfrac{\$430,000 - \$40,000}{12} = \$32,500$ depreciation for each of Years 1 through 3 using the straight-line method.

(b) $\dfrac{12 \times 13}{2} = 78$

12/78 X ($430,000 - $40,000) = $60,000   depreciation Year 1
11/78 X ($430,000 - $40,000) = $55,000   depreciation Year 2
10/78 X ($430,000 - $40,000) = $50,000   depreciation Year 3

(c) $\dfrac{100\%}{12} \times 2 = 16.67\%$

$430,000 X 16.67% = $71,681   depreciation Year 1
($430,000 - $71,681) X 16.67% = $59,732   depreciation Year 2
($430,000 - $71,681 - $59,732) X 16.67% = $49,774   depreciation Year 3

EXERCISE 11-2

Purpose: This exercise will provide an illustration of the computations for depreciation of partial periods using three common methods.

Scanlan Company purchased a new plant asset on April 1, 1992, at a cost of $690,000. It was estimated to have a service life of 20 years and a salvage value of $60,000. Scanlan's accounting period is the calendar year.

Instructions

(a) Compute the amount of depreciation for this asset for 1992 and 1993 using the straight-line method.

(b) Compute the amount of depreciation for this asset for 1992 and 1993 using the sum-of-the-years'-digits method.

(c) Compute the amount of depreciation for this asset for 1992 and 1993 using the double-declining balance method.

SOLUTION TO EXERCISE 11-2

(a) $\dfrac{\$690,000 - \$60,000}{20 \text{ years}} \times \dfrac{9}{12} = \underline{\$23,625}$ depreciation for 1992

$\dfrac{\$690,000 - \$60,000}{20 \text{ years}} = \underline{\$31,500}$ depreciation for 1993

(b) $\dfrac{20\,(20 + 1)}{2} = 210$

9/12 X 20/210 X ($690,000 - $60,000) = $\underline{\$45,000}$ depreciation for 1992

$\begin{aligned} 3/12 \text{ X } 20/210 \text{ X } (\$690,000 - \$60,000) = &\ \$15,000 \\ + \ 9/12 \text{ X } 19/210 \text{ X } (\$690,000 - \$60,000) = &\ \underline{\ \ 42,750} \\ &\ \overline{\$57,750} \quad \text{depreciation for 1993} \end{aligned}$

(c) Straight-line rate = $\dfrac{100\%}{20} = 5\%$;   5% X 2 = 10%

10% X $690,000 = $69,000 depreciation for asset's first year
10% X ($690,000 - $69,000) = $62,100 depreciation for asset's second year

9/12 X $69,000 = $\underline{\$51,750}$ depreciation for 1992

$\begin{aligned} 3/12 \text{ X } \$69,000 = &\quad \$17,250 \\ + \ 9/12 \text{ X } \$62,100 = &\quad \underline{\ \ 46,575} \\ &\quad \overline{\$63,825} \quad \text{depreciation for 1993} \end{aligned}$

Explanation and Approach:

(a) Write down and apply the formula for straight-line depreciation. Multiply the annual depreciation amount by the portion of the asset's year of service that falls in the given accounting period.

$$\frac{\text{Cost - Salvage Value}}{\text{Estimated Service Life}} = \text{Depreciation Charge}$$

(b) Write down and apply the formula for sum-of-the-years'-digits depreciation. Apportion the depreciation for the given asset year between the two accounting periods involved. The first nine months of the asset's first year of life fall in the 1992 calendar year. The last three months of the asset's first year of life and the first nine months of the asset's second year of life fall in the 1993 calendar year. There is no shortcut to the two-part computation of depreciation for 1993 as illustrated above.

Formula: $\dfrac{n\,(n+1)}{2}$ = Sum of the Years

$$\dfrac{\text{No. of Years Remaining at Beginning of Asset Year}}{\text{Sum of the Years}} \times (\text{Cost} - \text{Salvage}) = \text{Depreciation for Full Asset Year}$$

(c) Write down and apply the formula for the declining balance method. Apportion the depreciation for a given **asset year** between the two accounting periods involved.

$$\text{Constant Percentage} \times \begin{array}{c}\text{Book Value}\\ \text{at Beginning}\\ \text{of Asset Year}\end{array} = \text{Depreciation for Asset Year}$$

An alternative approach is as follows:
After the first partial year, calculate depreciation for a full **accounting year** by multiplying the constant percentage by the book value of the asset at the beginning of the accounting period.

Thus, the computation for 1993 would be as follows:
10% X ($690,000 - $51,750) = $63,825.

EXERCISE 11-3

Purpose: This exercise is designed to test your ability to solve for missing data by applying your knowledge regarding depreciation computations.

Landenberger Company acquired a plant asset at the beginning of Year 1. The asset has an estimated service life of 5 years. An employee has prepared depreciation schedules for this asset using three different methods to compare the results of using one method with the results of using other methods. You are to assume that the following schedules have been correctly prepared for this asset using (1) the straight-line method, (2) the sum-of-the-years'-digits method, and (3) the double-declining balance method (switching to the straight-line method after the mid-life of the asset).

Year	Straight-line	Sum-of-the Years'-Digits	Double-declining Balance
1	$ 6,000	$10,000	$14,400
2	6,000	8,000	8,640
3	6,000	6,000	5,184
4	6,000	4,000	888
5	6,000	2,000	888
Total	$30,000	$30,000	$30,000

Instructions
Answer the following questions:
(a) What is the cost of the asset being depreciated?
(b) What amount, if any, was used in the depreciation calculations for the salvage value of this asset?

(c)   Which method will produce the highest charge to income in Year 1?
(d)   Which method will produce the highest charge to income in Year 4?
(e)   Which method will produce the highest book value for the asset at the end of Year 3?
(f)   If the asset is sold at the end of Year 3, which method would yield the highest gain (or lowest loss) on disposal of the asset?

SOLUTION TO EXERCISE 11-3

(a)   If there is any salvage value and the amount is unknown (as is the case here), the cost would have to be determined by looking at the data for the double-declining balance method.

$$\frac{100\%}{5} = 20\%; \quad 20\% \times 2 = 40\%$$

Cost X 40% = $14,400; $14,400 ÷ .40 = $36,000 cost of asset.

(b) $36,000 cost (answer a) - $30,000 total depreciation = $6,000 salvage value.

(c)   The highest charge to income for Year 1 will be yielded by the double-declining balance method.

(d)   The highest charge to income for Year 4 will be yielded by the straight-line method.

(e)   The method to yield the highest book value at the end of Year 3 would be the method that yields the lowest accumulated depreciation at the end of Year 3 which is the straight-line method. Computations:
St.-line = $36,000 - ($6,000 + $6,000 + $6,000) = $18,000 book value at end of Year 3.
S.Y.D. = $36,000 - ($10,000 + $8,000 + $6,000) = $12,000 book value at end of Year 3.
D.D.B. = $36,000 - ($14,400 + $8,640 + $5,184) = $7,776 book value at end of Year 3.

(f)   The method that will yield the highest gain (or lowest loss) if the asset is sold at the end of Year 3 is the method which will yield the lowest book value at the end of Year 3. In this case it is the double-declining balance method.

Approach:
(a)   Write down the formula for each of the depreciation methods mentioned. Fill in the data given for Year 1.

Examine what remains to be solved.

$$\frac{\text{Cost - Salvage Value}}{\text{Estimated Service Life}} = \text{Straight-line Depreciation}$$

$$\frac{\text{Cost - Salvage Value}}{5} = \$6,000$$

$$\frac{\text{No. of Years Remaining at Beginning of Asset Year}}{\text{Sum of the Years}} \times (\text{Cost - Salvage}) = \text{SYD Depreciation}$$

5/15 X (Cost - Salvage) = $10,000

Constant Percentage X (Cost) = DDB Depreciation

40% X Cost = $14,400

There are two variables (cost and salvage value) unknown for each of the first two methods, and there is no way to solve for either of them. However, cost can easily be determined for the third method (DDB). Once you solve for cost, it is a simple matter to solve for salvage value.

(b)   The difference between the answer to part (a) and the total depreciation per the schedule ($30,000) is the salvage value used.

(c)   Examine the depreciation schedules. Notice the method that results in the highest deprecia-tion amount for Year 1.

(d)   Examine the depreciation schedules given. Notice the method that results in the highest depreciation amount for Year 4.

(e)   Write down the formula to compute book value: Cost - Accumulated Depreciation = Book Value. To obtain a high book value, you need a low accumulated depreciation. Examine the depreciation schedules to determine the method that would yield the lowest total depreciation for the first three years.

(f)   Write down the formula to compute gain or loss on disposal: Selling Price - Book Value = Gain (Loss). To obtain the highest gain, you need a low book value. Examine the formula for book value. To get a low book value, you need high depreciation charges. Use the deprecia-tion schedules to determine the method that would yield the highest accumulated depreciation balance at the end of three years.

EXERCISE 11-4

Purpose: This exercise will enable you to practice working with the composite method for comput-ing depreciation.

Presented below is information related to the Bosshardt Corporation (all assets are acquired at the beginning of Year 1):

Asset	Cost	Estimated Scrap	Estimated Life (in years)
A	$40,500	$5,500	10
B	33,600	4,800	9
C	36,000	3,200	8
D	19,000	1,500	7
E	23,500	2,500	6

Instructions
(a)   Compute the rate of depreciation per year to be applied to the plant assets under the compos-ite method.

(b) Compute the composite life.
(c) Prepare the adjusting entry necessary at the end of the year to record depreciation for Year 1.
(d) Prepare the entry at the end of Year 6 to record the sale of fixed asset D for cash of $5,000. It was used for 6 years, and depreciation was entered under the composite method.
(e) Prepare the adjusting entry necessary at the end of Year 7 assuming a new asset (F) costing $34,000 was acquired during Year 7. The salvage value estimated for this asset is $3,000.

SOLUTION TO EXERCISE 11-4

(a)

Asset	Cost	Estimated Scrap	Depreciable Cost	Estimated Life	Depreciation Per Year
A	$ 40,500	$ 5,500	$ 35,000	10	$ 3,500
B	33,600	4,800	28,800	9	3,200
C	36,000	3,200	32,800	8	4,100
D	19,000	1,500	17,500	7	2,500
E	23,500	2,500	21,000	6	3,500
	$152,600	$17,500	$135,100		$16,800

Composite rate = $16,800 ÷ $152,600, or 11.009%

(b) Composite life = $135,100 ÷ $16,800, or 8.04 years

(c)
End of Year 1

Depreciation Expense on Plant Assets	16,800	
Accumulated Depreciation on Plant Assets		16,800
($152,600 X 11.009% = $16,800)		

(d)
End of Year 6

Cash	5,000	
Accumulated Depreciation on Plant Assets	14,000	
Plant Assets		19,000

(e)
End of Year 7

Depreciation Expense on Plant Assets	18,451	
Accumulated Depreciation on Plant Assets		18,451
($152,600 - $19,000 (Asset D) + $34,000 (Asset F) = $167,600)		
($167,600 X 11.009% = $18,451)		

Explanation and Approach:

(a) Steps to compute the composite rate:
    1. Compute what would be the amount of annual straight-line depreciation for each asset by dividing each asset's **depreciable cost** by its estimated service life. Sum these amounts ($16,800).
    2. Compute the composite rate by dividing the total depreciation per year (results of Step 1-- $16,800) by the amount of **original cost.**
(b) Compute the composite life by dividing the total depreciable cost ($135,100) by the total annual depreciation charge ($16,800).
(c) & (e) Compute the depreciation for any given year by multiplying the composite rate (results of Step 2) by the balance in the asset account. The balance in the asset account will change

over time due to the acquisition of new assets and the disposal of old assets.

(d)   When using the group or composite method, no gain or loss on disposition is recorded. The difference between the proceeds (if any) on disposal and the original cost of the asset is debited (or credited) to the Accumulated Depreciation account. Thus if an asset is retired before, or after, the average service life of the group is reached, the resulting gain or loss is buried in the Accumulated Depreciation account.

EXERCISE 11-5

Purpose: This exercise will provide you with an illustration of how to handle a change in the estimated service life and salvage value of a plant asset due to an expenditure subsequent to acquisition.

The Russell Company purchased a machine at the very end of 1982 for $105,000. The machine was being depreciated using the straight-line method over an estimated life of 20 years, with a $15,000 salvage value. At the beginning of 1993, when the machine had been in use for 10 years, the company paid $25,000 to overhaul the machine. As a result of this improvement, the company estimated that the useful life of the machine would be extended an additional 5 years and the salvage value would be reduced to $10,000.

Instructions
Compute the depreciation charge for 1993.

SOLUTION TO EXERCISE 11-5

Cost	$105,000
Accumulated depreciation	45,000[a]
Book value	60,000
Additional expenditure capitalized (if any)	25,000
Revised book value	85,000
Current estimate of salvage	10,000
Remaining depreciable cost	75,000
Remaining years of useful life at 1/1/93	÷ 15[b]
Depreciation expense for 1993	$ 5,000

[a]Cost		$105,000
Original estimate of salvage		15,000
Original depreciable cost		90,000
Original service life in years	÷	20
Original depreciation per year		4,500
Number of years used	X	10
Accumulated depreciation --1/1/93		$ 45,000

[b]Original estimate of life in years	20
Number of years used	(10)
Additional years	5
Remaining years of useful life at 1/1/93	15

TIP: A change in the estimated useful life and/or salvage value of an existing depreciable asset is to be accounted for prospectively. Therefore, the book value at the beginning of the period of change, less the current estimate of salvage, is to be allocated over the remaining periods of life using the appropriate depreciation method. The book value at the beginning of the period of change is calculated using the original estimates of service life and salvage value.

TIP: The $25,000 cost of overhaul is capitalized in this case because the cost benefits the future. Therefore, the cost should be allocated to future periods by extending the useful life of the machine.

Approach: Whenever you have a situation that involves a change in the estimated service life and/or salvage value of a depreciable asset, use the format shown above to compute the remaining depreciable cost and allocate that amount over the remaining useful life using the given depreciation method.

EXERCISE 11-6

Purpose: This exercise will allow you to practice using various depreciation methods and it will also give you the opportunity to compare the results of using one method to the results of using another method.

On January 1, 1992, Irish Company, a machine-tool manufacturer, acquires for $1,000,000 a piece of new industrial equipment. The new equipment has a useful life of five years and the salvage value is estimated to be $100,000. Irish estimates that the new equipment can produce a total of 40,000 units and expects it to produce 10,000 machine tools in its first year. Production is then estimated to decline by 1,000 units per year over the remaining useful life of the equipment.

The following depreciation methods may be used:
- Double-declining-balance
- Straight-line
- Sum-of-the-years'-digits
- Units-of-output

Instructions
(a) Identify which depreciation method would result in the maximization of profits for financial statement reporting for the **three**-year period ending December 31, 1994. Prepare a schedule showing the amount of accumulated depreciation at December 31, 1994, under the method selected. Show supporting computations in good form. Ignore present value and income tax considerations in your answer.

(b) Identify which depreciation method would result in the minimization of profits for the **three**-year period ending December 31, 1994. Prepare a schedule showing the amount of accumulated depreciation at December 31, 1994, under the method selected. Show supporting computations in good form. Ignore present value and income tax considerations in your answer.

(AICPA Adapted)

SOLUTION TO EXERCISE 11-6

(a) The straight-line method of depreciation would result in the maximization of profits for financial statement reporting for the three-year period ending December 31, 1994.

Irish Company
ACCUMULATED DEPRECIATION USING STRAIGHT-LINE METHOD
December 31, 1994

$$\frac{\text{Cost - Salvage Value}}{\text{Estimated Service Life}}$$

$$\frac{\$1,000,000 - \$100,000}{5 \text{ years}} = \$180,000$$

Year	Depreciation Expense	Accumulated Depreciation
1992	$180,000	$180,000
1993	180,000	$360,000
1994	180,000	$540,000
	$540,000	

(b) The double-declining-balance method of depreciation would result in the minimization of profits for the three-year period ending December 31, 1994.

Irish Company
ACCUMULATED DEPRECIATION USING DOUBLE-DECLINING-BALANCE METHOD
December 31, 1994

Straight-line rate is 5 years or 20%. Double-declining balance rate is 40% (20% X 2). Ignore salvage value.

Year	Book Value at Beginning of Year	Depreciation Expense	Accumulated Depreciation
1992	$1,000,000	$400,000	$400,000
1993	600,000	240,000	$640,000
1994	360,000	144,000	$784,000
		$784,000	

Other supporting computations:

Irish Company
ACCUMULATED DEPRECIATION USING SUM-OF-THE-YEARS'-DIGITS METHOD
December 31, 1994

$$\frac{n(n + 1)}{2} = \frac{5(5 + 1)}{2} = 15$$

5/15 X ($1,000,000 - $100,000) = $300,000
4/15 X ($1,000,000 - $100,000) = $240,000
3/15 X ($1,000,000 - $100,000) = $180,000

Year	Depreciation Expense	Accumulated Depreciation
1992	$300,000	$300,000
1993	240,000	$540,000
1994	180,000	$720,000
	$720,000	

Irish Company
ACCUMULATED DEPRECIATION USING UNITS-OF-OUTPUT METHOD
December 31, 1994

$$\frac{\text{Cost - Salvage Value}}{\text{Total Units of Output}} = \frac{\$1,000,000 - \$100,000}{40,000} = \$22.50$$

10,000 X $22.50 = $225,000
9,000 X $22.50 = $202,500
8,000 X $22.50 = $180,000

Year	Depreciation Expense	Accumulated Depreciation
1992	$225,000	$225,000
1993	202,500	$427,500
1994	180,000	$607,500
	$607,500	

EXERCISE 11-7

Purpose: This exercise will give you practice in computing depletion.

During 1992, Alston Corporation acquired a mineral mine for $2,700,000 of which $450,000 is attributable to the land value after the mineral has been removed. Engineers estimate that 15 million units of mineral can be recovered from this mine. During 1992, 1,200,000 units were extracted and 800,000 units were sold.

Instructions
Compute the depletion for 1992.

SOLUTION TO EXERCISE 11-7

$$\frac{\$2,700,000 - \$450,000}{15,000,000} = \$.15$$

$.15 X 1,200,000 = $180,000 Depletion for 1992

Explanation and Approach: Write down the formula to compute depletion, enter the data given, and solve.

$$\frac{\text{Acquisition Cost} + \text{Costs to Explore and Develop} - \text{Residual Value of Land} + \text{Costs to Restore Land to Alternative Use}}{\text{Number of Units to be Extracted}} = \text{Depletion Cost Per Recoverable Unit}$$

$$\begin{matrix} \text{Depletion Cost} \\ \text{Per Recoverable} \\ \text{Unit} \end{matrix} \quad X \quad \begin{matrix} \text{Units Extracted} \\ \text{During} \\ \text{Period} \end{matrix} \quad = \quad \begin{matrix} \text{Depletion} \\ \text{for the} \\ \text{Period} \end{matrix}$$

Note: The depletion cost is the amount to be removed from the property, plant, and equipment classification ($180,000 in this case). It is based on the units extracted from the earth during the period. The portion of this $180,000 which gets to the income statement is dependent upon the number of units sold. When the number of units extracted exceed the number sold, as in this exercise, a portion of the depletion costs goes into the Inventory account on the balance sheet.

ANALYSIS OF MULTIPLE-CHOICE TYPE QUESTIONS

Question

1. A machine was purchased for $8,000,000 on January 1, 1992. It has an estimated useful life of 8 years and a residual value of $800,000. Depreciation is being computed using the sum-of-the-years'-digits method. What amount should be shown for this machine, net of accumulated depreciation, in the company's December 31, 1993 balance sheet?
   a. $4,200,000.
   b. $5,000,000.
   c. $6,300,000.
   d. $6,600,000.

Solution = b.

Explanation and Approach: Write down the formula to compute book value and the formula to compute depreciation using the sum-of-the-years'-digits method. Fill in the data from the scenario at hand and solve. Be careful that you don't get so involved with the computation of depreciation that you lose sight of the question--and that is, to compute the book value of the equipment. It would be helpful to underline the middle of the last sentence of the stem of the question in order to keep your focus on what is being asked.

$$\text{Cost} - \text{Accumulated Depreciation} = \text{Book Value}$$

$$\frac{\text{No. of Years Remaining Life}}{\text{Sum of the Years}} \text{ X Depreciable Cost} = \text{Depreciation Charge}$$

$$\frac{n(n + 1)}{2} = \text{Sum of the Years}$$

$$\frac{8(9)}{2} = 36$$

8/36 X ($8,000,000 - $800,000) = $1,600,000 depreciation for 1992.
7/36 X ($8,000,000 - $800,000) = $1,400,000 depreciation for 1993.

Depreciation for 1992	$1,600,000
Depreciation for 1993	1,400,000
Accumulated depreciation	$3,000,000

Cost	$8,000,000
Accumulated depreciation	3,000,000
Book value	$5,000,000

Question

2. Tammy Company purchased a machine on July 1, 1992 for $900,000. The machine has an estimated life of five years and a salvage value of $120,000. The machine is being depreciated by the 150% declining-balance method. What amount of depreciation should be recorded for the year ended December 31, 1993?
   a. $229,500.
   b. $198,900.
   c. $189,000.
   d. $163,800.

Solution = a.

Explanation and Approach: Write down the formula to use for the declining-balance approach. (Notice the facts indicate there is a partial period for the first year (1992) and the question asks for the depreciation for the 1993 reporting period.) Compute the rate that is 150% of the straight-line rate. Apply the formula to the facts given. Remember that salvage value is not used with this method in computing depreciation in the early years of the asset's life.

Constant Percentage X Book Value at Beginning of Year = Depreciation

$$\frac{100\%}{Life} = \frac{100\%}{5 \ years} = 20\% \quad 20\% \ X \ 150\% = 30\% \ constant \ percentage$$

30% X $900,000 = $270,000 First year
30% X ($900,000 - $270,000) = $189,000 Second year

1/2 X $270,000 = $135,000 for 1992
1/2 X $270,000 + 1/2 X $189,000 = $229,500 for 1993

OR

30% X ($900,000 - $135,000) = $229,500 for 1993

Question

3. A plant asset with a five-year estimated useful life and no salvage value is sold during the second year. How would the use of the straight-line method of depreciation instead of an accelerated depreciation method affect the amount of gain or loss on the sale of the plant asset?

	Gain	Loss
a.	Increase	Decrease
b.	Decrease	Increase
c.	No Effect	Increase
d.	No Effect	No Effect

Solution = b.

Explanation and Approach: An accelerated method would result in more accumulated depreciation and, therefore, less book value. In contrast, the straight-line method results in less accumulated depreciation and more book value. This means a lower gain or a higher loss is computed if the asset is sold and the straight-line method is in use.

One way you can prove this to yourself is to make up a set of facts (cost, service life, accelerated method to use) and assume the asset is sold for a given amount at the end of the second year. Compare that gain or loss with the gain or loss that would result if the straight-line method is used.

Question

4. Roberts Truck Rental uses the group depreciation method for its fleet of trucks. When it retires one of its trucks and receives cash from a salvage company, the carrying value of property, plant, and equipment will be decreased by the
    a. original cost of the truck.
    b. original cost of the truck less the cash proceeds.
    c. cash proceeds received.
    d. cash proceeds received and original cost of the truck.

Solution = c.

Explanation and Approach: Write down the journal entry to record the disposal of the truck and analyze its effect. Remember that no gain or loss is recorded on the disposal when the group or composite method is used.

Cash .... Proceeds
Accumulated Depreciation .... Plug
    Truck .... Original Cost

In analyzing the entry's net effect on the book value (carrying amount) of property, plant, and equipment we find the following: (1) The decrease in Truck will reduce PP&E by the truck's original cost. (2) The debit to Accumulated Depreciation will increase PP&E by the excess of the truck's original cost over the proceeds from disposal. (3) Therefore, the net effect is to decrease PP&E by the amount of the cash proceeds from the sale.

Question

5. The Schoen Company purchased a piece of equipment at the beginning of 1983 for $60,000. The equipment was being depreciated using the straight-line method over an estimated life of 20 years, with no salvage value. At the beginning of 1993, when the equipment had been in use for 10 years, the company paid $10,000 to overhaul the equipment. As a result of this improvement, the company estimates that the useful life of the equipment will be extended an additional five years. What should be the depreciation expense for this equipment in 1993?
    a. $2,000.
    b. $2,667.
    c. $3,000.
    d. $1,867.

Solution = b.

Explanation and Approach: Write down the model or format to compute depreciation whenever there has been a change in the estimated service life and/or salvage value. Fill in the data of the case at hand and solve:

Cost	$60,000
Accumulated depreciation	30,000[a]
Book value (before overhaul)	30,000
Additional expenditure capitalized (if any)	10,000
Revised book value (after overhaul)	40,000
Current estimate of salvage	-0-
Remaining depreciable cost	40,000
Remaining years of useful life at 1/1/93	÷ 15[b]
Depreciation expense for 1993	$ 2,667

[a]Cost	$60,000
Original estimate of salvage	-0-
Original depreciable cost	60,000
Original service life in years	÷ 20
Original depreciation per year	3,000
Number of years used	X 10
Accumulated depreciation --1/1/93	$30,000

[b]Original estimate of life in years	20
Number of years used	(10)
Additional years	5
Remaining years of useful life at 1/1/93	15

TIP: Be careful when computing the length of time between two dates. The length of time between the beginning of 1983 and the beginning of 1993 is 10 years; whereas, the length of time between the end of 1983 and the beginning of 1993 is nine years. It is a common mistake to deduct one year from the other (1993 - 1983 = 10 years). As you can see from the foregoing, that will not always work. It is wise to write down the years that fall between the two dates and then count those years on your list. For example, the length of time between the end of 1989 and the beginning of 1992 is two years and is determined as follows:

1990	1
1991	2

CHAPTER 12

INTANGIBLE ASSETS

OVERVIEW

The balance sheet classification for intangible assets is used to report assets which lack physical existence and are not properly classifiable elsewhere. For instance (1) bank deposits and accounts receivable both are intangible by a legal definition but they are properly classifiable as current assets for accounting purposes, and (2) investment in stock is intangible in nature but should be classified as either a current asset or a long-term investment for accounting purposes. Assets such as patents, trademarks, copyrights, and franchises are intangible in nature and are classified in the intangible asset section of a balance sheet. Intangible assets are discussed in this chapter.

TIPS ON CHAPTER TOPICS

TIP: An intangible asset is to be amortized over its useful life; however, the amortization period should not exceed 40 years. This rule applies even to assets which may appear to have an unlimited life (such as organization costs and goodwill).

TIP: Research and development (R & D) costs are to be expensed in the period incurred. The FASB established this guideline after a study revealed that very few R & D projects ever culminate in a successfully marketed product. When great uncertainty exists, the principle of convervatism dictates that we choose the alternative with the least favorable effect on net income and on assets.

TIP: To capitalize earnings means to discount or calculate the present worth of the projected future earnings of an asset or business. If the earnings are assumed to continue indefinitely, the present value is determined by dividing the appropriate earnings figure by the appropriate rate.

EXERCISE 12-1

Purpose: This exercise will give you practice in identifying items that are to be classified as costs associated with various intangible assets.

The Redskins Corporation incurred the following costs during January 1992:
1.	Attorney's fees in connection with organization of the corporation	$12,000
2.	Meetings of incorporators, state filing fees, and other organizational costs	3,000
3.	Improvements to leased offices prior to occupancy	29,000
4.	Costs to design and construct a prototype	50,000
5.	Testing of prototype	5,000
6.	Troubleshooting breakdowns during production	5,500
7.	Fees paid to engineers and lawyers to prepare patent application; patent granted January 22.	22,000
8.	Payment of six months rent on leased facilities	42,000

9.	Stock issue costs	11,000
10.	Payment for a copyright.	44,000
11.	Materials purchased for future research and development projects; materials have alternative use.	70,000
12.	Costs to advertise new business.	16,000

Instructions

(a) For each item above, identify what account should be debited to record the expenditure.

(b) Indicate in what subclassification the related account will be reported when it is time to issue financial statements.

SOLUTION TO EXERCISE 12-1

	Account to Debit	Classification
1.	Organization Costs	Intangible Asset
2.	Organization Costs	Intangible Asset
3.	Leasehold Improvements	Property, Plant, and Equipment (or Intangible Asset)
4.	Research and Development Expense	Operating Expense
5.	Research and Development Expense	Operating Expense
6.	Factory Overhead	Allocated to Inventory and Cost of Goods Sold
7.	Patent	Intangible Asset
8.	Prepaid Rent	Current Asset
9.	Organization Costs (or reduction of Additional Paid-in Capital)	Intangible Asset (or reduction of Additional Paid-in Capital)
10.	Copyright	Intangible Asset
11.	Raw Materials Inventory	Current Assets
12.	Advertising Expense	Operating Expense

EXERCISE 12-2

Purpose: This exercise will review the accounting guidelines related to three types of intangible assets--franchise, patent, and trademark.

Information concerning Linda Heckenmueller Corporation's intangible assets follows:

1. On January 1, 1992, Heckenmueller signed an agreement to operate as a franchisee of Speedy Copy Service, Inc. for an initial franchise fee of $75,000. Of this amount, $15,000 was paid when the agreement was signed and the balance is payable in 4 annual payments of $15,000 each, beginning January 1, 1993. The agreement provides that the down payment is not refundable and no future services are required of the franchisor. The present value at January 1, 1992, of the 4 annual payments discounted at 14% (the implicit rate for a loan of this type) is $43,700. The agreement also provides that 5% of the revenue from the franchise must be paid to the franchisor annually. Heckenmueller's revenue from the franchise for 1992 was $900,000. Heckenmueller estimates the useful life of the franchise to be 10 years.

2. Heckenmueller incurred $65,000 of experimental and development costs in its laboratory to develop a patent which was granted on January 2, 1992. Legal fees and other costs associated with registration of the patent totaled $13,200. Heckenmueller estimates that the useful life of the patent will be 8 years.

3. A trademark was purchased from Walton Company for $32,000 on July 1, 1989. Expenditures for successful litigation in defense of the trademark totaling $8,000 were paid on July 1, 1992. Heckenmueller estimates that the useful life of the trademark will be 20 years from the date of acquisition.

Instructions
(a) Prepare a schedule showing the intangible asset section of Heckenmueller's balance sheet at December 31, 1992. Show supporting computations in good form.
(b) Prepare a schedule showing all expenses resulting from the transactions that would appear on Heckenmueller's income statement for the year ended December 31, 1992. Show supporting computations in good form.

(AICPA adapted)

SOLUTION TO EXERCISE 12-2

(a)

Linda Heckenmueller Corporation
Intangible Assets
December 31, 1992

Franchise, net of accumulated amortization of $5,870 (Schedule 1)	$52,830
Patent, net of accumulated amortization of $1,650 (Schedule 2)	11,550
Trademark, net of accumulated amortization of $5,835 (Schedule 3)	34,165
Total intangible assets	$98,545

Schedule 1   Franchise

Cost of franchise on 1/1/92 ($15,000 + $43,700)	$58,700
1992 amortization ($58,700 X 1/10)	(5,870)
Cost of franchise, net of amortization	$52,830

Schedule 2   Patent

Cost of securing patent on 1/2/92	$13,200
1992 amortization ($13,200 X 1/8)	(1,650)
Cost of patent, net of amortization	$11,550

Schedule 3   Trademark

Cost of trademark on 7/1/89	$32,000
Amortization, 7/1/89 to 1/1/92 ($32,000 X 1/20 X 2.5)	(4,000)
Book value on 1/1/92	28,000
Cost of successful legal defense on 7/1/92	8,000
Book value after legal defense	36,000
Amortization, 1/1/92 to 12/31/92 (Schedule 4)	(1,835)
Cost of trademark, net of amortization	$34,165

(b)

Linda Heckenmueller Corporation
Expenses Resulting from Selected Intangibles Transactions
For the Year Ended December 31, 1992

Interest expense ($43,700 X 14%)	$ 6,118
Franchise amortization (Schedule 1)	5,870
Franchise fee ($900,000 X 5%)	45,000
Patent amortization (Schedule 2)	1,650
Trademark amortization (Schedule 4)	1,835
Total expenses	$60,473

Note: The $65,000 of research and development costs incurred in developing the patent would have been expensed prior to 1992 (per *SFAS No. 2*).

Schedule 4	Trademark Amortization	
Amortization of original cost ($32,000 X 1/20)		$1,600
Amortization of legal fees ($8,000 X 1/17 X 6/12)		235
Total trademark amortization		$1,835

Explanation:

1. The franchise rights will benefit future periods. Therefore, the costs associated with obtaining those rights should be capitalized and amortized over future periods. The acquisition cost is determined by the cash given (down payment of $15,000) and the cash equivalent of the related payable (present value of the four annual payments at 14%--$43,700). The fact that "the down payment is not refundable and no future services are required of the franchisor" has no impact on how the franchisee accounts for the franchise. The provision in the agreement which calls for the franchisee to pay 5% of the annual revenue from the franchise to the franchisor does not initially require any accounting treatment; an expense accrues as revenues are earned from use of the franchise. The capitalized franchise costs are to be amortized over the useful period of 10 years. The interest expense resulting from deferred payment is to be recognized annually by applying the implicit rate of 14% to the outstanding payable balance.

2. Research and development costs are to be expensed in the period incurred. Thus, the $65,000 of experimental and development costs incurred in developing the patent would have been expensed prior to 1992. Legal fees and other costs associated with obtaining the patent should be matched with each of the eight years estimated to be benefited; therefore, the $13,200 of legal fees and registration costs should be capitalized and amortized.

3. The purchase price of the trademark ($32,000) was capitalized in mid-1989 when the trademark was acquired. That cost is being amortized over the 20-year useful life. (Note that only one-half year of amortization was recorded in 1989.) Expenditures of $8,000 for successful litigation in defense of the trademark rights are to be charged to the Trademark account because such a suit establishes the legal rights of the holder of the patent (which benefits future periods). Because the litigation was settled in the middle of 1992, only one-half year of amortization of these legal costs is recorded for 1992. The $8,000 is to be amortized over the remaining useful life of the trademark (17 years in this case).

Approach: The ideal approach would be to prepare the journal entries associated with the facts given and post them to T-accounts to determine the balances to be reported on the income statement for the year ending December 31, 1992 and on the balance sheet at December 31, 1992. Under some circumstances (such as exam conditions), time may not permit these additional steps. You should at least think about and visualize the flow of the information through the accounts. This will greatly aid the successful completion of the schedules required.

EXERCISE 12-3

Purpose: This exercise reviews the subject of leasehold improvements.

On January 1, Year 1, Mr. Howard Anderson's Prize Paints entered into a lease contract with the Regency Mall Corp. The agreement provides for a ten-year lease on store space in a suburban mall. Mr. Anderson is leasing the space for his wholesale paint business. In order to prepare the facilities for his purpose, Mr. Anderson constructed several partitions at a cost of $3,200 and lowered the ceiling at a cost of $1,400. The partitions and ceiling revert to the owner of the property at the end of the lease term. Mr. Anderson assumes they will last as long as the building, which he estimates to have a twenty-year life.

Instructions

(a) Prepare the journal entry to record the payment to the builder who put in the partitions and ceiling.
(b) Identify the period of time over which the improvements should be amortized. Explain why.
(c) Prepare the related adjusting entry (if any) at the end of Year 1.
(d) Explain how the improvements would appear on the balance sheet at the end of the third year of the lease.

SOLUTION TO EXERCISE 12-3

(a) Leasehold Improvements 4,600
         Cash 4,600

(b) Leasehold improvements are to be amortized over their useful life or the remaining term of the lease, whichever is less. In this scenario, the remaining term of the lease is ten years which is less than the twenty-year useful life of the improvements. The ten year period should be used.

(c) The adjusting entry to amortize the improvements would be:
Amortization of Leasehold Improvements Expense 460
         Leasehold Improvements ($4,600 ÷ 10 years = $460) 460

(d) Leasehold Improvements would most likely appear in the property, plant, and equipment section of Prize Paints' balance sheet at an amount of $3,220 [$4,600 - 3($460) = $3,220] at the end of the third year of the lease although some accountants would prefer to report this item in the intangible asset classification.

EXERCISE 12-4

Purpose: This exercise will give you practice in identifying activities that constitute R & D activities.

Listed below are four independent situations involving research and development costs:

1. During 1992 Bebe Co. incurred the following costs:

Research and development services performed by Way Company for Bebe	$325,000
Testing for evaluation of new products	300,000
Laboratory research aimed at discovery of new knowledge	375,000
Research and development services performed by Bebe for Elway Company	220,000

For the year ended December 31, 1992, Bebe should report research and development expense of how much?

2. Holly Corp. incurred the following costs during the year ended December 31, 1992:

Design, construction, and testing of preproduction prototypes and models	$220,000
Routine, on-going efforts to refine, enrich, or otherwise improve upon the qualities of an existing product	250,000
Quality control during commercial production including routine testing of products	300,000
Laboratory research aimed at discovery of new knowledge	360,000

What is the total amount to be classified and expensed as research and development for 1992?

3. Polaski Company incurred costs in 1992 as follows:

Equipment acquired for use in various research and development projects	$890,000
Depreciation on the equipment above	135,000
Materials used in R & D	300,000
Compensation costs of personnel in R & D	400,000
Outside consulting fees for R & D work	150,000
Indirect costs appropriately allocated to R & D	260,000

What is the total amount of research and development expense that should be reported in Polaski's 1992 income statement?

4. Liverpool Inc. incurred the following costs during the year ended December 31, 1992:

Laboratory research aimed at discovery of new knowledge	$175,000
Radical modification to the formulation of a chemical product	125,000
Research and development costs reimbursable under a contract to perform research and development for Johnathon King Inc.	350,000
Testing for evaluation of new products	275,000

What is the total amount to be classified and expensed as research and development for 1992?

Instructions

Provide the correct answer to each of the four situations.

SOLUTION TO EXERCISE 12-4

1.

Research and development services performed by Way Company for Bebe	$ 325,000
Testing for evaluation of new products	300,000
Laboratory research aimed at discovery of new knowledge	375,000
Total R & D expense	$1,000,000

R & D costs related to R & D activities conducted for other entities are classified as a receivable (because of the impending reimbursement).

2.

Design, construction, and testing of preproduction prototypes and models	$220,000
Laboratory research aimed at discovery of new knowledge	360,000
Total R & D expense	$580,000

3.
Depreciation on the equipment acquired for use in various R & D projects	$ 135,000
Materials used in R & D	300,000
Compensation costs of personnel in R & D	400,000
Outside consulting fees for R & D work	150,000
Indirect costs appropriately allocated to R & D	260,000
Total R & D expense	$1,245,000

Equipment that has alternative future uses (in other R & D projects or otherwise) is to be capitalized; the related depreciation is to be classified as R & D.

4.
Laboratory research aimed at discovery of new knowledge	$175,000
Radical modification to the formulation of a chemical product	125,000
Testing for evaluation of new products	275,000
Total R & D expense	$575,000

Approach: Read the requirement of each situation before you begin detailed work on the first one. Notice that all four items deal with research and development costs. Therefore, review in your mind the definitions of the words research and development. Recall what you can from the list of activities considered to be R & D and the list of activities which are **not** considered to be R & D. Think of why the items logically appear on the particular list. It is important to think about these items **before** you dig into the questions because details in the situations may mislead you. To minimize confusion, organize your thoughts and recall what you know about the subject before you begin to process the data at hand.

To differentiate research and development costs from other similar costs, the FASB issued the following definitions in *SFAS No. 2*:

Research is planned search or critical investigation aimed at discovery of new knowledge with the hope that such knowledge will be useful in developing a new product or service . . . or a new process or technique . . . or in bringing about a significant improvement to an existing product or process.

Development is the translation of research findings or other knowledge into a plan or design for a new product or process or for a significant improvement to an existing product or process whether intended for sale or use. It includes the conceptual formulation, design, and testing of product alternatives, construction of prototypes, and operation of pilot plants. It does not include routine or periodic alterations to existing products, production lines, manufacturing processes, and other on-going operations even though those alterations may represent improvements; it does not include market research or market testing activities.

Many costs have characteristics similar to those of research and development costs, for instance, costs of relocation and rearrangement of facilities, start-up costs for a new plant or new retail outlet, marketing research costs, promotion costs of a new product or service, and costs of training new personnel. To distinguish between R & D and these other similar costs, the following schedule (from *SFAS No. 2*) provides (1) examples of activities that typically would be **included** in research and development, and (2) examples of activities that typically would be **excluded** from research and development.

1. **R & D Activities**	2. **Activities Not Considered R & D**
(a) Laboratory research aimed at discovery of new knowledge.	(a) Engineering follow-through in an early phase of commercial production.
(b) Searching for applications of new research findings.	(b) Quality control during commercial production including routine testing.
(c) Conceptual formulation and design of possible product or process alternatives.	(c) Trouble-shooting breakdowns during production.
(d) Testing in search for or evaluation of product or process alternatives.	(d) Routine, on-going efforts to refine, enrich, or improve the qualities of an existing product.
(e) Modification of the design of a product or process.	(e) Adaptation of an existing capability to a particular requirement or customer's need.
(f) Design, construction, and testing of preproduction prototypes and models.	(f) Periodic design changes to existing products.
(g) Design of tools, jigs, molds, and dies involving new technology.	(g) Routine design of tools, jigs, molds, and dies.
(h) Design, construction, and operation of a pilot plant not useful for commercial production.	(h) Activity, including design and construction engineering related to the construction, relocation, rearrangement, or startup of facilities or equipment.
(i) Engineering activity required to advance the design of a product to the manufacturing stage.	(i) Legal work on patent applications, sale, licensing, or litigation.

ILLUSTRATION 12-1
DETERMINATION OF GOODWILL AND PURCHASE PRICE

Step 1: **Determine an estimate of future average annual earnings.** This is usually done by computing the adjusted average net earnings of the firm in the past. Adjust for accounting changes, extraordinary items, and other such special items.

Step 2: **Determine normal earnings.** Multiply **the industry average rate of return** times **the fair market value of the identifiable net assets** of the firm.

Step 3: **Determine excess earnings.** This is the average earnings from Step 1 less the normal earnings from Step 2.

Step 4: **Determine the value of goodwill.** This can be done by using an appropriate discount rate and choosing the number of periods for which the excess earnings will be maintained. It could be treated as a perpetuity by capitalizing the excess earnings (dividing excess earnings by an appropriate capitalization rate). Alternatively, the number of years method could be used.

Step 5: **Determine purchase price.** This will be the sum of the value of goodwill and the fair value of identifiable net assets of the firm.

EXERCISE 12-5

Purpose: This exercise illustrates the steps in estimating the value of goodwill.

Mr. Judski is contemplating the sale of his business, Classic Vettes. The following data are available:

Book value of tangible & identifiable intangible assets less liabilities	$185,000
Market value of tangible & identifiable intangible assets less liabilities	200,000
Estimated average future annual income for Classic Vettes	28,000
Normal rate of return for the industry	10%

Instructions
(a) Compute the estimated value of goodwill if excess income is capitalized at a 10% rate.
(b) Compute the estimated value of goodwill if excess income is capitalized at a 25% rate.

SOLUTION TO EXERCISE 12-5

(a) $200,000 X 10% = $20,000 normal earnings.
$28,000 - $20,000 = $8,000 excess earnings
$8,000 ÷ 10% = $80,000 goodwill

(b) $200,000 X 10% = $20,000 normal earnings
$28,000 - $20,000 = $8,000 excess earnings
$8,000 ÷ 25% = $32,000 goodwill

Explanation and Approach: Perform the applicable steps described in **Illustration 12-1**:
(a) Step 1: Determine an estimate of future average annual earnings. This is given data in the exercise at hand--$28,000.

Step 2: Determine normal earnings. Multiply the industry average rate of return times the fair market value of the identifiable net assets of the firm.
10% X $200,000 = $20,000 Normal earnings

Step 3: Determine excess earnings. Deduct normal earnings from future average annual earnings.
$28,000 - $20,000 = $8,000 Excess earnings

Step 4: Determine the value of goodwill. Capitalize excess earnings by dividing excess earnings by the chosen capitalization rate .
$8,000 ÷ 10% = $80,000 goodwill

TIP: The higher the capitalization rate, the lower the resulting value for goodwill.

TIP: Excess earnings are often referred to as superior earnings.

TIP: Net identifiable assets are determined by deducting total liabilities from total identifiable (tangible and intangible) assets.

TIP: Fair value, market value, and fair market value are terms which are often used interchangeably.

EXERCISE 12-6

Purpose: This exercise will provide an example of how to use the present value method to estimate the value of goodwill.

As the president of Winnie Records Corp., you are considering purchasing Winkle Tape Corp., whose balance sheet is summarized as follows:

Current assets	$ 300,000	Current liabilities	$ 300,000
Fixed assets (net of depreciation)	700,000	Long-term liabilities	500,000
Other assets	300,000	Common stock	400,000
		Retained earnings	100,000
Total	$1,300,000	Total	$1,300,000

The fair market value of current assets is $600,000. The normal rate of return on net assets for the industry is 15%. The average expected annual earnings projected for Winkle Tape Corp. is $140,000.

Instructions
Assuming that the excess earnings continue for 5 years, determine the value for goodwill.

SOLUTION TO EXERCISE 12-6

Step 1: Average expected annual earnings are $140,000 (data given).

Step 2:	Fair market value of net assets	$800,000*
	Normal rate of return	15%
	Normal earnings	$120,000

Step 3:	Expected earnings	$140,000
	Normal earnings	(120,000)
	Excess earnings	$ 20,000

Step 4:	Excess earnings	$ 20,000
	Present value of an annuity of 1 factor, 5 years @ 15%	3.35216
	Estimated goodwill	$67,043.20

*Book value of total assets	$1,300,000
Excess fair market value over book value of current assets	300,000**
Fair value of total assets	1,600,000
Total liabilities ($300,000 + $500,000)	800,000
Fair market value of net assets of Winkle	$ 800,000

**Fair market value of current assets	$600,000
Book value of current assets	300,000
Excess fair market value over book value of current assets	$300,000

Approach: Apply the steps listed in Illustration 12-1.

ANALYSIS OF MULTIPLE-CHOICE TYPE QUESTIONS

Question

1. The adjusted trial balance of the Laventhal Corporation as of December 31, 1992 includes the following accounts:

Trademark	$ 30,000
Discount on bonds payable	37,500
Organization costs	12,500
Excess of cost over fair value of identifiable net assets of acquired business	175,000
Advertising costs (to promote goodwill)	20,000

What should be reported as total intangible assets on Laventhal's December 31, 1992 balance sheet?
   a. $217,500.
   b. $230,000.
   c. $237,500.
   d. $275,000.

Solution = a.

Explanation and Approach: Identify the classification of each item listed. Sum the ones you identify as being intangible assets.

Trademark	$ 30,000
Organization costs	12,500
Excess of fair value of identifiable net assets of acquired business	175,000
Total intangible assets	$217,500

Discount on bonds payable is to be classified as a contra liability. Advertising costs incurred are to be reported as an expense on the income statement. The costs to develop and maintain goodwill are not to be capitalized. Only the costs to acquire goodwill with a going business can be recorded as goodwill. The "excess of fair value of net identifiable net assets of acquired business" is a technical term referring to goodwill.

Question

2. A patent with a remaining legal life of 12 years and an estimated useful life of 8 years was acquired for $288,000 by Bradley Corporation on January 2, 1988. In January 1992, Bradley paid $18,000 in legal fees in a successful defense of the patent. What should Bradley record as patent amortization for 1992?
   a. $24,000.
   b. $36,000.
   c. $38,250.
   d. $40,500.

Solution = d.

Explanation and Approach: Analyze the Patent account. Use the data given to compute the amounts reflected therein and the resulting amortization for 1992.

Beginning of 1988, patent cost	$288,000
Estimated years of service life	÷ 8
Annual amortization for 1988-1991	36,000
Number of years used	4
Total amortization 1988-1991	144,000

Cost at beginning of 1988	288,000
Amortization for 1988-1991	(144,000)
Book value at beginning of 1992	144,000
Legal fees capitalized	18,000
Revised book value, beginning of 1992	162,000
Remaining years of life	÷ 4
Amortization for 1992	$ 40,500

Question

3. On January 1, 1992, Teeple Corporation incurred organization costs of $30,000. For financial reporting purposes, Teeple is amortizing these costs on the same basis as the maximum allowable for federal income tax purposes. What portion of the organization costs will Teeple defer to years subsequent to 1992?

 a. $0.
 b. $6,000.
 c. $24,000.
 d. $30,000.

Solution = c.

Explanation: The maximum amount of amortization will result from using the minimum amortization period which, for tax purposes, is 60 months (5 years).
$30,000 ÷ 5 yrs. = $6,000 amortization per year.
If $6,000 is amortized, then the amount to defer is computed as follows:

Total organization costs	$30,000
Amount amortized in 1992	(6,000)
Amount to defer to subsequent periods	$24,000

TIP: Note the importance of reading the question carefully. An intermediate step--the computation of the $6,000 amortization amount for 1992--is one of the distractors. You should read the last line of the paragraph first to understand the essence of the problem. It is wise to write down the essential computation to keep your focus:

   Total Organization Costs
   Less: Amount to Amortize in 1992
   = Amount to Defer

Question

4. In 1992, Barry Sanders Corporation incurred research and development costs as follows:

Materials and equipment	$200,000
Personnel	300,000
Indirect costs	100,000
Total	$600,000

These costs relate to a product that will be marketed in 1993. It is estimated that these costs will be recouped by December 31, 1995. The materials and equipment have no alternative future uses. What is the amount of research and development costs that should be charged to income in 1992?

a. $0.
b. $100,000.
c. $400,000.
d. $600,000.

Solution = d.

Explanation: All R & D costs are to be expensed in the period incurred. Equipment used in R & D activities that has alternative uses would be capitalized and depreciated. This equipment has no alternative use so it is expensed immediately. A reasonable allocation of indirect costs should be included in R & D. Costs of personnel engaged in R & D activities are to be expensed in the period incurred.

Question

5. The owners of Tellmart Shoe Store are contemplating selling the business to new interests. The cumulative earnings for the past 5 years amounted to $750,000 including extraordinary gains of $25,000. The annual earnings based on an average rate of return on investment for this industry would have been $115,000. If excess earnings are to be capitalized at 15%, then implied goodwill should be

a. $175,000.
b. $233,334.
c. $200,000.
d. $725,000.

Solution = c.

Explanation and Approach: Follow the steps in **Illustration 12-1.**

1. Cumulative earnings over 5 years | $750,000
    Extraordinary gains included in above | (25,000)
    Total earnings excluding extraordinary items | 725,000
    Number of years included above | ÷ 5
    Average earnings in past 5 years assumed to be average future annual earnings | 145,000

2. Normal earnings = $115,000.

3. Expected average earnings | $145,000
    Normal earnings | (115,000)
    Excess earnings | $ 30,000

4. Excess earnings | $ 30,000
    Capitalization rate | ÷ 15%
    Estimated value of goodwill | $200,000

CHAPTER 13

CURRENT LIABILITIES AND CONTINGENCIES

OVERVIEW

Initially, the resources (assets) of a business have to come from an entity outside of the particular organization. Two main sources of resources are creditor sources (liabilities) and owners' sources (owners' equity). In this chapter, we begin our in-depth discussion of liabilities.

Due to the nature of some business activities, it is common to find some goods and services being received while payment for these items is made days or weeks later. Therefore, at a specific point in time, such as a balance sheet date, we may find that a business has obligations for merchandise received from suppliers (accounts payable), for money it has borrowed (notes payable), for interest incurred (interest payable), for property taxes (property taxes payable), for sales tax charged to customers which has not yet been remitted to the government (sales taxes payable), for salaries and wages (salaries and wages payable), and for other amounts due to government agencies in connection with employee compensation. Such payables are reported as current (short-term) liabilities, because they will fall due within the next 12 months and will require the use of current assets (cash, in these cases) to liquidate them. Accounting for current liabilities is discussed in this chapter.

TIPS ON CHAPTER TOPICS

TIP: Current liabilities are often called short-term liabilities or short-term debt. Noncurrent liabilities are often called long-term liabilities or long-term debt.

TIP: Current liabilities are obligations whose liquidation is reasonably expected to require the use of existing resources properly classifiable as current assets, or the creation of other current liabilities. Noncurrent liabilities are obligations which do not meet the criteria to be classified as current.

TIP: An estimated loss from a loss contingency should be accrued by a charge to expense and a credit to a liability if both of the following conditions are met: (1) it is **probable** that a liability has been incurred at the date of the balance sheet, and (2) the amount of the loss can be **reasonably estimated.** If the loss is either probable or estimable but not both, and if there is at least a **reasonable possibility** that a liability has been incurred, the contingency must be disclosed in the notes (but not accrued). If it is only **remotely possible** that a liability has been incurred, no accrual nor note disclosure is required (there are some exceptions to this guideline).

EXERCISE 13-1

Purpose: This exercise tests your ability to distinguish between current and long-term liabilities.

Instructions

Indicate how each of the following items would be reported on a balance sheet being prepared at December 31, 1993.

1. Obligation to supplier for merchandise purchased on credit. (Terms 2/10, n/30)
2. Note payable to bank maturing 90 days after balance sheet date.
3. Bonds payable due January 1, 1998.
4. Property taxes payable.
5. Interest payable on long-term bonds payable.
6. Income taxes payable.
7. Portion of lessee's lease obligations due in years 1995 through 1999.
8. Revenue received in advance, to be earned over the next six months.
9. Salaries payable.
10. Rent payable.
11. Short-term notes payable.
12. Pension obligations maturing in ten years.
13. Installment loan payment due three months after balance sheet date.
14. Installment loan payments due after one year.
15. Portion of lessee's lease obligations due within a year after the December 31, 1993 balance sheet date.
16. Bank overdraft.
17. Accrued officer bonus.
18. Premium offers outstanding.
19. Cash dividends declared but not paid.
20. Deferred rent revenue.
21. Stock dividends payable.
22. Bonds payable due June 1, 1994.
23. Bonds payable due July 1, 1994 for which a sinking fund will be used to pay off the debt. The sinking fund is classified as a long-term investment.
24. Discount to the bonds payable in item 3 above.
25. Current maturities of long-term debt.
26. Accrued interest on notes payable.
27. Customer deposits.
28. Sales taxes payable.
29. FICA withholdings.
30. Contingent liability (reasonable possibility of loss).
31. Contingent liability (probable and estimable).
32. Obligation for warranties.
33. Unearned warranty revenue.
34. Gift certificates outstanding.
35. Loan from stockholder.

SOLUTION TO EXERCISE 13-1

TIP: Apply the definition of a current liability. Analyze each situation and determine if the liability will fall due within a year (or operating cycle) of the balance sheet date and whether it will require the use of current assets or the incurrence of another current liability to be liquidated. If so, it is current; if not, it is long-term. Recall that current assets include cash and assets expected to be converted to cash or sold or consumed within the next year or operating cycle, whichever is longer.

1. Current liability (called Accounts Payable).
2. Current liability.
3. Noncurrent liability.
4. Current liability.
5. Current liability; interest is usually due monthly, quarterly, or annually.
6. Current liability.
7. Noncurrent liability.
8. Current liability.
9. Current liability.
10. Current liability.
11. Current liability.
12. Noncurrent liability.
13. Current liability.
14. Noncurrent liability.
15. Current liability.
16. Current liability (assuming no other bank accounts with positive balances in same bank).
17. Current liability.
18. Current liability; may also have a portion as a noncurrent liability.
19. Current liability
20. Current liability or noncurrent liability, depending on when the revenue is expected to be earned.
21. Paid-in capital; it does not meet the definition of a liability.
22. Current liability.
23. Noncurrent liability; even though it is coming due within a year, it will not require the use of current assets to be liquidated.
24. Contra noncurrent liability (deducted from the related bonds payable).
25. Current liability.
26. Current liability.
27. Current liability or noncurrent liability, depending on the time left before they are to be returned.
28. Current liability.
29. Current liability.
30. Note disclosure only.
31. Current liability or noncurrent liability, depending on the date settlement is expected.
32. Current liability or noncurrent liability, depending on term of warranty; (this title is used with the expense warranty method).
33. Current liability or noncurrent liability, depending on length of warranty; (this title is used with the sales warranty method).
34. Current liability, most likely; could have a portion as a noncurrent liability.
35. Current liability or noncurrent liability, depending on the due date of the loan; loans with related parties are required to be separately disclosed; if this loan is due on demand, the payable must be classified as a current liability.

EXERCISE 13-2

Purpose: This exercise will provide you with two examples of the proper treatment of short-term debt expected to be refinanced.

Situation 1
On December 31, 1991, Mayor Frederick Specialty Foods Company had $1,200,000 of short-term debt in the form of notes payable due February 2, 1992. On January 21, 1992, the company issued 25,000 shares of its common stock for $40 per share, receiving $975,000 proceeds after brokerage fees and other costs of issuance. On February 2, 1992, the proceeds from the stock sale, supplemented by an additional $225,000 cash, are used to liquidate the $1,200,000 debt. The December 31, 1991, balance sheet is issued on February 23, 1992.

Instructions
Show how the $1,200,000 of short-term debt should be presented on the December 31, 1991, balance sheet, including note disclosure.

Situation 2
Included in Hubbard Corporation's liability account balances at December 31, 1991, were the following:

14% note payable issued October 1, 1991, maturing September 30, 1992	$500,000
16% note payable issued April 1, 1989, payable in six annual installments of $200,000 beginning April 1, 1990	800,000

Hubbard's December 31, 1991 financial statements were issued on March 31, 1992. On January 13, 1992, the entire $800,000 balance of the 16% note was refinanced by issuance of a long-term obligation payable in a lump-sum. In addition, on March 8, 1992, Hubbard consummated a noncancelable agreement with the lender to refinance the 14%, $500,000 note on a long-term basis, with readily determinable terms that have not yet been implemented. Both parties are financially capable of honoring the agreement, and there have been no violations of the agreement's provisions.

Instructions
Explain how the liabilities should be classified on the December 31, 1991, balance sheet. How much should be classified as a current liability?

SOLUTION TO EXERCISE 13-2

Situation 1

Mayor Frederick Specialty Foods Co.
Partial Balance Sheet
December 31, 1991

Current liabilities:	
Notes payable (Note 1)	$225,000
Long-term debt:	
Notes payable refinanced in February 1992 (Note 1)	975,000

Note 1--Short-term debt refinanced
  As of December 31, 1991, the Company had notes payable totaling $1,200,000 due on February 2, 1992. These notes were refinanced on their due date to the extent of $975,000 received from the issuance of common stock on January 21, 1992. The balance of $225,000 was liquidated using current assets.

Current liabilities:

Notes payable (Note 1)	$225,000
Short-term debt expected to be refinanced (Note 1)	975,000
Long-term debt	XXX,XXX
(Same Note as above.)	

Situation 2

The entire $800,000 balance of the 16% note is properly excluded from short-term obligations since before the balance sheet was issued, Hubbard refinanced the note by issuance of a long-term obligation. The $500,000, 14% note is properly excluded from short-term obligations due to the fact that, before the balance sheet was issued, Hubbard entered into a financing agreement that clearly permits Hubbard to refinance the short-term obligation on a long-term basis with terms that are readily determinable, and all of the following conditions are met:

1.   The agreement is noncancelable as to all parties and extends beyond one year.
2.   At the balance sheet date and at the date of its issuance, Hubbard is not in violation of the agreement.
3.   The lender is financially capable of honoring the agreement.

Explanation and Approach:

Review the criteria which will require an enterprise to exclude a short-term obligation from current liabilities and apply the criteria to the situation at hand.

In accordance with *SFAS No. 6*, an enterprise is required to exclude a short-term obligation from current liabilities only if both of the following conditions are met:

1.   It must **intend to refinance** the obligation on a long-term basis, and
2.   It must **demonstrate an ability** to consummate the refinancing.

Intention to refinance on a long-term basis means the enterprise intends to refinance the short-term obligation so that the use of working capital will not be required during the ensuing fiscal year or operating cycle, if longer. The **ability** to consummate the refinancing may be demonstrated by:

(a)   **Actually refinancing** the short-term obligation by issuance of a long-term obligation or equity securities after the date of the balance sheet but before it is issued; or

(b)   Entering into a **financing agreement** that clearly permits the enterprise to refinance the debt on a long-term basis with terms that are readily determinable.

If an actual refinancing occurs, the portion of the short-term obligation to be excluded from current liabilities may not exceed the proceeds from the new obligation or equity securities issued that are to be used to retire the short-term obligation.

When a financing agreement is relied upon to demonstrate ability to refinance a short-term obligation on a long-term basis, the agreement must meet all of the following conditions:

(a)   The agreement must be noncancelable as to all parties and must extend beyond the normal operating cycle of the company or one year, whichever is longer.

(b)   At the balance sheet date and at the date of its issuance, the company must not be in violation of the agreement.

(c)   The lender or investor is expected to be financially capable of honoring the agreement.

The amount of short-term debt that can be excluded from current liabilities:

1.   Cannot exceed the amount available for refinancing under the agreement.
2.   Must be adjusted for any limitations or restrictions in the agreement which indicate that

the full amount obtainable will not be available to retire the short-term obligations.

3.   Cannot exceed a reasonable estimate of the **minimum** amount expected to be available, if the amount available for refinancing will fluctuate (that is, the most conservative estimate must be used).

If any of these three amounts cannot be reasonably estimated, the entire amount of the short-term debt must be included in current liabilities.

EXERCISE 13-3

Purpose: This exercise will provide an example of the proper accounting for an obligation to an agency of the state government--unremitted sales taxes.

During the month of June, Chelsea's Boutique had cash sales of $234,000 and credit sales of $137,000, both of which include the 6% sales tax that must be remitted to the state by July 15. Sales taxes on June sales were lumped with the sales price and recorded as a credit to the Sales Revenue account.

Instructions
(a) Prepare the adjusting entry that should be recorded to fairly present the financial statements at June 30.
(b) Prepare the entry to record the remittance of the sales taxes on July 5 if a 2% discount is allowed for payments received by the State Revenue Department by July 10.

SOLUTION TO EXERCISE 13-3

(a) 6/30 Sales Revenue   21,000
               Sales Taxes Payable   21,000

               Computation:

Sales plus sales tax	$371,000	
Sales exclusive of tax ($371,000 ÷ 1.06)	350,000	
Sales tax	$ 21,000	

(b) 7/5   Sales Taxes Payable   21,000
               Cash (98% X $21,000)   20,580
               Gain on Sales Tax Collections (2% X $21,000)..........   420

Explanation: Sales taxes on transfers of tangible personal property and on certain services must be collected from customers and remitted to the proper governmental authority. A liability is set up to provide for taxes collected from customers but as yet unremitted to the tax authority. The Sales Taxes Payable account should reflect the liability for sales taxes due to the government.

When the sales tax collections credited to the liability account are not equal to the liability as computed by the governmental formula, an adjustment of the liability account may be made by recognizing a gain or a loss on sales tax collections.

EXERCISE 13-4

Purpose: This exercise will show you how to compute a bonus under two different agreements.

Merry Rawls, president of the Merry Music Company, has a bonus arrangement with the company under which she receives 15% of the net income (after deducting taxes and bonus) each year. For the current year, the net income before deducting either the provision for income taxes or the bonus is $239,800. The bonus is deductible for tax purposes, and the effective tax rate is 40%.

Instructions
(a)   Compute the amount of Merry's bonus.
(b)   Compute the appropriate provision for federal income taxes for the year.
(c)   Recompute the amount of Merry's bonus if the bonus is to be 15% of income after bonus but before tax. (Round to the nearest dollar.)

SOLUTION TO EXERCISE 13-4

(B = bonus; T = taxes)

(a)

$$B = .15 (\$239,800 - B - T)$$
$$T = .40 (\$239,800 - B)$$
$$B = .15 [\$239,800 - B - .4 (\$239,800 - B)]$$
$$B = .15 (\$239,800 - B - \$95,920 + .4B)$$
$$B = .15 (\$143,880 - .6B)$$
$$B = \$21,582 - .09B$$
$$1.09B = \$21,582$$
$$\text{Bonus} = \underline{\$19,800}$$

(b)

$$T = .40 (\$239,800 - B)$$
$$T = .40 (\$239,800 - \$19,800)$$
$$T = .40 (\$220,000)$$
$$\text{Taxes} = \underline{\$88,000}$$

(c)

$$B = .15 (\$239,800 - B)$$
$$B = \$35,970 - .15B$$
$$1.15B = \$35,970$$
$$\text{Bonus} = \underline{\$31,278}$$

TIP: Examine the equation to compute the bonus. Make sure it is consistent with the wording of the agreement. For instance, if the bonus is based on income **after** bonus and **after** taxes, then income must be reduced by both bonus and taxes in your formula (Income - B - T) [see part (a)]. But if the bonus is to be based on income after bonus and before taxes, then taxes are **not** part of your equation [see part (c)].

TIP: Always "prove" the bonus figure computed.

Proof--parts (a) and (b)

Income before bonus and before taxes	$239,800
Bonus	(19,800)
Income before taxes	220,000
Income taxes (40% X $220,000) [agrees with (b)]	(88,000)
Income after bonus and after taxes	132,000
Bonus rate	15%
Bonus [agrees with (a)]	$ 19,800

Proof--part (c)

Income before bonus and before taxes	$239,800
Bonus	31,278
Income before taxes	208,522
Bonus rate	15%
Bonus [agrees with (c)]	$ 31,278

ILLUSTRATION 13-1
ACCOUNTING TREATMENT OF LOSS CONTINGENCIES

Loss Related to	Usually Accrued	Not Accrued	Maybe Accrued*
1. Collectibility of receivables	X		
2. Obligations related to product warranties and product defects	X		
3. Premiums offered to customers	X		
4. Risk of loss or damage of enterprise property by fire, explosion, or other hazards		X	
5. General or unspecified business risks		X	
6. Risk of loss from catastrophes assumed by property and casualty insurance companies including reinsurance companies		X	
7. Threat of expropriation of assets			X
8. Pending or threatened litigation			X
9. Actual or possible claims and assessment**			X
10. Guarantees of indebtedness of others			X
11. Obligations of commercial banks under "standby letters of credit"			X
12. Agreements to repurchase receivables (or the related property) that have been sold			X

* Should be accrued when both criteria are met (probable and reasonably estimable).

**Estimated amounts of losses incurred prior to the balance sheet date but settled subsequently should be accrued as of the balance sheet date.

Source: Kieso and Weygandt, *Intermediate Accounting,* Seventh Edition.

EXERCISE 13-5

Purpose: This exercise will review accounting for compensated absences.

Marsha Diebler Company began operations on January 2, 1991. It employs 9 individuals who work 8-hour days and are paid hourly. Each employee earns 10 paid vacation days and 6 paid sick days annually. Vacation days may be taken after January 15 of the year following the year in which they are earned. Sick days may be taken as soon as they are earned; unused sick days accumulate. Additional information is as follows:

Actual Hourly Wage Rate		Vacation Days Used by Each Employee		Sick Days Used by Each Employee	
1991	1992	1991	1992	1991	1992
$6.00	$7.00	0	9	4	5

Marsha Diebler has chosen not to accrue paid sick leave until used, and has chosen to accrue paid vacation time at expected future rates of pay without discounting. The company used the following projected rates to accrue vacation time:

Year in Which Vacation Time Was Earned	Projected Future Pay Rates Used to Accrue Vacation Pay
1991	$6.90
1992	7.60

Instructions
(a) Prepare journal entries to record transactions related to compensated absences during 1991 and 1992.
(b) Compute the amounts of any liability for compensated absences that should be reported on the balance sheet at December 31, 1991 and 1992.

SOLUTION TO EXERCISE 13-5

(a)

1991

To accrue the expense and liability for vacations:	Wages Expense	4,968.00(1)	
	Vacation Wages Payable		4,968.00
To record sick time paid:	Wages Expense	1,728.00(2)	
	Cash		1,728.00
To record vacation time paid:	No entry.		

1992

To accrue the expense and liability for vacations:	Wages Expense	5,472.00(3)	
	Vacation Wages Payable		5,472.00
To record sick time paid:	Wages Expense	2,520.00(4)	
	Cash		2,520.00

To record vacation time paid: Wages Expense   64.80
                                            Vacation Wages Payable   4,471.20(5)
                                            Cash   4,536.00(6)

(1)   9 employees X \$6.90/hr. X 8 hrs./day X 10 days = \$4,968.00.
(2)   9 employees X \$6.00/hr. X 8 hrs./day X 4 days = \$1,728.00.
(3)   9 employees X \$7.60/hr. X 8 hrs./day X 10 days = \$5,472.00.
(4)   9 employees X \$7.00/hr. X 8 hrs./day X 5 days = \$2,520.00.
(5)   9 employees X \$6.90/hr. X 8 hrs./day X 9 days = \$4,471.20.
(6)   9 employees X \$7.00/hr. X 8 hrs./day X 9 days = \$4,536.00.

(b)   Accrued liability at year-end:

	1991 Vacation Wages Payable		1992 Vacation Wages Payable	
Jan. 1 balance	\$ 0		\$4,968.00	
+ accrued	4,968.00		5,472.00	
- paid	(0)		(4,471.20)	
Dec. 31 balance	\$4,968.00	(1)	\$5,968.80	(2)

(1)   9 employees X \$6.90/hr. X 8 hrs./day X 10 days   = \$4,968.00

(2)   9 employees X \$6.90/hr. X 8 hrs./day X 1 day   = \$ 496.80
       9 employees X \$7.60/hr. X 8 hrs./day X 10 days   = \$5,472.00
                                                    \$5,968.80

TIP: The expense and related liability for compensated absences should be recognized in the year in which the employees earn the rights to those absences.

EXERCISE 13-6

Purpose: This exercise will enable you to practice analyzing situations to determine whether a liability should be reported, and if so, at what amount.

John Cleese Inc., a publishing company, is preparing its December 31, 1992, financial statements and must determine the proper accounting treatment for each of the following situations:

1.   Cleese sells subscriptions to several magazines for a one-year, two-year, or three-year period. Cash receipts from subscribers are credited to Magazine Subscriptions Collected In Advance, and this account had a balance of \$2,300,000 at December 31, 1992. Outstanding subscriptions at December 31, 1992, expire as follows:

                              During 1993--\$600,000
                              During 1994-- 500,000
                              During 1995-- 800,000

2. On January 2, 1992, Cleese discontinued collision, fire, and theft coverage on its delivery vehicles and became self-insured for these risks. Actual losses of $50,000 during 1992 were charged to Delivery Expense. The 1991 premium for the discontinued coverage amounted to $80,000, and the controller wants to set up a reserve for self-insurance by a debit to Delivery Expense of $30,000 and a credit to Reserve for Self-insurance of $30,000.

3. A suit for breach of contract seeking damages of $1,000,000 was filed by an author against Cleese on July 1, 1992. The company's legal counsel believes that an unfavorable outcome is probable. A reasonable estimate of the court's award to the plaintiff is in the range between $200,000 and $700,000. No amount within this range is a better estimate of potential damages than any other amount.

4. During December 1992, a competitor company filed suit against Cleese for industrial espionage claiming $1,500,000 in damages. In the opinion of management and company counsel, it is reasonably possible that damages will be awarded to the plaintiff. However, the amount of potential damages awarded to the plaintiff cannot be reasonably estimated.

Instructions

For each of the situations above, prepare the journal entry that should be recorded as of December 31, 1992, or explain why an entry should not be recorded. Show supporting computations in good form.

(AICPA adapted)

SOLUTION TO EXERCISE 13-6

1. Magazine Subscriptions Collected in Advance 400,000
   Magazine Subscriptions Revenue 400,000
   (To adjust the unearned revenue account
   Liability account:

Book balance at December 31, 1992	$2,300,000
Adjusted balance	
($600,000 + $500,000 + $800,000)	1,900,000
Adjustment required	$ 400,000)

2. No entry should be made to accrue for an expense because the absence of insurance coverage does not mean that an asset has been impaired or a liability has been incurred as of the balance sheet date. Cleese may, however, appropriate retained earnings for self-insurance as long as actual costs or losses are not charged to the appropriation of retained earnings and no part of the appropriation is transferred to income. Appropriation of retained earnings and/or disclosure in the notes to the financial statements are not required, but are recommended.

3. Estimated Loss from Pending Lawsuit 200,000
   Estimated Liability from Pending Lawsuit 200,000
   (To record estimated minimum damages on breach-of-contract litigation)

This situation involves a contingent liability. Because it is **probable** that a liability has been incurred and the loss is reasonably estimable, the loss should be accrued. When the expected loss amount is in a range, the best estimate within the range is used for the accrual. When no amount within the range is a better estimate than any other amount, the dollar amount at the low end is accrued and the dollar amount at the high end of the range is disclosed in the notes.

4. No entry should be made for this loss contingency, because it is not probable that an asset has been impaired or a liability has been incurred and the loss cannot be reasonably estimated as of the balance sheet date. The loss contingency should be disclosed in the notes to financial statements because the likelihood of loss is judged to be reasonably possible.

EXERCISE 13-7

Purpose: This exercise will provide an example of accounting for premium claims outstanding.

Jo-Ann Beiler Company includes 1 coupon in each box of soap powder that it packs, and 10 coupons are redeemable for a premium (a kitchen utensil). In 1992, Jo-Ann Beiler Company purchased 8,800 premiums at 88 cents each and sold 110,000 boxes of soap powder at $3.30 per box; 44,000 coupons were presented for redemption in 1992. It is estimated that 60% of the coupons will eventually be presented for redemption.

Instructions
Prepare all the entries that would be made relative to sales of soap powder and to the premium plan in 1992.

SOLUTION TO EXERCISE 13-7

Inventory of Premiums (8,800 X $.88)	7,744	
Cash		7,744
Cash (110,000 X $3.30)	363,000	
Sales		363,000
Premium Expense	3,872	
Inventory of Premiums [(44,000 ÷ 10) X $.88]		3,872
Premium Expense	1,936*	
Estimated Liability for Premiums		1,936

*[(110,000 X 60%) - 44,000] ÷ 10 X $.88 = $1,936

Explanation: The first entry records the purchase of 8,800 kitchen utensils which will be used as premiums. The second entry records the sales of soap powder (110,000 boxes). The third entry records the redemption of 44,000 coupons with customers receiving one premium for every 10 coupons. The cost of the 4,400 kitchen utensils distributed to these customers is recorded by a debit to expense. The fourth entry is an adjusting entry at the end of the accounting period to accrue the cost of additional premiums included in boxes of soap sold this period that are likely to be redeemed in future periods. This is an application of the matching principle. The expense of a premium should be recognized in the same period as the related revenue which, in this case, is from the sale of soap boxes containing the coupons that customers will redeem for a premium.

EXERCISE 13-8

<u>Purpose</u>: This exercise will provide an example of the journal entries involved in accounting for a warranty that is included with the sale of a product (warranty is not sold separately). Two methods are examined--the cash basis and the expense warranty method (an accrual method).

Colleen Mahla Corporation sells portable computers under a two-year warranty contract that requires the corporation to replace defective parts and to provide the necessary repair labor. During 1991 the corporation sells for cash 300 computers at a unit price of $2,500. On the basis of past experience, the two-year warranty costs are estimated to be $110 for parts and $130 for labor per unit. (For simplicity, assume that all sales occurred on December 31, 1991.)

Instructions
(a) Record any necessary journal entries in 1991, applying the cash basis method.
(b) Record any necessary journal entries in 1991, applying the expense warranty accrual method.
(c) What liability relative to these transactions would appear on the December 31, 1991 balance sheet and how would it be classified if the cash basis method is applied?
(d) What liability relative to these transactions would appear on the December 31, 1991 balance sheet and how would it be classified if the expense warranty accrual method is applied?

In 1992 the actual warranty costs to Colleen Mahla Corporation were $15,300 for parts and $17,800 for labor.
(e) Record any necessary journal entries in 1992, applying the cash basis method.
(f) Record any necessary journal entries in 1992, applying the expense warranty accrual method.
(g) Under what conditions is it acceptable to use the cash basis method? Explain.

SOLUTION TO EXERCISE 13-8

(a) Cash (300 X $2,500) 750,000
       Sales of Computers 750,000

(b) Cash (300 X $2,500) 750,000
       Sales of Computers 750,000

    Warranty Expense [300 X ($110 + $130)]..................................... 72,000
       Estimated Liability Under Warranties 72,000

(c) No liability would be disclosed under the cash basis method relative to future costs due to warranties on past sales.

(d) Current Liabilities:
    Estimated Liability Under Warranties $36,000

    Long-term Liabilities:
    Estimated Liability Under Warranties $36,000

(e) Warranty Expense 33,100
       Parts Inventory 15,300
       Wages Payable 17,800

(f) Estimated Liability Under Warranties 33,100
         Parts Inventory 15,300
         Wages Payable 17,800

(g) The cash basis is used for income tax purposes. Theoretically, the accrual basis (expense warranty method in this case) should be used for financial reporting purposes. However, the cash basis is often justifiably used for accounting purposes when warranty costs are immaterial or when the warranty period is relatively short.

EXERCISE 13-9

Purpose: This exercise will exemplify the journal entries involved in accounting for a warranty that is sold separately from the related product. The sales warranty method is used for such situations.

Terence Trent Company sells electric typewriters for $700 each and offers to each customer a three-year warranty contract for $75 that requires the company to perform periodic services and to replace defective parts. During 1991, the company sold 300 typewriters and 250 warranty contracts for cash. It estimates the three-year warranty costs as $20 for parts and $40 for labor and accounts for warranties on the sales warranty accrual method. Assume all sales occurred on December 31, 1991, and revenue on the sale of the warranties is to be recognized on a straight-line basis over the life of the contract.

Instructions
(a) Record any necessary journal entries in 1991.
(b) What liability relative to these transactions would appear on the December 31, 1991, balance sheet and how would it be classified?

In 1992, Terence Trent Company incurred actual costs relative to 1991 typewriter warranty sales of $2,000 for parts and $3,000 for labor.
(c) Record any necessary journal entries in 1992 relative to 1991 typewriter warranties.
(d) What amounts relative to the 1991 typewriter warranties would appear on the December 31, 1992, balance sheet and how would they be classified?

SOLUTION TO EXERCISE 13-9

(a) Cash 228,750
         Sales of Typewriters (300 X $700) 210,000
         Unearned Warranty Revenue (250 X $75) 18,750

(b) Current Liabilities:
         Unearned Warranty Revenue $ 6,250
             (Note: Warranty costs are assumed to be incurred equally
                     over the three-year period)

     Long-term Liabilities:
         Unearned Warranty Revenue $12,500

(c) Warranty Expense	5,000	
Parts Inventory..		2,000
Wages Payable		3,000
Unearned Warranty Revenue	6,250	
Revenue from Warranties		6,250

(d) Current Liabilities:

Unearned Warranty Revenue$6,250

Long-term Liabilities:

Unearned Warranty Revenue$6,250

ANALYSIS OF MULTIPLE-CHOICE TYPE QUESTIONS

Question

1. Included in Arnold Company's liability accounts at December 31, 1992 was the following:

    12% Note payable issued in 1990 for cash and due in May 1993 $2,000,000

    On February 1, 1993, Arnold issued $5,000,000 of five-year bonds with the intention of using part of the bond proceeds to liquidate the $2,000,000 note payable maturing in May. On March 2, 1993, Arnold used $2,000,000 of the bond proceeds to liquidate the note payable. Arnold's December 31, 1992 balance sheet is being issued on March 15, 1993. How much of the $2,000,000 note payable should be classified as a current liability on the balance sheet?
    a. $0.
    b. $800,000.
    c. $1,000,000.
    d. $2,000,000.

Solution = a.

Explanation and Approach: Mentally review the definition of a current liability and the guidelines for reporting short-term debt expected to be refinanced. At the date the balance sheet is issued, we have evidence of the intent and ability to refinance the debt on a long-term basis. That evidence is the post balance sheet issuance of long-term debt securities. Therefore, the $2,000,000 note payable should be classified as a long-term liability.

Question

2. D. Scott Corporation provides a two-year warranty with the sale of its product. Scott estimates that warranty costs will equal 4% of the selling price the first year after sale and 6% of the selling price the second year after the sale. The following data are available:

	1991	1992
Sales	$400,000	$500,000
Actual warranty expenditures	10,000	38,000

The balance of the warranty liability at December 31, 1992 should be
a. $12,000.
b. $42,000.
c. $44,000.
d. $50,000.

Solution = b.

Explanation and Approach: Draw a T-account and enter the amounts that would be reflected in the account and determine its balance.

Warranty Obligation

(2)	10,000	(1)	40,000
(4)	38,000	(3)	50,000
		Balance, 12/31/92	42,000

(1) $400,000 X (4% + 6%) = $40,000 expense for 1991.
    The total warranty cost related to the products sold during 1991 should be recognized in the period of sale (matching principle).
(2) Given data. Actual expenditures during 1991.
(3) $500,000 X (4% + 6%) = $50,000 expense for 1992.
(4) Given data. Actual expenditures during 1992.

Question
3.   A contingent loss which is judged to be reasonably possible and estimable should be

	Accrued	Disclosed
a.	Yes	Yes
b.	Yes	No
c.	No	Yes
d.	No	No

Solution = c.

Explanation: A contingent loss that is probable and estimable is to be accrued. A contingent loss that is reasonably possible should be disclosed, but it should not be accrued. A contingent loss that is remotely possible can be ignored (unless it is one of the items on a list of contingencies that must always be disclosed, regardless of the likelihood of loss occurrence, such as guarantees of indebtedness of others).

Question
4.   Garth Brooks, a manager of a local business, is to receive an annual bonus equal to 10% of the company's income in excess of $100,000 before income tax but after deduction of the bonus. If income before income tax and bonus is $820,000 and the tax rate is 40%, the amount of the bonus would be
a. $22,800.
b. $36,981.
c. $65,455.
d. $72,000.

Solution = c.

Explanation and Approach: Carefully write an equation that expresses the agreement. Notice what should be deducted from income before the bonus percentage is applied--$100,000 and the bonus (but **not** taxes). Solve for bonus. Prove your answer.

$$B = 10\% (\$820,000 - \$100,000 - B)$$
$$B = \$82,000 - \$10,000 - .1B$$
$$1.1B = \$72,000$$
$$B = \$72,000 \div 1.1$$
$$B = \underline{\$65,455}$$

Proof:
$$\begin{array}{r} \$820,000 \\ - 100,000 \\ \underline{- 65,455} \\ 654,545 \\ \underline{10\%} \\ \underline{\$ 65,455} \end{array}$$

Question

5.   Martha's Boutique sells gift certificates. These gift certificates have no expiration date. Data for the current year are as follows:

Gift certificates outstanding, January 1	$225,000
Gift certificates sold	750,000
Gift certificates redeemed	660,000
Gross profit expressed as percentage of sales	40%

At December 31, Martha should report unearned revenue of
a. $90,000.
b. $126,000.
c. $261,000.
d. $315,000.

Solution = d.

Explanation and Approach: Draw a T-account for the liability and enter the data given.

Gift Certificates Outstanding

Redeemed	660,000	Beginning Balance	225,000
		Sold	750,000
		Ending Balance	315,000

The gross profit percentage is not used in the solution for the balance of unearned revenue.

CHAPTER 14

LONG-TERM LIABILITIES

OVERVIEW

Sources of assets include current liabilities, long-term liabilities, and owners' equity. Liabilities are considered a "temporary" source of assets, whereas owners' equity is a more "permanent" source of resources. When a company borrows money, it does so with the expectation of using the borrowed funds to acquire assets that can be used to generate more income. The objective is to generate an amount of additional income which exceeds the cost of borrowing the funds (interest).

Long-term debt consists of probable future sacrifices of economic benefits arising from present obligations that are not payable within a year or the operating cycle of the business, whichever is longer. Bonds payable, long-term notes payable, mortgages payable, pension liabilities, and lease obligations are examples of long-term liabilities. This chapter will focus on the first two of these.

Although the subject of accounting for bonds is included in the principles of accounting course, many intermediate students don't remember the details of the procedures and look upon this topic as one of the most difficult they have encountered. Perhaps they have problems with the material because they try to memorize their way through the topic. As a result, it is imperative that you think about the time value of money concepts introduced in Chapter 6 and grasp how they are applied in the computations involved in accounting for long-term debt. When you see the logic and rationale of the accounting procedures, you will find it easier to recall these guidelines years from now.

TIPS ON CHAPTER TOPICS

TIP: The denomination of a bond is called the **face value.** Synonymous terms are **par value, principal amount, maturity value,** and **face amount.**

TIP: Bond prices are quoted in terms of percentage of par. Thus a bond with a par value of $4,000 and a price quote of 102 is currently selling for a price of $4,080 (102% of $4,000). A bond with a quote of 100 is selling for its par value.

TIP: The bond contract is called an **indenture.** This term is often confused with the term debenture. A **debenture** bond is an unsecured bond.

TIP: The interest rate written in the bond indenture and ordinarily appearing on the bond certificate is known as the **stated rate.** Synonymous terms are **coupon rate, nominal rate,** and **contract rate.**

TIP: The rate of interest actually earned by bondholders is called the **effective, yield,** or **market rate.**

TIP: A bond's **issuance price** is determined by the present value of all of the future cash flows promised by the bond indenture. The future cash flows include the face value and interest payments. The bond's present value is determined by using the market rate of interest at the date of issuance. An excess of the issuance price over par is called a **premium;** an excess of par value over the issuance price is called a **discount.**

TIP: In computing the present value of a bond's (1) maturity value and (2) interest payments, the **same** interest rate is used. That rate is the effective interest rate on a per interest period basis. As an example, if a ten-year bond has a stated rate of 10%, pays interest semiannually, and is issued to yield 12%, a 6% rate is used to perform all of the present value calculations.

TIP: Bond prices vary inversely with changes in the market rate of interest. This means that as the market rate of interest goes down, bond prices go up; and as the market rate of interest goes up, bond prices go down. It also means that at the date of issuance, if the market rate of interest is below the stated rate, the price will be above par; likewise, if the market rate is above the stated rate, the issuance price will be below par. Hence, a premium or a discount is an adjustment to interest via an adjustment to price.

TIP: Interest payments on notes payable are generally made on a monthly or quarterly basis. Interest payments on bonds payable are usually made semiannually. Despite these common practices, interest rates generally are expressed on an annual basis. Therefore, care must be taken that the annual rate be converted to a "rate per period" before other computations are performed.

TIP: A bond's **carrying value (book value, carrying amount)** is equal to the (1) par value plus any unamortized premium, or (2) par value minus any unamortized discount. When the effective interest method of amortization is used, the bond's carrying value will equal its present value (assuming the amortization is up to date). A bond's **net carrying value** is equal to its carrying value minus any related unamortized bond issuance costs.

TIP: An **interest payment** promised by a bond is computed by multiplying the bond's par value by its stated interest rate. This amount is often referred to as the **cash interest** or **stated interest.** The **effective interest expense** (interest expense using the effective interest method of amortization) for the same period of time is determined by multiplying the bond's carrying value at the beginning of the period by the effective interest rate. The difference between the interest payment (cash interest) and the effective interest expense for a period is the amount of premium or discount amortization for the period. The amount of amortization for a period causes the carrying value to change.

TIP: Using the **straight-line method of amortization,** interest expense is determined by either adding the amount of discount amortization to the cash interest or deducting the amount of premium amortization from the cash interest. The periodic amount of amortization is determined by dividing the issuance premium or discount by the number of periods in the bond's life.

TIP: The **life** of a bond is measured by the time between the date of issuance and the date of maturity. The bond's life is shorter than the term of the bond if the bond is issued on a date later than it is dated.

TIP: Regardless of whether the straight-line method of amortization or the effective interest method of amortization is used, the following will occur:
1. The amount of cash interest (stated interest) is a constant amount each period.
2. The bond's carrying amount increases over the bond's life if it is issued at a discount, due to the amortization of the discount.
3. The bond's carrying amount decreases over the bond's life if it is issued at a premium, due to the amortization of the premium.

TIP: If the straight-line method of amortization is used, the following relationships will exist:
1. The amount of amortization is a constant amount each period.
2. The amount of interest expense is a constant amount each period.

TIP: If the effective interest method of amortization is used, the following relationships will exist:
1. The interest rate is constant each period.
2. The interest expense is an increasing amount each period if the bond is issued at a discount (because a constant rate is applied to an increasing carrying amount each period).
3. The interest expense is a decreasing amount each period if the bond is issued at a premium (because a constant rate is applied to a decreasing carrying amount each period).
4. The amount of amortization increases each period because the difference between the effective interest expense and the cash interest widens each period.

TIP: The pattern of interest expense using the effective interest method may be compared to the pattern of interest expense using the straight-line method for both a bond issued at a discount and a bond issued at a premium by reference to the graph in **Illustration 14-1**. The relationship between interest expense and cash interest should also be noted. The difference between the cash interest and interest expense for a period is the amount of amortization for the period. The pattern of the periodic amount of amortization is also depicted by the graph.

TIP: The Discount on Bonds Payable account is a contra liability account so its balance should be deducted from Bonds Payable on the balance sheet. The Premium on Bonds Payable account is an adjunct type valuation account so its balance should be added to the balance of Bonds Payable on the balance sheet. Unamortized Bond Issuance Costs are to be classified as a deferred charge in the "Other Assets" classification on the balance sheet; they may be amortized over the bond's life using the straight-line method.

TIP: The **effective interest method** of amortization is sometimes called the **interest method** or the **present value** method or the **effective method**.

TIP: If you use the effective interest rate (at the date of a bond's issuance) to compute the (1) present value of the bond at the beginning of a given period, and (2) the present value of the same bond at the end of the given period, the difference between the two present value figures equals the amortization of the bond's premium or discount during that same period. This is true because the effective interest method results in reporting the present value of the liability at a balance sheet date. That's why the effective interest method is the only method that is GAAP.

TIP: When the accounting period ends on a date other than an interest date, the amortization schedule for a bond or a note payable is unaffected by this fact. That is, the schedule is prepared and computations are made according to the bond periods, ignoring the details of the accounting period. The interest expense amounts shown in the amortization schedule are then apportioned to the appropriate accounting period(s). As an example, if the interest expense for the six months ending April 30, 1993, is $120,000, then $40,000 of that amount would go on the income statement for the 1992 calendar year and $80,000 of it should be reflected on the income statement for the 1993 calendar year.

ILLUSTRATION 14-1
GRAPH TO DEPICT INTEREST PATTERNS FOR BONDS

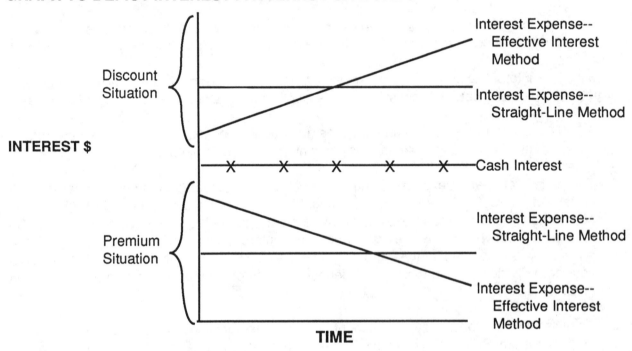

ILLUSTRATION 14-2
FORMATS FOR COMMON COMPUTATIONS INVOLVING BONDS PAYABLE

1. Cash Interest Per Period.

        Par value   Cash interest is always a
   X   Stated rate of interest per period   constant amount each period.
   =   Cash interest per period

2. Interest Expense Using Straight-line Amortization Method.

        Cash interest for the period   Interest expense is a
    +   Discount amortization for the period   constant amount each period
 OR -   Premium amortization for the period   using this method.
    =   Interest expense for the period

3. Amortization Amount Using Straight-line Method.
    Issuance premium or discount ÷ Periods in bond's life = Amortization per period.

4. Interest Expense Using Effective Interest Method.
          Carrying value at the beginning of the period
      X <u>Effective rate of interest per interest period</u>
      = Interest expense for the interest period

The carrying value changes each interest period so the interest expense changes each period.

5. Amortization Amount Using Effective Interest Method.
          Interest expense for the interest period
      - <u>Cash interest for the interest period</u>
      = Amortization of discount for the interest period

Interest expense is greater than cash interest for bonds issued at a discount.

OR

      Cash interest for the interest period
  - <u>Interest expense for the interest period</u>
  = Amortization of premium for the interest period

Cash interest is greater than interest expense for bonds issued at a premium.

6. Carrying Value and Net Carrying Value.
          Par value
      - Unamortized discount
    OR + <u>Unamortized premium</u>
      = Carrying value
      - <u>Unamortized debt issue costs</u>
      = Net carrying amount

The process of amortization decreases the unamortized amount of discount or premium; hence the carrying amount moves toward the par value.

7. Gain or Loss on Redemption.
          Net carrying amount
      - <u>Redemption price</u>
      = Gain if positive, that is, if net carrying value is the greater.
      = Loss if negative, that is, if redemption price is the greater.

ILLUSTRATION 14-3
COMPUTATION AND PROOF OF BOND ISSUANCE PRICE

Guemple Company issues a 5-year bond on January 1, 1992 (maturity date is January 1, 1997), with a stated interest rate of 6%. The market rate of interest at the date of issuance is 5%, the par value is $1,000, and interest is due annually on January 1.

The bond is a promise to pay $1,000 on January 1, 1997, and $60 (6% X $1,000) every January 1 from January 1, 1992 to January 1, 1997. The price of the bond is determined by the present value of all future cash flows related to the bond. The present value of the bond is found by discounting all of the promised payments at the market rate of interest (5%). This process is illustrated by the following:

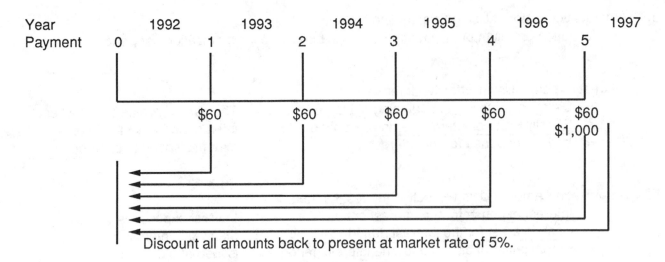

Year	1992	1993	1994	1995	1996	1997
Payment	0	1	2	3	4	5

$60 $60 $60 $60 $60

$1,000

Discount all amounts back to present at market rate of 5%.

Present value of $1,000 due in 5 periods at 5% interest ($1,000 X .78353).	$ 783.53
Present value of an ordinary annuity of $60 per period for 5 years at 5% interest ($60 X 4.32948)	259.77
Total present value	$1,043.30

Note: The factor of .78353 was derived from the Present Value of 1 table and the factor of 4.32948 was derived from the Present Value of an Ordinary Annuity of 1 table.

Thus, the bond price would be $1,043.30. Theoretically, this is the sum that would be required to be invested now at 5% compounded annually (market rate) to allow for the periodic (annual in this case) withdrawal of $60 (stated amount of interest) at the end of each of 5 years and the withdrawal of $1,000 at the end of 5 years. The following is proof that $1,043.30 is the amount required in this case.

Jan. 1, 1992	$1,043.30		$1,043.30	
	+ 52.17	interest at 5%	.05	market rate
	1,095.47		52.1650	effective interest
1st interest	- 60.00			
payment on 1/1/93	1,035.47		1,035.47	
	+ 51.77		.05	
	1,087.24		51.7735	
2nd interest	- 60.00			
payment on 1/1/94	1,027.24		1,027.24	
	+ 51.36		.05	
	1,078.60		51.3620	
3rd interest	- 60.00			
payment on 1/1/95	1,018.60		1,018.60	
	+ 50.93		.05	
	1,069.53		50.9300	
4th interest	- 60.00			
payment on 1/1/96	1,009.53		1,009.53	
	+ 50.48		.05	
	1,060.01		50.4765	
5th interest	- 60.00			
payment on 1/1/97				
Principal payment	1,000.00			
	.01	Rounding error		

EXERCISE 14-1

Purpose: This exercise will illustrate (1) the computations and journal entries throughout a bond's life for a bond issued at a discount and (2) the accounting required when bonds are called prior to their maturity date.

Arnold Howell Company issued bonds with the following details:

Face value	$100,000
Stated interest rate	7%
Market interest rate	10%
Maturity date	January 1, 1996
Date of issuance	January 1, 1993
Bond issue costs	$8,000
Call price	102
Interest payments due	Annually on January 1
Method of Amortization	Effective Interest

Instructions
(a)   Compute the amount of issuance premium or discount.
(b)   Prepare the journal entry for the issuance of the bonds.
(c)   Prepare the amortization schedule for these bonds.
(d)   Prepare all of the journal entries (subsequent to the issuance date) for 1993 and 1994 that relate to these bonds. Assume the accounting period coincides with the calendar year. Assume reversing entries are not used.
(e)   Prepare the journal entry to record the retirement of the bonds assuming they are called on January 1, 1995.

SOLUTION TO EXERCISE 14-1

(a) $100,000 par X 7% stated rate = $7,000 annual cash interest.

Factor for present value of a single sum, i = 10%, n = 3	.75132
Factor for present value of an ordinary annuity, i = 10%, n = 3	2.48685

$100,000 X .75132 =	$75,132.00
$7,000 X 2.48685 =	17,407.95
Issuance price	$92,539.95

Face value	$100,000.00
Issuance price	92,539.95
Discount on bonds payable	$ 7,460.05

(b)

Cash ($92,539.95 - $8,000.00)	$84,539.95	
Discount on Bonds Payable	7,460.05	
Unamortized Bond Issue Costs	8,000.00	
Bonds Payable		100,000.00

Explanation and Approach: Always start with the easiest part of a journal entry. The issuance of a bond is **always** recorded by a credit to the Bonds Payable account for the par value of the bonds ($100,000 in this case). Because the issuance price is less than par, a contra type valuation account must be established; it is titled Discount on Bonds Payable and is debited for the issuance discount of $7,460.05. The $8,000 issuance costs are to be amortized over the periods benefited by the loan in order to comply with the matching principle; hence they are initially charged to an asset account. Cash was received for the issuance price less the issuance costs (fees to attorneys, accountants, printers, and underwriters) so debit Cash for the net proceeds of $84,539.95.

TIP: The Unamortized Bond Issue Costs account can be titled Bond Issue Costs. The Discount on Bonds Payable account is sometimes called Unamortized Bond Discount. Regardless of whether the word unamortized appears in the account titles or not, the balances of these accounts at a balance sheet date (after adjustments) represent the unamortized amounts.

(c)

Date	7% Stated Interest	10% Interest Expense	Discount Amortization	Carrying Value
1/1/93				$ 92,539.95
1/1/94	$ 7,000.00	$ 9,254.00	$2,254.00	94,793.95
1/1/95	7,000.00	9,479.40	2,479.40	97,273.35
1/1/96	7,000.00	9,726.65[a]	2,726.65	100,000.00
	$21,000.00	$28,460.05	$7,460.05	

[a]Includes rounding error of 69¢.

Explanation: Stated interest is determined by multiplying the par value ($100,000) by the contract rate of interest (7%). Interest expense is computed by multiplying the carrying value at the beginning of the interest period by the effective interest rate. The amount of discount amortization for the period is the excess of the interest expense over the stated interest (cash interest) amount. The carrying value at an interest payment date is the carrying value at the beginning of the interest period plus the discount amortization for the period.

TIP: The amount of interest expense of $9,479.40 appearing on the "1/1/95" payment line is the amount of interest expense for the interest period ending on that date. Thus, in this case, $9,479.40 is the interest expense for the twelve months preceding the date 1/1/95 which would be the calendar year of 1994.

TIP: Any rounding error should be plugged to (included in) the interest expense amount for the last period. Otherwise, there would forever be a small balance left in the Discount on Bonds Payable account long after the bonds were extinguished.

TIP: Notice that the total interest expense ($28,460.05) over the three-year period equals the total cash interest ($21,000.00) plus the total issuance discount ($7,460.05). Thus, you can see that the issuance discount represents an additional amount of interest to be recognized over the life of the bonds.

(d)   December 31, 1993

Interest Expense	9,254.00	
Interest Payable		7,000.00
Discount on Bonds Payable		2,254.00

Bond Issue Expense	2,666.67	
Unamortized Bond Issue Costs		2,666.67
($8,000.00 ÷ 3 = $2,666.67)		

January 1, 1994

Interest Payable	7,000.00	
Cash		7,000.00

December 31, 1994

Interest Expense	9,479.40	
Interest Payable		7,000.00
Discount on Bonds Payable		2,479.40
Bond Issue Expense	2,666.67	
Unamortized Bond Issue Costs		2,666.67

(e)
January 1, 1995

Interest Payable	7,000.00	
Bonds Payable	100,000.00	
Loss on Redemption of Bonds	7,393.31	
Discount on Bonds Payable		2,726.65
Unamortized Bond Issue Costs		2,666.66
Cash ($102,000 + $7,000)		109,000.00

($7,460.05 - $2,254.00 - $2,479.40 = $2,726.65 unamortized discount)
($8,000.00 - $2,666.67 - $2,666.67 = $2,666.66 unamortized issue costs)
($100,000.00 X 102% = $102,000.00 price to retire)
($100,000.00 - $2,726.65 = $97,273.35 carrying value)
($97,273.35 - $2,666.66 = $94,606.69 net carrying value)
($102,000.00 - $94,606.69 = $7,393.31 loss)

TIP: There was a call premium (amount in excess of par required) of $2,000.00 in this situation.

TIP: Gains or losses on extinguishment of debt are to be classified as extraordinary items on the income statement (even though they may not meet the criteria of being unusual in nature and infrequent in occurrence) because of the guidelines contained in *SFAS No. 4.*

EXERCISE 14-2

Purpose: This exercise will serve as an example of bonds issued between interest payment dates and the straight-line method of amortization.

Presented below are selected transactions on the books of the Peter Pan Tools Corporation.

May 1, 1991   Bonds payable with a par value of $700,000, which are dated January 1, 1991, are sold at 104 plus accrued interest. They are coupon bonds, bear interest at 12% (payable annually at January 1), and mature January 1, 2001.

Dec. 31   Adjusting entries are made to record the accrued interest on the bonds, and the amortization of the proper amount of premium. The straight-line method of amortization is used.

Jan. 1, 1992   Interest on the bonds is paid.
April 1   Bonds with par value of $420,000 are purchased at 102 plus accrued interest, and retired. (The company's policy is to record bond premium amortization only at the end of each year.)
Dec. 31   Adjusting entries are made to record the accrued interest on the bonds, and the proper amount of premium amortization.

Instructions

Prepare journal entries for the transactions above. Assume reversing entries are not used and collections of accrued interest are recorded in the Interest Expense account.

SOLUTION TO EXERCISE 14-2

May 1, 1991

Cash	756,000.00	
Bonds Payable		700,000.00
Premium on Bonds Payable		28,000.00
Interest Expense		28,000.00

($700,000 X 104% = $728,000 issuance price)
($728,000 - $700,000 par = $28,000 premium)
($700,000 X 12% X 4/12 = $28,000 accrued interest)
($728,000 + $28,000 = $756,000 total proceeds)

December 31, 1991

Interest Expense...	84,000.00	
Interest Payable		84,000.00

($700,000 X 12% = $84,000 interest for one year)

Premium on Bonds Payable	1,931.03	
Interest Expense		1,931.03

(From May 1, 1991 to January 1, 2001 = 116 months for the bond's total life) ($28,000 X 8/116 = $1,931.03 amortization of premium)

January 1, 1992

Interest Payable...	84,000.00	
Cash		84,000.00

April 1, 1992

Bonds Payable	420,000.00	
Premium on Bonds Payable	15,206.90*	
Interest Expense ($420,000 X 12% X 3/12)	12,600.00	
Cash ($420,000 X 102% + $12,600)		441,000.00
Gain on Retirement of Bonds		6,806.90**

*[($420,000 ÷ $700,000) X $28,000 X 105/116 = $15,206.90]

**		
Par value of bonds redeemed	$420,000.00	
Unamortized premium on bonds redeemed	15,206.90	
Carrying value of bonds redeemed	435,206.90	
Reacquisition price ($420,000 X 102%)	(428,400.00)	
Gain on redemption	$ 6,806.90	

December 31, 1992

Interest Expense ($280,000 X 12%)	33,600.00	
Interest Payable		33,600.00
Premium on Bonds Payable	1,593.10	
Interest Expense		1,593.10

Amortization per year on $280,000 bonds
   ($28,000 X 12/116 X .4)* $1,158.62
Amortization on $420,000 bonds for 3 mo.
   ($28,000 X 3/116 X .6)** 434.48
Total premium amortization for 1992...............$1,593.10

*$700,000 - $420,000 = $280,000; $280,000 ÷ $700,000 = .4
**$420,000 ÷ $700,000 = .6

TIP: The computations are tedious in this exercise because the bonds were issued between interest payment dates and only a portion of them were retired. Because the bonds were dated January 1, 1991, but were not sold until May 1, 1991, the life of the bonds is 116 months (rather than ten full years or 120 months). The 116 months is used for the allocation of the issuance premium. Because $420,000 par value bonds were retired on April 1, 1992, only $280,000 (or 40%) par value bonds remain at the end of 1992.

EXERCISE 14-3

Purpose: This exercise will illustrate the computation of the bond price when interest is due semiannually. Additionally, it will present the accounting for bonds where the effective interest method of amortization is used and the end of the accounting period does not coincide with the end of an interest period.

P & J Chase Company sells $500,000 of 10% bonds on November 1, 1992. The bonds pay interest on May 1 and November 1 and are to yield 12%. The due date of the bonds is May 1, 1996. The accounting period is the calendar year. No reversing entries are made. Bond premium or discount is to be amortized at interest dates and at year-end.

Instructions
(a) Compute the price of the bonds at the issuance date.
(b) Prepare the amortization schedule for this issue.
(c) Prepare all of the relevant journal entries for this bond issue from the date of issuance through May 1994.

SOLUTION TO EXERCISE 14-3

(a) Factor for present value of a single sum, i = 6%, n = 7   .66506
Factor for present value of an ordinary annuity, i = 6%, n = 7   5.58238
$500,000 X 5% = $25,000 interest per period

$500,000 X .66506 =	$332,530.00
$25,000 X 5.58238 =	139,559.50
Issuance price	$472,089.50

14-11

(b)

Date	5% Stated Interest	6% Interest Expense	Discount Amortization	Carrying Value
11/1/92				$472,089.50
5/1/93	$ 25,000.00	$ 28,325.37	$ 3,325.37	475,414.87
11/1/93	25,000.00	28,524.89	3,524.89	478,939.76
5/1/94	25,000.00	28,736.39	3,736.39	482,676.15
11/1/94	25,000.00	28,960.57	3,960.57	486,636.72
5/1/95	25,000.00	29,198.20	4,198.20	490,834.92
11/1/95	25,000.00	29,450.10	4,450.10	495,285.02
5/1/96	25,000.00	29,714.98*	4,714.98	500,000.00
	$175,000.00	$202,910.50	$27,910.50	

*Includes a rounding error of $2.12.

TIP: There are two interest periods per year; therefore, the stated interest rate per interest period is the annual rate (10%) divided by 2 which is 5%.

TIP: If you round all of your computations to the nearest cent, your rounding error will be small. A small (less than $5.00) rounding error provides some sense of comfort that the amortization schedule is largely correct. A large rounding error (more than $10.00) indicates that one or more mistakes are likely included in the computations within the schedule or in the determination of the starting point (issuance price of the debt).

TIP: The amortization schedule displays amounts according to bond periods. If one interest period overlaps into two different accounting periods, the amount of expense and amortization for that interest period must be appropriately allocated to the respective accounting periods.

TIP: Instead of just memorizing what goes on an amortization schedule, think about the reason the amounts have been included. That will help you to construct a schedule without much effort. In the date column, start with the issuance date, followed by each interest date. The stated interest amount is computed by multiplying the face value of the instrument by the stated rate of interest per period. Interest expense is computed by multiplying the carrying value at the beginning of the period (end of the last line on the amortization schedule) by the market rate of interest per period. The difference between the stated interest and the interest expense for the period is the amount of the amortization for the period. Discount amortization is added to the previous carrying value (or premium amortization is deducted from the previous carrying value) to arrive at the carrying value at the end of the interest period (interest payment date).

(c)   November 1, 1992

Cash	472,089.50	
Discount on Bonds Payable	27,910.50	
Bonds Payable		500,000.00

December 31, 1992

Interest Expense	9,441.79	
Discount on Bonds Payable		1,108.46
Interest Payable		8,333.33

      ($28,325.37 X 2/6 = $9,441.79)
      ($3,325.37 X 2/6 = $1,108.46)
      ($25,000.00 X 2/6 = $8,333.33)

May 1, 1993

Interest Payable	8,333.33	
Interest Expense	18,883.58	
Discount on Bonds Payable		2,216.91
Cash		25,000.00

      ($28,325.37 - $9,441.79 = $18,883.58)
      ($3,325.37 - $1,108.46 = $2,216.91)

November 1, 1993

Interest Expense	28,524.89	
Discount on Bonds Payable		3,524.89
Cash		25,000.00

December 31, 1993

Interest Expense	9,578.80	
Discount on Bonds Payable		1,245.47
Interest Payable		8,333.33

      ($28,736.39 X 2/6 = $9,578.80)
      ($3,736.39 X 2/6 = $1,245.46 + $.01 to balance)
      ($25,000.00 X 2/6 = $8,333.33)

May 1, 1994

Interest Expense	19,157.59	
Interest Payable	8,333.33	
Discount on Bonds Payable		2,490.92
Cash		25,000.00

      ($28,736.39 - $9,578.80 = $19,157.59)
      ($3,736.39 - $1,245.47 = $2,490.92)

EXERCISE 14-4

Purpose: This exercise will enable you to practice identifying data required to perform comput-ations involving bonds payable and applying the terminology associated with bonds.

On January 1, 1992, Tuna Fishery sold $100,000 (face value) worth of bonds. The bonds are dated January 1, 1992 and will mature on January 1, 1997. Interest is paid annually on January 1. Issue costs related to these bonds amounted to $2,000, and these costs are being amortized by the straight-line method. The following amortization schedule was prepared by the accountant for the first 2 years of the life of the bonds:

Date	Stated Interest	Effective Interest	Amortization	Carrying Value of Bonds
1/1/92				$104,212.37
1/1/93	$7,000.00	$6,252.74	$747.26	103,465.11
1/1/94	7,000.00	6,207.91	792.09	102,673.02

Instructions

On the basis of the information above, answer the following questions (round your answers to the nearest cent or percent) and explain the reasoning or computations, as appropriate:

(a) What is the nominal or stated rate of interest for this bond issue?

(b) What is the effective or market rate of interest for this bond issue?

(c) Prepare the journal entry to record the sale of the bond issue on January 1, 1992, including the issue costs.

(d) Prepare the appropriate entry(ies) at December 31, 1994, the end of the accounting year.

(e) Show how the account balances related to the bond issue will be presented on the December 31, 1994 balance sheet. Indicate the major classification(s) involved.

(f) What is the book value of the bonds at December 31, 1994?

(g) What is the net book value of the bonds at December 31, 1994?

(h) If the bonds are retired for $100,500 (excluding interest) at January 1, 1995, will the bonds be retired at a gain or a loss? What is the amount of that gain or loss? Where will it be reported on the income statement for the year ending December 31, 1995?

SOLUTION TO EXERCISE 14-4

(a) Stated interest = Stated rate of interest X Par
$7,000 = Stated rate of interest X $100,000
$7,000 ÷ $100,000 = Stated rate of interest
7% = Stated rate of interest

(b) Effective interest = Market rate X Carrying value at beginning of period
$6,252.74 = Market rate X $104,212.37
$6,252.74 ÷ $104,212.37 = Market rate
6% = Market rate

(c)

Cash		102,212.37	
Unamortized Bond Issue Costs		2,000.00	
Bonds Payable			100,000.00
Premium on Bonds Payable			4,212.37

(d)

Interest Expense		6,160.38	
Premium on Bonds Payable		839.62	
Interest Payable			7,000.00
($102,673.02 X 6% = $6,160.38)			
Bond Issue Expense		400	
Unamortized Bond Issue Costs			400

(e) Other assets
        Unamortized bond issue costs $800

Long-term liabilities
    Bonds payable, 7%, due 1/1/97 $100,000.00
    Unamortized premium*   1,833.40
                                              $101,833.40

*$4,212.37 - $747.26 - $792.09 - $839.62 = $1,833.40.

(f) $101,833.40 [See solution for part (e).]
        Book value is another name for carrying value.
        The amount, $101,833.40, can also be computed by:

Carrying value at 1/1/94 per schedule	$102,673.02
Amortization for 1994 (part d)	(839.62)
Carrying value at 12/31/94	$101,833.40

(g)

Bonds payable balance	$100,000.00
Premium on bonds payable balance	1,833.40
Book value	101,833.40
Unamortized bond issue costs	(800.00)*
Net book value at 12/31/94	$101,033.40

*[$2,000 - 3($400) = $800]

(h)   Gain. A gain will result because the retirement price is less than the net carrying value at the date of retirement.

Net carrying value at 1/1/95 [part (g)]	$101,033.40
Retirement price	100,500.00
Gain on retirement of debt	$ 533.40

This gain from retirement of debt should be classified as an extraordinary item on the income statement; therefore, it is to be reported net of any related income tax effect.

EXERCISE 14-5

Purpose: This exercise will illustrate the accounting for a transfer of noncash assets to settle a debt obligation in a troubled debt situation.

Navajo Co. owes $180,000 plus $14,400 of accrued interest to Mohawk, Inc. The debt is a 10-year, 8% note. Because Navajo Co. is in financial trouble, Mohawk, Inc. agrees to accept some property and cancel the entire debt. The property has a cost of $150,000, accumulated depreciation of $80,000, and a fair market value of $110,000.

Instructions
(a)   Prepare the journal entry on Navajo's books for the debt settlement.
(b)   Prepare the journal entry on Mohawk's books for the debt settlement.

SOLUTION TO EXERCISE 14-5

(a) <u>Navajo's entry:</u>

Notes Payable	180,000	
Interest Payable	14,400	
Accumulated Depreciation	80,000	
Property		150,000
Gain on Property Disposition (Not extraordinary)		40,000*
Gain on Settlement (Extraordinary)		84,400**

*$110,000 - ($150,000 - $80,00) = $40,000
**($180,000 + $14,400) - $110,000 = $84,400

(b) <u>Mohawk's entry:</u>

Property	110,000	
Allowance for Doubtful Accounts	84,400	
(or Loss on Settlement of Receivable)		
Notes Receivable		180,000
Interest Receivable		14,400

<u>Explanation to (a):</u> The debtor is required to determine the excess of the carrying amount of the payable ($180,000 + $14,400 = $194,400) over the fair value of the assets transferred ($110,000) and report that difference as an extraordinary gain ($84,400). The difference between the fair value of those assets and their carrying amounts is to be recognized as a gain or loss on disposition of assets. In this case, the fair value of $110,000 exceeds the carrying amount of $70,000; therefore, a gain of $40,000 is to be recognized. Although the gain on troubled debt restructuring is to be classified as an extraordinary item, the gain (or loss) from disposition of assets is to be classified as other revenues and gains (or other expenses and losses) on the debtor's income statement.

<u>Approach to (a):</u> (1) Begin with the easiest part of the journal entry. Remove the debt amounts by a debit to Notes Payable for $180,000 and a debit to Interest Payable for $14,400. (2) Remove the carrying value of the property by a debit to Accumulated Depreciation for $80,000 and a credit to Property for $150,000 cost. (3) Compute and record the gain from settlement ($84,400 credit) and, (4) compute and record the gain from disposition of assets ($40,000). (5) Double check the entry to make sure it balances.

<u>Explanation to (b):</u> The creditor is required to determine the excess of the carrying amount of the receivable over the fair value of the assets being transferred to the creditor and record it as a charge against the Allowance for Doubtful Accounts account or to a loss account (such a loss is not to be classified as an extraordinary item).

<u>Approach to (b):</u> (1) Remove the carrying amount of the receivable from the accounts by a credit to Notes Receivable for $180,000 and a credit to Interest Receivable for $14,400. (2) Record the acquisition of the property by a debit to Property for its fair value of $110,000. (3) Record the loss on settlement of $84,400 by a debit to Allowance for Doubtful Accounts or to a loss account. (4) Double check the entry to make sure it balances.

EXERCISE 14-6

Purpose: This exercise will illustrate the accounting for a troubled debt restructuring involving a modification of terms of an existing debt arrangement.

Pawnee Corp. owes $150,000 plus $15,000 of accrued interest to Mohawk Trust Co. The debt is a 10-year, 10% note due December 31, 1992. Because Pawnee Corp. is in financial trouble, Mohawk agrees to extend the maturity date to December 31, 1994, reduce the interest rate to 4%, payable annually on December 31 and forgive the accrued interest.

Instructions
(a) Prepare the journal entries on Pawnee's books on December 31, 1992, 1993, and 1994.
(b) Prepare the journal entries on Mohawk's books on December 31, 1992, 1993, and 1994.

SOLUTION TO EXERCISE 14-6

(a) Pawnee's entries:

1992	Interest Payable	15,000	
	Gain on Restructuring (Extraordinary)		3,000
	Notes Payable		12,000
1993	Notes Payable	6,000	
	Cash (4% X $150,000)		6,000
1994	Notes Payable	156,000	
	Cash [$150,000 + (4% X $150,000)]		156,000

(b) Mohawk's entries:

1992	Allowance for Doubtful Accounts*	3,000	
	Notes Receivable	12,000	
	Interest Receivable		15,000
1993	Cash	6,000	
	Notes Receivable		6,000
1994	Cash	156,000	
	Notes Receivable		156,000

*Or, Loss on Restructuring (not classified as extraordinary).

Explanation: The profession takes the position that a troubled debt restructuring involving a modification of terms is a continuation of an existing debt arrangement and does not transfer economic resources on the restructure date. The effects from these types of restructurings should be accounted for prospectively (over future years) by both the debtor and the creditor. Unless the carrying amount at the time of restructure exceeds the undiscounted total future cash flows, the debtor will not change the carrying amount of the payable and the creditor will not change the recorded investment in the receivable. But, when the carrying amount of the debt at the time of restructure is greater than the undiscounted total future cash flows (as it is in this situation), both the debtor and the creditor adjust the carrying amount. The debtor recognizes a gain, the creditor recognizes a loss, and neither recognizes interest as part of the future payments or receipts.

Pawnee's carrying amount of the debt of $165,000 ($150,000 + $15,000 = $165,000) exceeds the total future cash flows of $162,000 [$150,000 + ($6,000 X 2) = $162,000]. Therefore, a $3,000 gain on restructuring is to be recognized and classified as an extraordinary item on the debtor's income statement. The payments made subsequent to the restructure date are all recorded as a reduction in principal because no interest is to be recognized.

Mohawk's carrying amount of the receivable of $165,000 exceeds the total future cash flows of $162,000. Therefore, a $3,000 difference is charged to the Allowance for Doubtful Accounts or to a loss account (not extraordinary). None of the subsequent receipts are recognized as interest.

In the journal entry on Pawnee's books at the restructure date, the accrued interest being forgiven is eliminated from the Interest Payable account, the computed gain is recorded, and the difference is recorded as an adjustment to the note's principal balance in the Notes Payable account.

ANALYSIS OF MULTIPLE CHOICE TYPE QUESTIONS

Question
1. If bonds are initially sold at a discount and the straight-line method of amortization is used, interest expense in the earlier years of the bond's life will
   a. be less than the amount of interest actually paid.
   b. be less than it will be in the latter years of the bond's life.
   c. be the same as what it would have been had the effective interest method of amortization been used.
   d. exceed what it would have been had the effective interest method of amortization been used.

Solution = d.

Explanation and Approach: Quickly sketch the graph that shows the patterns of and relationships between interest paid, interest expense using the straight-line method, and interest expense using the effective interest method. The graph appears in **Illustration 14-1.** Treat each of the possible answer selections as a True-False question. Look at the graph after reading each of the answer selections to determine if it is a correct statement.

Selection a. is False because interest expense for a bond issued at a discount will be greater than interest actually paid throughout the bond's entire life, regardless of the amortization method used. Selection b. is False because interest expense is a constant amount each period when the straight-line method is used; hence, interest expense will be the same amount in the latter years as it is in the earlier years. Selection c. is False because in the earlier years of life for a bond issued at a discount, interest expense computed using the straight-line method is greater than interest expense computed using the effective interest method. Selection d. is True. The interest expense will increase over a bond's life when the bond is issued at a discount and the effective interest method of amortization is used. In the earlier years of life that expense amount is less than interest expense computed using the straight-line method, and in the latter years of life, that expense amount is more than interest expense computed using the straight-line method.

Question

2. A large department store issues bonds with a maturity date that is twenty years after the issuance date. If the bonds are issued at a discount, this indicates that at the date of issuance, the
    a. nominal rate of interest and the stated rate of interest coincided.
    b. nominal rate of interest exceeds the yield rate.
    c. yield rate of interest exceeds the coupon rate.
    d. stated rate of interest exceeds the effective rate.

Solution = c.

Explanation and Approach: Before reading the answer selections, write down the relationship that causes a bond to be issued at a discount: market rate of interest exceeds the stated rate of interest. Then list the synonymous terms for market rate and for stated rate: (1) market rate, effective rate, and yield rate; (2) stated rate, coupon rate, nominal rate, and contract rate. Section a. is incorrect because the nominal rate and the stated rate are just different names for the same thing. Selections b. and d. are incorrect because an excess of nominal rate (stated rate) over the yield rate (effective rate) will result in a premium, not a discount. When the yield rate (market rate) exceeds the coupon rate (stated rate), an issuance discount will result.

Question

3. At the beginning of 1992, the Alston Corporation issued 10% bonds with a face value of $400,000. These bonds mature in five years, and interest is paid semiannually on June 30 and December 31. The bonds were sold for $370,560 to yield 12%. Alston uses a calendar-year reporting period. Using the preferable method of amortization, what amount of interest expense should be reported for 1992? (Round all computations to the nearest dollar.)
    a. $44,333.
    b. $44.467.
    c. $44,601.
    d. $45,888.

Solution = c.

Explanation and Approach: Write down the formula for computing interest using the effective method of amortization. Use the data in the question to work through the formula.

	Carrying value at the beginning of the period	$370,560.00
X	Effective rate of interest per interest period	6%
	Interest expense for the first interest period	22,233.60
-	Cash interest for the interest period	20,000.00*
	Amortization of discount for the first interest period	2,233.60
+	Carrying value at the beginning of the first period	370,560.00
	Carrying value at the beginning of the second period	372,793.60
X	Effective rate of interest per interest period	6%
	Interest expense for the second interest period	22,367.62
+	Interest expense for the first interest period	22,233.60
=	Interest expense for the calendar year of 1992	$ 44,601.22

*$400,000 X $\frac{10\%}{2}$ = $20,000.

TIP: The interest must be computed on a per interest period basis. In this question, the interest period is six months. The interest for 1992 is comprised of the interest for the bond's first two interest periods.

Question

4. At December 31, 1992, the following balances existed on the books of the Malloy Corporation:

Bonds Payable	$500,000
Discount on Bonds Payable	40,000
Interest Payable	12,500
Unamortized Bond Issue Costs	30,000

If the bonds are retired on January 1, 1993, at 102, what will Malloy report as a loss on redemption?

a. $92,500.
b. $80,000.
c. $67,500.
d. $50,000.

Solution = b.

Explanation and Approach: Write down the format for the computation of the gain or loss on redemption and plug in the amounts from this question.

	Par value	$500,000
-	Unamortized discount	40,000
	Carrying amount	460,000
-	Unamortized debt issue costs	30,000
	Net carrying amount	430,000
-	Redemption price	510,000*
=	Gain (Loss) on redemption	$ (80,000)

*$500,000 X 102% = $510,000.

Question

5. A debtor in a troubled debt restructuring has debt that is settled by a transfer of land with a fair value that is less than the carrying amount of the debt but is more than the book value of the land. Should a gain or loss on debt settlement be recognized? Should a gain or loss on the disposition of assets be recognized?

	Gain or Loss on Debt Settlement	Gain or Loss on Disposition of Assets
a.	Gain	Gain
b.	Gain	Loss
c.	Loss	Loss
d.	Loss	Gain

Solution = a.

14-20

Explanation and Approach: Assign amounts to the (1) carrying amount of the debt, (2) carrying amount of the land, and (3) fair value of the land. Be sure your assigned amounts maintain the relationships stated in the question. Then use a journal entry approach to solve. For instance: Fair value of land, $100,000; carrying amount of debt, $127,000; and book value of land, $65,000. For the journal entry, debit the debt account(s) for $127,000; credit Land for $65,000; credit Gain on Disposition for $35,000 (an excess of the fair value over the book value indicates that a gain has been experienced on the old asset). The rest of the entry is due to a gain or loss on settlement. A credit for $27,000 is needed for the entry to balance; hence, there is a gain on settlement. If you are able to settle a debt by giving an asset with a value that is less than the carrying amount of the debt, you have an advantageous settlement of debt; hence a gain on settlement should be recognized.

Debt	127,000	
Land		65,000
Gain on Disposition of Assets		35,000
Gain on Settlement of Debt		27,000